Yes!
A MEMOIR OF MODERN HAWAII

This book has been financed
privately and net proceeds of sales
will go to the Aloha United Way.

By Walter A. Dods Jr.
with Gerry Keir and Jerry Burris

© 2015 Walter A. Dods Jr.

All rights reserved. No part of this book may be reproduced in any form or by any electronic or mechanical means, including information retrieval systems, without prior written permission from the publisher, except for brief passages quoted in reviews.

ISBN 978-1-935690-76-4

Library of Congress Control Number: 2015953115

Legacy Isle Publishing
1000 Bishop St., Suite 806
Honolulu, HI 96813
www.legacyislepublishing.net
info@legacyislepublishing.net

Printed in Korea

Cover and book design by Stacey Leong Design, Honolulu, Hawaii

Dedicated with love to my Mom and Dad, who sacrificed so much for all seven of us Dods kids; to Diane, an accomplished woman, a wonderful wife and mother; to our four children, Walter III, Chris, Peter and Lauren; and to our daughter-in-law Starr and grandchildren Dylan, Sawyer and Finley.

FOREWORD

> "The most powerful word in the English language has three letters and thousands of meanings. It's the word 'Yes.' Before any mountain... or heart... was ever moved, someone had to utter the magic word. Yes."
>
> —1969 First Hawaiian Bank ad launching my first marketing campaign, "The Bank That Says Yes"

I've lived a very unlikely life by saying "Yes!" Yes, to job promotions that put me in over my head. Yes, to involvement in political campaigns. Yes, to community service and charity fundraising.

I say my life is an "unlikely" story because I came from a blue-collar, working-class background. One of the many homes my Dad moved us into over the years was a Quonset hut in the back of Kuliouou Valley on Oahu. Dad, a cop, would always tell us seven kids that we were middle class and proud of it.

Over the years, I developed a reputation—largely undeserved—as a political insider and powerbroker who could make or break political careers. I wish!

If you read some of the commentary about me, including topping a couple of silly "Most Powerful" lists, I come across as something akin to one of the doges of historical Venice—political and commercial rulers of all they could see. What a joke. If anything, I was a man who worked to make the community he lived in and the bank he worked for be as successful as possible. In fact, throughout my career, I saw those goals as one and the same.

To be sure, along the way things worked out pretty well for me, too. As a result, I occasionally found myself a long, long way from my roots.

Soon after the merger of First Hawaiian Bank with San Francisco's Bank of the West, I was in Venice, sitting down for dinner inside the Palazzo Ducale, the palace where the ancient doges ruled. I was representing First Hawaiian, meeting with top global executives from BNP Paribas, one of the biggest banks in the world, which had owned Bank of the West since 1980. At these annual dinners, everything is first class, including the locations.

The Bridge of Sighs goes across to the palazzo, a 600-year-old masterpiece of Gothic architecture right on Saint Mark's Square. It has a lacy marble façade, painted and gilded ceilings, walls covered with priceless art and huge murals. There are gorgeous marble doors, grand staircases, huge meeting halls full of artwork and statues. On the night of our formal BNP dinner, we were sitting at the table in the museum; next to us on the wall was a world-famous painting of a woman covered in unbelievable jewels. On the table in front of us were the actual jewels from the painting!

At another dinner meeting, at a museum in Amsterdam, I was sitting so close to Van Gogh's famous painting *The Boy with the Blue Cap* that I could have touched it. I'll never forget the scene at a working dinner in Paris. We were in a fog because their custom is cigars and brandy after dinner; you could hardly see the people through the cloud of cigar smoke. It took me several dry cleanings to get the smell out of my shirts, ties and suits.

It's been an amazing ride for a guy who began his career as a lowly dead-files clerk in an insurance company in Honolulu. There were times at those fancy European events when I would say to myself, *What's a kid who struggled through Saint Louis School doing in a place like this?*

That, actually, is one of the reasons I wanted to write this book: to show other local kids of modest means that, yes, you can dream big dreams, too. And make them come true.

CONTENTS

Foreword 6
CHAPTER 1 — Little Buster Grows Up, Must Drive with Pillow 10
CHAPTER 2 — Tire Marks on My Foot for a Year 22
CHAPTER 3 — Saying "Yes" to a Career in Banking 34
CHAPTER 4 — Oh, Johnny! The Bellinger Years 46
CHAPTER 5 — Manoa Finance: Digging out of a Deep Hole 56
CHAPTER 6 — Politics: Building a Community 68
CHAPTER 7 — Japan Deal Could Have Killed Bank 80
CHAPTER 8 — A Sudden Death, a Coup Attempt 92
CHAPTER 9 — We Were No. 2; We Had to Try Harder 98
CHAPTER 10 — Reaching for the Downtown Sky 112
CHAPTER 11 — Two Jacks: Shock on Bishop Street 128
CHAPTER 12 — Ssshhh! ABA President Asleep on Sofa 138
CHAPTER 13 — Project Rainbow: Getting in Bed with the French 146
CHAPTER 14 — Bidding in Barcelona: How to Sell a Bank on a Napkin 160
CHAPTER 15 — When Banking Could Extend a Hand 172
CHAPTER 16 — "If You Run, It's Gonna Kill You" 178
CHAPTER 17 — Our Man in Washington 184
CHAPTER 18 — From the Banking Frying Pan into a Telecom Fire 196
CHAPTER 19 — Trust, Friendship and the Art of the Deal 202
CHAPTER 20 — People I've Known 212
CHAPTER 21 — Most Powerful? Nah! 226
CHAPTER 22 — Local Boys (and Girls) Can Succeed. Here's How 232
Acknowledgments: Mahalo Plenty 246
APPENDIX A: Family Trees 247
APPENDIX B: Walter Dods Jr. Career Highlights 249
APPENDIX C: Let's Make a Deal 251
Index 253

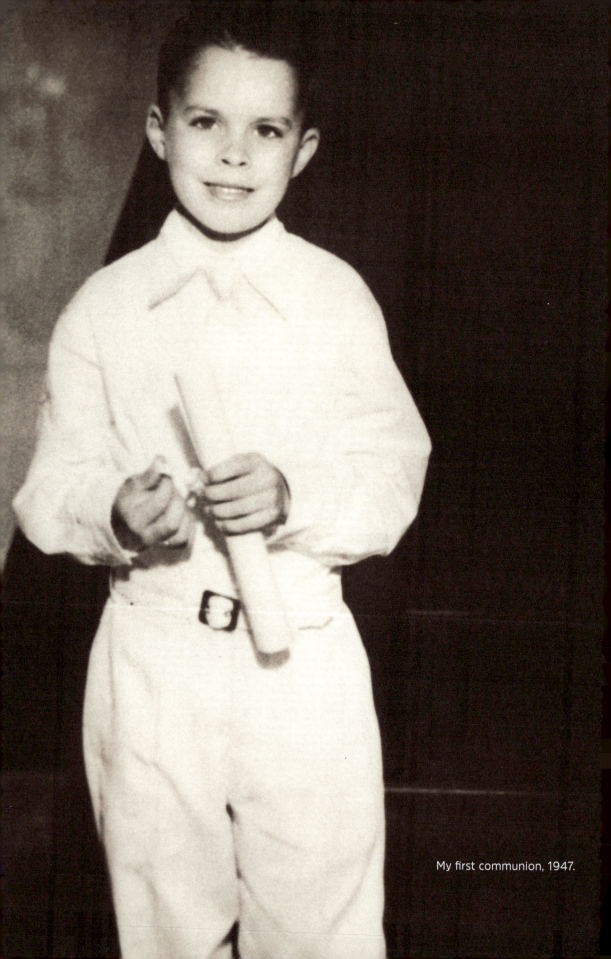

My first communion, 1947.

CHAPTER 1

Little Buster Grows Up, Must Drive with Pillow

"To understand Walt, you have to know his background."
Wesley Park, longtime friend, retired First Hawaiian board member

I wasn't born with a silver spoon. Far from it. My childhood was filled with love, discipline at home and at school and a sense that paying bills was a struggle every month for my parents.

Maybe it was inevitable that I would end up working in a bank, working with numbers. My Dad's father, who died before I was born, was an accountant and worked at sugar plantations and other companies on Oahu and the Big Island. He apparently was the kind of guy who worked around the clock. But obviously not all the time because he had eight children.

My great-great-grandfather, James Dods, born in Scotland in 1810, was an adventurer. With four young kids in tow in 1853, he left on a difficult three-month journey by clipper ship to Australia. Later he moved to Fiji, where he worked as a sugar planter and died at the age of 86.

His second son, Archibald, spent many of his young years in Fiji and Australia. Like his father, Archibald was eager to see the world and, at age 22, set off to strike it rich in the western Canada gold rush of 1862. That didn't work out, but he stayed on to teach at a boy's school in British Columbia. In 1867, he married a woman from New Orleans with the colorful name of Mary Tennessee Williams.

Still restless, Archibald eventually moved to the Kingdom of Hawaii where he ended up as a teacher at Lahainaluna, a boarding school above the port town of Lahaina on Maui, one of the better public schools at the time. Over the years, the family sailed back and forth several times between Hawaii and Canada. In 1908, Archibald finally moved back to Victoria to stay, and my great-grandfather passed away there in 1915, leaving seven grown children, one of whom was my grandfather, Robert. Archibald's obituary in the *Victoria Daily Colonist*, complete with a huge picture of him and his bushy mustache, described him as a "splendid type of Victoria pioneer." He was reported to have been friendly with Queen Liliuokalani and had her autograph.

All of my grandfather's siblings were with Archibald in Victoria when he died, but Robert had planted his roots in Hawaii. In 1904, he was living in North Kohala on the Big Island as a plantation bookkeeper. He met and married a Hawaii-born woman named Mary Irene Sutherland. He later worked as a bookkeeper at other sugar plantations, at a railroad company on the Big Island and the Wahiawa Water Company on Oahu.

Unfortunately, Robert died in 1926 at the age of 47 of a collapsed lung, a complication of tuberculosis, leaving my grandmother, Mary Irene, with eight kids and no breadwinner. My father, Walter Dods Sr., was 10 years old at the time. His mother had a nervous breakdown and was institutionalized at the Territorial Mental Hospital in Kaneohe on Oahu. When I was a small kid, Dad would bring her home on weekends for visits. She never had much to say and died in 1955 at the age of 71.

After their father died, the Dods brothers were sent to an orphanage in Hilo called Father Louis Boys' Home. It was right next to what today is Hilo High School. Around age 15, Dad ended up at Hilo Boarding School as a boarder. He attracted a fair amount of attention. A school official wrote a letter describing him as a "fine, wide-awake boy and a good worker." The school was near Lyman House—it's there to this day as a museum, in beautiful condition. The man who ran it was particularly admiring of this orphan kid, who was out cleaning the yards every day at Lyman House; he wrote a letter saying how somebody ought to help this kid, my dad, get an education.

My great-grandpa, Archibald Dods.

Dad's brother Chester was a little older and a great athlete. Neal Blaisdell (who later went on to become Honolulu mayor) recruited Chester out of Hilo High to play football for McKinley High on Oahu. The team was nicknamed the "Wonder Team" and was one of the all-time great Island football teams. The 1933 McKinley team traveled to the Mainland and defeated Weber College (now known as Weber State University) and BYU's freshman team. Ricks College (now called BYU-Idaho) traveled to Honolulu and lost to McKinley in a game attended by 19,000 fans.

After high school Uncle Chester joined the Honolulu Police Department and eventually rose to captain. One of his closest friends, also a captain, was Jack Burns, later a three-term governor. They knew each other way back before I was a twinkle in anyone's eye. My father was still at Hilo High at the time and was a pretty good athlete himself—but not as good as the most famous Island basketball player of the time, the great Ah Chew Goo, a starting guard; the other guard was my father.

Around that time Dad earned the nickname "Buster." It's a nickname for Walter, apparently. Think of Buster McGuire, the great old Punahou football player. Dad was "Big Buster" and I was "Little Buster" my whole life. My brothers and sisters still call me that.

Eventually Uncle Chester pulled Dad out of the Hilo orphanage to live with him in Kaimuki on Oahu. At about the age of 20, Dad became a policeman like his brother and shortly met and married a pretty young Portuguese girl who was working as a drugstore soda jerk. She had attended Maryknoll until she dropped out around the 10th grade. That was my mom, Mildred Vivian Phillips.

I joke a lot about my Portuguese blood on my mother's side. One time, after I was inducted into the Bank Marketing Hall of Fame, I kidded my mother—who was in the audience—telling her, "Now we'll have to start calling ourselves *Mediterranean*, not *Portuguese*."

All of Mom's great-grandparents were born in the Azores, Portuguese-owned islands in the North Atlantic from which they immigrated to Hawaii in the late 1800s during the early waves of Portuguese laborers recruited for the plantations. The migration began in the 1870s and picked up steam in the 1880s after King Kalakaua visited Portugal on a trip around the world and met King Dom Luis. The two nations signed a friendship and immigration treaty, which triggered a flow of immigrants from impoverished Portugal to labor-short Hawaii.

> "Hello, Walter. Well hello, Walter. It's so nice to run a bank that speaks some French. Your birthday's near, Walter. Sixty years, Walter . . . Promise that you won't go away; Portuguese CEOs are scarce today."
>
> —Jimmy Borges at Walt's 60th birthday party

Manuel Phillips, my great-grandfather, was born around 1860. His actual name is a moving target. Immigration records show he was named Filippe (or Felipe) Manuel, but soon after getting to Hawaii he flipped the order and became Manuel Phillips. He and his wife sailed from the Azores to Hawaii in 1882 aboard the steamship SS *Hansa*, along with 1,100 other Portuguese immigrants. He was 24, she 18, and they were newlywed. Her name, too, is a little fuzzy. Immigration records show her as Alexandrina Augusta (maiden name Santos), but later Census records list her name as Hannabela.

Manuel was a carpenter with no formal education; both he and his wife were illiterate. Their primary language was Portuguese, though they did eventually learn English. They had 12 children; by the 1900 Census, 10 were still living. Number 8 among the living was my grandfather, David Phillips, born in Honolulu in 1895.

My other Portuguese great-grandparents were Antone and Marianne Botelho. Both came to Hawaii in the 1870s as infants. They were married in the Republic of Hawaii in 1894 when both were in their early 20s. They lived on Beretania Street in Honolulu, and he worked as a boilermaker in an ironworks. Neither could read nor write. Antone and Marianne had 12 children, but child mortality was high; as of 1900 only three were still living. The oldest was my grandmother, Minnie Botelho, born in Honolulu in 1895.

David Phillips and Minnie Botelho married in 1919 and had 11 children, including Mildred, my mother, born in 1922. David worked as a janitor in a store.

My ancestors came from different sides of the tracks; one grandfather was educated, a schoolteacher; the other was a laborer.

Since my mother came from a big family, she had to drop out of school to work and help support the family. After they were married my mom and dad lived in an apartment on Tusitala Street in Waikiki, when I was born. My father was never very religious, but he allowed my mother to raise us as Catholics and go to Catholic schools.

Our family quickly grew to seven kids, and I guess you could say we were poor, getting by on my father's police salary until Mom could go to work as a cashier in a coffee shop, first at Rexall Drugs and then mostly at the Minute Chef in the Princess Kaiulani Hotel in Waikiki.

Half a year after I was born in May 1941 came the attack on Pearl Harbor, a traumatic time for my family and everybody else on Oahu. Dad was immediately called to work and was gone for a week or two. My mother never saw him, didn't know whether he was alive or dead. He was put in charge of the emergency room at Queens Hospital where they'd bring the Pearl Harbor victims. If "no chance," they'd put them in one corner, and if "chance," they'd put them in another corner. Just body after body after body. One time he was making his rounds and he heard a noise in the pile of bodies in the "dead" corner. He looked around. Nothing. After three or four times hearing this noise, he went back and dug around and found a guy alive at the bottom of the pile.

> "Once when we were kids in Aina Haina I said to Walt, 'We're both *haoles*.' And he said, 'No, I'm Portagee.'"
>
> —Paul Mullin Ganley, Damon Estate trustee

After Waikiki, my family moved to Puunui, right below Oahu Country Club at the entrance to Nuuanu Valley. At the end of Wyllie Street, there was an old beaten-down house that somebody rented to my father when we were young. I can remember the blackouts during the war and I vaguely remember Dad being the most popular person in the neighborhood because, as a cop, he had gas, which was rationed. He would let neighbors come by and siphon a pint or two out of his tank.

After Puunui, we moved to Kailua, which was inexpensive back then. Realty offices had little tract houses on Oneawa Street in an area called Coconut Grove that they specialized in selling to cops and firemen. After a while, I think the commute from Kailua was too much for Mom and Dad, so we moved to a Quonset hut in Kuliouou and spent quite a few years there.

I think the Quonset was war surplus; it had three bedrooms—one for my parents, a second for the boys and the third for the girls. Actually, they weren't really rooms; there were dividers separating the rooms, and if you stood up you could see into the

All nine of us in the Dods family lived in this Quonset hut in Kuliouou.

next room. It sounds as if we were poor, but we never felt that way. Everybody was like that. We'd go into each other's houses, and if there was food around, we'd share it.

The Reeves and Correa clans kind of controlled that neighborhood. Naomi "Sister" Correa was *the* political power in that area and later became a leader within the Hawaii Democratic Party. Her son, Butch, became adjutant general for the State of Hawaii.

Growing up in a family of seven was easier on me than the other six, because I was the oldest. I could get my share of food at the table. The bathroom was the hardest. In both our Quonset hut and later when we moved into a real house in Aina Haina, there were nine of us and one bathroom. In the morning, we were crammed in—Dad putting on his police uniform, Mom getting ready for work, one of us on the toilet, another brushing his teeth, somebody showering. We were close-knit, but it was so crowded that I tried to go to friends' houses when I could.

We older ones took turns changing the younger ones' diapers, rinsing the diapers in the toilet, carrying the babies around and feeding them. We'd have a pot boiling all the time on the stove, sterilizing nipples for the bottles. Whoever was around would mix the formula.

On Sunday nights, Mom would make chocolate pudding for us, and we'd all fight to lick the spoon and lick the inside of the pot. On a special Sunday, we'd get the pudding on top of a little pound cake. That was an extra treat.

My father was deathly afraid of having his service revolver around with seven kids in the house. Every night he would dismantle the gun, hide the revolver in one place, the pistol in another and the bullets in different places. In the morning, he would be swearing: "Goddammit, I can't find the bullets!" Half the time he would go to work with just the gun butt sticking out of his holster.

My father, having been an orphan, had very strong feelings that what he most wanted for his kids was love and a good education—because he didn't have either. He sent almost all of us to Catholic schools (Saint Louis School and Sacred Hearts Academy). And with seven kids, he struggled. Private school tuition was like $200 a year. That was big money in those days. Money was always a big problem.

That was kind of my first introduction to banking. True story: He would borrow from the credit union to pay the tuitions, and when the credit union notes came due, he'd borrow from Budget Finance to pay off the credit unions and then from Beneficial Finance to pay off Budget. He ran a modified Ponzi scheme back in those days.

The bill collectors would call all the time for their payments, and my father would take his big old police hat, turn it upside down and put all the bills in it and he'd pick, randomly, which ones he would pay each month. One night this bill collector called him and my father told him, word for word, "Look, you call me one more time and I'm not going to put your name in the hat this month." I *vividly* remember that story. He really struggled to get us to Saint Louis, but we did get that good education.

> "Walt's brother Bob told me that as a teenager, Walter played banker for a while—although not a very good one. His friends from Saint Louis School would go to the gas station where he worked in Aina Haina and he'd put some gas on the cuff for them. I'm not sure if they ever paid their bill later."
>
> —Jack Hoag,
> *retired president of
> First Hawaiian Bank*

We also got discipline. Saint Louis was totally different than it is today. It was a very, very strict school, run by the brothers and priests. The discipline was hard and firm. I remember our principal, Brother Aiu, a big Hawaiian who looked like Kamehameha, handsome, with silver hair. Every year, the first day of school we'd *run* down to the lockers and he would stand in the middle of the hallway and punch the first guy that came sprinting down the hall—I mean *knock* him to the floor—and the rest of the year we would *walk* to our lockers. It was justice, old style.

We Dods boys credit Saint Louis and the brothers for keeping us out of jail. I mean, we were wild kids. Teachers were dedicated. Class sizes were a minimum of 45 students, and they had iron control over us. They were good teachers, inspirational, and we learned a lot from them.

If my life had taken a different turn, I might have become a priest. It's kind of embarrassing to say because I was certainly not a devout guy and I don't even go to church anymore. But I went to an all-boys school and the brothers preached religion a lot. I was an altar boy and the priests kept talking to me. One of them took me to the seminary on the Pali, St. Stephens, to visit and tried to convince me to go into the priesthood. I told my parents I was interested, but he got to me too late. Right about that time I was turning into a young man with a car and a girlfriend, so my interest didn't last very long.

In my teenage years, I was a big-time hot-rodder. My friends and I would drag race every night. We'd, well, *borrow* tires from cars and trucks around the streets. If it weren't for the brothers, I probably would have gotten into serious trouble.

Cars were a big thing for me, but first I had to earn some money.

When I was about 12, because we were seven kids with no money, I started working as a yard boy in the neighborhood and then babysat. As soon as I was 15 and could legally work, I worked 40 hours a week, or more, for the rest of my high school career. The first job was in the pineapple cannery. Every kid in Hawaii who had any kind of a connection—and my dad knew somebody in the Human Resources department—worked in the cannery. I was a steam cleaner, the hardest of all jobs. At night, the cannery would shut down and just a skeleton crew would come in. We'd take this huge steam hose and clean all the pineapple and grease off the machines. It was hard work.

> "Buster's cars were an expensive hobby. My dad used to tell me that when Buster was in high school and working at Aina Haina Chevron, he did so much with his cars that every paycheck he owed the station money!"
>
> —*brother Tommy Dods*

Even then we'd get into trouble. We'd take the big pineapple juice containers, clean them out and fill them with cold water and then, hot and sweaty from all the steaming, we'd all jump into the pineapple containers. I could never drink pineapple juice, for like 30 years, after I finished working in the cannery.

Later, I worked three jobs: Monday through Thursday at Aina Haina Foodland, in the '50s, as a bag boy; Saturday and Sunday at Aina Haina Service Station; and Sunday nights, late, I'd go to Aina Haina Chop Suey and wash dishes for the entire night. That was the hardest. I wanted to cry every time I'd walk in there. The dishes would be piled up, all those little plates. In the beginning I would get yelled at a lot, but eventually the old Chinese man who was the owner took a liking to me and he'd cook for me—pork hash and some noodles. That would be the only good meal I'd have all week.

I eventually had enough money to get my first car, a big, ugly old Chrysler that one neighbor was going to throw away but gave to me. It had the fluid drive, automatic. It was a tank. But I only had that for a little while. My first real car was a '49 Ford. I made a makeshift stick shift on the floor for it. It was a piece of junk, but I was hooked.

When I got my first driver's license at age 15, I was only 4 feet 10 inches and weighed 80 pounds. And, I had a restriction written on my license—"*Must Drive with Pillow*"—because I couldn't see over the dashboard without one. I grew a foot between my sophomore year and the time I was 20, but in between I was very skinny.

Sometimes I think being the smallest boy in the class gave me that competitive nature, but back then I was not ambitious. My biggest goal was maybe to become manager of the Aina Haina Service Station. That would be my life's dream when I was going to high school. If I could do that, I would have accomplished something in life. I *never, ever* had any other dreams.

Millie and Walter Dods Sr.

When I was working at the service station, there were a couple of guys who had fast cars. They would take me out at night after work and we'd go drag racing on the Mauka Arterial. The Mauka Arterial started where the Oasis nightclub used to be. The H-1 freeway started there and ended at Kapiolani Hospital. That was the first section of the freeway and that's where we'd drag. We'd meet at Scotty's Drive Inn on Keeaumoku Street, then drive up to Kaimuki late at night and get some guys to block the freeway. Mostly, I was a rider in a friend's car who had a new Plymouth Fury with dual quad carburetors.

I loved my hot rods as a kid, but none seemed right when it came time to go to the school prom. I asked my dad if I could use his car, which he used for official police work. He was reluctant, but finally gave in after sternly warning me to drive it cautiously and sensibly. After all I would be representing the police department. Prom night came and I proudly headed off in the grown-up car. After the prom, lots of people headed off to Kelly's Drive-In out near the airport to get something to eat. We did too. My friends still remember that night as I pulled up to that old green-and-white building, loud police siren wailing away.

That was quite an entrance, but at least I didn't speed!

I was a straight-A student in first through eighth grades at St. Louis, contrary to popular opinion. In my freshman year I started to discover girls and cars, and I started to get A-minuses. My sophomore year my grades went down more and junior year down even further because I'd be drag racing too much. I'd get home at 2 or 3 in the morning and then go to school. After working after school, I'd pick up my books and scramble to get my homework done. It was all last minute.

I got out of Saint Louis School by the hair of my chin. The classes had levels A, B, C and so forth depending on your grades. I started off at 9-A and then I went down to 10-C, then 11-D and 12-F, something like that, because I was just winging it all the way through school. There was not a whole lot of scholarly work

"I met Walt's mom in the early 1960s long before I met Walt. I was at the Aina Haina branch, and one of my main jobs was to approve or disapprove potential checking account overdrafts. One of the regular overdrafts was Millie Dods, a lovely lady. Once or twice a week I was calling her and she would come in dutifully with some cash and cover the overdraft. That went on for quite some time and we got along fine.

"Fast forward 20 years, I was at a party at the Halekulani Hotel celebrating Walter's promotion to president of the bank. Millie was there and went up to him and said: 'Buster, you may be president but you take care of Jack Hoag because he took care of me when you were in high school.'"

—Jack Hoag

that went on, but the teachers said I had an aptitude for speaking so I did well in the debates. I loved to argue, and I guess I was quick on my feet.

At one point in my youth I wanted to become a professional clarinetist and move to New Orleans to be in a jazz band. All I had was a crappy metal clarinet they give you in school, so my folks borrowed money to buy me a wooden clarinet, the proper equipment. "OK, if you are going to run away and become a jazz player, you need the right instrument," Mom said.

Mom had outfoxed me because two days later I decided it wasn't such a good idea to leave home and become a clarinetist. I don't play today. I wish I did.

At home, Mom was the disciplinarian. She would spank us with wooden hangers. This could happen at any time and she'd say, "Well, I'm doing this now because I know you are going to do something bad today and I want to get it out of the way."

Mom was a pistol. Years later when she was a cashier at the Minute Chef, she would help this security guard who had no money and was starving. She would get leftover food, still good food, and feed him every night. Later on, that man became well-known in Hawaii: Larry Price, former University of Hawaii head football coach and now a radio personality. One day, Larry was attacking me on his morning radio show over something or other and my mother called him and said, "Don't you *ever, ever* say anything bad about my son again or I will tell everybody how I fed you your whole life!"

"Oh, Auntie Millie, I will never, ever criticize Walter again on the radio."

My Mom loved Las Vegas. She liked to go and play the slots in her senior years. She had free airfare from my sister who worked at Hawaiian Airlines, and the hotels loved her because she always lost, so they would give her a free room downtown.

All the banks would send her unsolicited credit cards and she would max one out, then max the next one and pay from the next one, almost like Dad's Ponzi scheme. Every Christmas I would go to her house and say, "OK, Mom, put all your charge cards on the table." I would pay all her bills, clean all her cards out. Toward the end of her life, it was more than $50,000 every Christmas.

I'd write the checks, pay them off, and then cut all the cards up in front of her. She would swear that she'd never use a charge card again, and for a month or so that would happen. Then they would start coming in the mail again. When my father was still alive, he would shake his head at me and say, "Why are you doing that?" But that was something I could do for her later in life in return for all she did for me.

Every year, *The Honolulu Advertiser* would run a story about all the top corporate executives' pay, and the first call I would get would be from Mom chuckling and saying, "I always thought you were a good, generous son but, by your pay, I see I'm not getting my cut."

> "All his life, Buster has made a point of taking care of his family. If anything happens in our family, whenever we need help, we go to him for advice. But where does he go? Who helps Buster?"
>
> —Tommy Dods

Photo taken about 1945. Left to right are myself, brother Bobby and sister Suzanne.

My father was a quiet, humble man and rarely ever got angry. But if he did, you really knew it. He put a hand on me maybe once or twice in my life, and both times I deserved it. Once, I got caught drag racing with another cop's son. I was coming down Kalanianaole Highway with a friend and a cop pulls me over.

"Are you Sergeant Dods' son?"

"Yessir."

He calls into dispatch and we're listening on the motorcycle speaker, and he says, "Patch me through to Sergeant Dods." I hear my father get on and the officer says, "Sergeant, shall I take them down and book them, or bring them home?" And I'm praying he's going to take me down and book me. But I hear coming over this little speaker on the motorcycle: "Bring the son of a bitch home." Dad pulled me up against the wall and gave me one whack and took away my license for like six months. That was a tough time.

Overall, through my teenage years, the dominant factor was Saint Louis. I think the values you learned there were really, really good. We weren't Punahou or Iolani, not the cream of the crop. We were blue-collar kids and so we were all close. Lifelong friends. That was the goal, trying to create character and keep us out of jail.

I don't regret a second of Saint Louis School. It, and the values my parents taught me, are the foundation of all that followed.

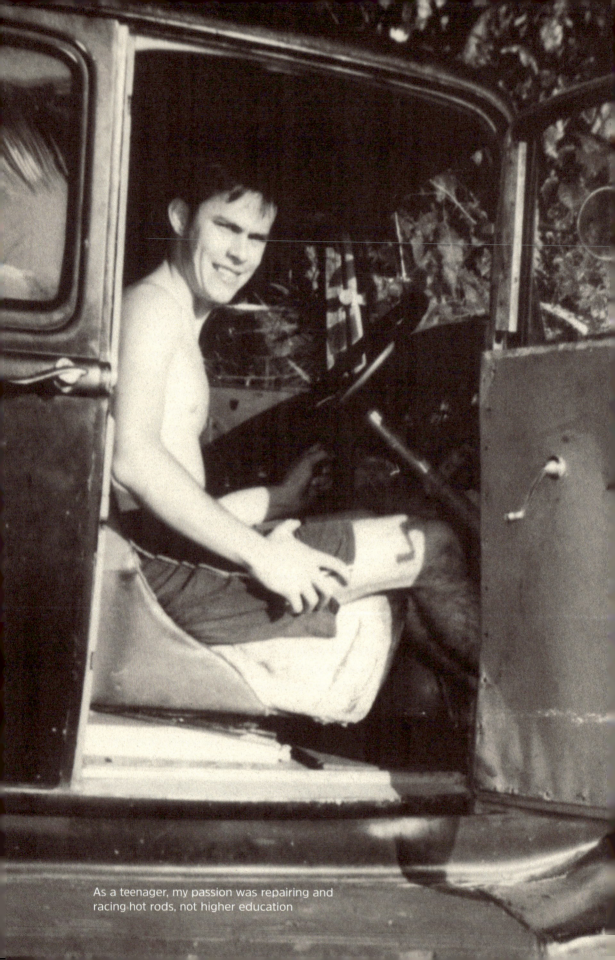

As a teenager, my passion was repairing and racing hot rods, not higher education

CHAPTER 2

Tire Marks on My Foot for a Year

When I got out of high school, I still was more focused on my wheels than on my future. Ambition was not my strong suit.

I had an old '51 Ford that I had dropped the front end on and I had put in a makeshift floor shift that would lock in gear every once in a while. When that happened, I would have to go under the car and fix it myself. I would drop the drive shaft to unlock the transmission, then put the shaft back up. It wasn't much of a car, but I loved it.

I remember one night making out with a gal on a hill in Manoa Valley and the car got stuck, the transmission was locked, and it was pitch dark. I climbed under the car to go through my fix-it routine, but the bearings all dropped out. When the drive shaft dropped, the car with its lowered front end started rolling down on me and I screamed. My date, who was in the front seat, hit the foot brake and the car stopped —right on my foot in the soft dirt. I told her to release the brake one second, then stop again. She did and I rolled out. She released the brake and the car rolled down the hill, up the hill, down the hill, over and over. For a year I had tire marks across my foot. I could very easily have been killed that night. Then, I had to walk her home—late— and her father gave both of us bloody hell. The next day, my hot rod buddies helped me tow the car to a repair shop.

I graduated from Saint Louis the year Hawaii became a state, 1959. It was August, right after graduation, that we had the big Statehood celebration in Waikiki, which at that time was just the Royal Hawaiian, Halekulani and Moana Hotels—pretty low-rise.

Kalakaua Avenue was all closed off. They put out these little stands, they had Hawaiian entertainment and the whole of Kalakaua Avenue was packed from corner to corner. It was a joyous time. The vote was 94 percent in favor of Statehood, and the turnout was the highest in history. It was a heady time; Hawaiians, haoles, locals, everybody was thrilled. We all went in our hot rods down to Waikiki and cruised the side streets.

Statehood wasn't a burning issue for us high school kids. We were much more interested in girls and hot rods. I was aware that we had been waiting a long time, in part because we were viewed as having too many Asians, but many people in Washington were concerned about the influence of the ILWU, the dockworkers' union, which was regarded by its critics as a communist sympathizer. We had gone through that big dock strike in 1949 and they felt Hawaii was going to be Democrat all the way and too liberal.

Our delegate to Congress, Jack Burns, finally realized that, took a big gamble and cut a deal to let Alaska go first and Hawaii would be second. He risked his entire career, threw it all on the line and was heavily criticized. There was deep-seated fear in Congress about Hawaii changing the balance of the Senate between Republicans and Democrats and they figured if Alaska came in first, heavily Republican, it would offset Hawaii.

After I graduated from Saint Louis, I continued to work those three jobs that summer—Foodland, Aina Haina Service Station and the Chinese restaurant. Then in September I went to the University of Hawaii. I did one semester and realized that there wasn't enough money for me to do my hot rods and everything else and go to school. I had to pay my way through so, after the first semester, I dropped out and applied for a better-paying job.

I went all over town applying and finally got one as a "dead-files clerk" at what was then called Home Insurance Company of Hawaii, which was where Bank of Hawaii is now at the corner of King and Bishop Streets. (Home Insurance later changed its name to First Insurance Co. of Hawaii.) Home Insurance's headquarters were all little buildings before the Financial Plaza was built.

A dead-files clerk filed the expired insurance policies that became dead files. I put them in boxes in an attic. I had to climb up a ladder and go into the ceiling, take up the files, and it was almost like an *ukupau* system—work 'til you're finished. I'd finish early, close the ceiling trapdoor and take my naps up there.

I was promoted to mail boy and worked hard. I got close to the guy who was building the company's new building, which still houses First Insurance at Thomas Square. I was a 19-year-old mailroom assistant in 1960 when they put me in charge of coordinating the move of all the crated boxes from downtown in pickup trucks.

I needed more money. My starting salary in 1959 was $195 a month, less than $50 a week. That still wasn't enough for my drag racing and hot rodding, so I cut a deal with the building manager to make extra money at night by washing the windows of the new building on Ward. I would go up on the catwalk every day after work and wash. It was like painting the Golden Gate Bridge. By the time I finished, the windows I had already washed would be dirty. It was a four-story building with just me washing, so when I finished, I would start all over again.

On the fourth floor was a company called Beam and Milici, an advertising agency run by Paul Beam and Ray Milici. While washing windows, I used to look in and watch these people and I was so fascinated by the artwork they drew. One of them was the late Tom Lee, who ultimately was the artist who designed the "helmet" logo we still use today at First Hawaiian. Small world.

> "I was Buster's assistant mechanic, helping change engines and carburetors. Once, an engine fell on him while we were working on his Ford. It's amazing that we all came through our small-kid times in one piece. I'm sure we had guardian angels."
>
> —sister Suzanne Dods Chong Kee

Jerry Beam, Paul's son, and I would get together for coffee and we became good friends. Ultimately, when I got to the bank, one of the conditions I asked for was to pick my own advertising agency. I picked Milici's firm based on my observation of them through the window, and Milici picked up one of the largest advertising accounts in Hawaii.

At First Insurance, I moved beyond office boy and started becoming an underwriter, learning how to underwrite automobile, fire, liability and personal insurance policies. My biggest break in my career came when I met an insurance agent named Richard Akamine, who told me, at my age of 20 or 21, "Hey, you've got to get off your ass and stop playing with your hot rod and grow up." I was a hard worker, but I had no ambitions of any kind. I needed money for my car and rent and stuff, but I didn't think past that.

Richard asked me to attend a Junior Chamber of Commerce meeting. At that point, the Jaycees were active in the community, doing community service, leadership, things I knew nothing about. Even simple things like learning Robert's Rules of Order, which helped me the rest of my life. I got *really* active in lots of community projects to the point I won an award for the Outstanding First-Year Jaycee for Hawaii. I was sent to the nationals. There were three of us picked for the whole country and I won the national award, called the SPOKE award: Service, Participation, Organization, Knowledge and Enthusiasm.

Being in the Jaycees and winning that award changed my life. It taught me about leadership and public speaking. I recognized for the first time in my life that I could be more than just an office boy.

I started to advance at First Insurance. I went through every underwriting department. I had to go door-to-door selling insurance. It was a great sales experience but miserable going through it. It forced me to cold-call on people—*very* difficult. I learned how to handle rejection.

At the same time, I was growing in the Jaycees. By the time I was 25, I was president of the Honolulu Jaycees. It was the largest chapter in Hawaii and I had won just about every award, which changed my outlook and created a desire to do more, do better.

We did the 50th State Fair and Miss Hawaii Pageant, which at that time was a big project. I also was chairman of a committee called the Nimitz Beautification Project in which we convinced all the landowners from the airport to downtown to pay voluntary assessments to plant the whole middle of Nimitz Highway with bougainvillea trees. It was beautiful at one point back in the early '60s.

That was my first taste of politics because we would compete against all the other chapters to run for statewide office. I had a mentor at Hawaiian Telephone Company named Joe Kiehm. We would compete against the Chinese Jaycees, the Japanese Jaycees, the Bayanihan Jaycees, Kaimuki Jaycees. Joe taught me how to count votes,

YES! A MEMOIR OF MODERN HAWAII

TIRE MARKS ON MY FOOT FOR A YEAR

Cartoon by Corky Trinidad.
Reprinted with permission of
Honolulu Star-Advertiser.

put coalitions together and win. I ended up being campaign manager for some of the fellows who then became statewide presidents of the Jaycees. Kind of funny that 50 years later I'd still be doing that kind of stuff.

That led to my first exposure to real politicians. I remember as president of the Jaycees taking a proclamation for the State Jaycees for some project to Iolani Palace and meeting Gov. Jack Burns for the first time. He said to me, "Are you Sergeant Dods' son?" I said, "Yes." He said, "I used to carry you when you were a little baby. I used to change your diapers!" He was embarrassing me in front of everybody. Burns had been a police captain, and my father's older brother, Chester, was a captain, too. Burns and Chester were very close.

Politics was different then, real grass roots. I remember the rallies in parks and on school grounds. Politicians would speak without microphones as neighborhood folks would gather 'round. The big thing for us kids was to collect the voting cards they'd hand out—a picture on the front and a few words on the back about their backgrounds. We used to collect them and bet—"match, no match"—with the cards. If two faces came out and you said "match," you won the other guy's voting card. The goal was to see who could get the most cards. We didn't understand the politics of it at all.

The first real campaign I worked on was for Mayor Neal Blaisdell. I got drafted into going to his house in Kaimuki to help. I don't remember if they were making yard signs, or whatever, but I was part of that. I did some door-to-door for Blaisdell when he was running for mayor. It's ironic that my first campaign was for a Republican, but he was like a Burns Republican. Burns and Blaisdell were really close and campaigned for each other across party lines.

And then, through the Jaycees, the second campaign I worked on was for Democrat Walter Heen, who ran against Patsy Mink for Congress in 1964. He didn't win, but I worked on that campaign going door to door, low-level grunt work.

I found I got a lot more satisfaction out of the community service than I did from selling insurance or underwriting. I was making decent money by then, but I didn't feel challenged or satisfied. I started working fewer and fewer hours. I didn't like it.

During that same time, I started going to night school at UH. When I got into the Jaycees, I began to realize that I needed a college education, so, along with my job and community work, I started going to night classes. I kept at it for years. When I say "night," I use the term loosely; sometimes it would be a 4 o'clock class and I'd cut out of work early. The company would reimburse me for that course if I passed it. It wasn't a well-thought-out plan, but I stuck with it and finally earned a bachelor's degree from UH in 1967—eight years after graduating from Saint Louis. My major was business with an emphasis on personnel and industrial relations. Why PIR? Nights didn't offer all the courses you need and you had to catch as catch can. PIR classes were the easier classes to sign up for at night.

TIRE MARKS ON MY FOOT FOR A YEAR

Yes, sigh, there was a time when I had hair.

I was at First Insurance during a time when young men were looking over their shoulders, worrying about the military draft. One guy who helped me was Ron Hashimoto, the chief underwriter for casualty, who said to me, "Hey, you better get your ass in gear or you're going to get drafted. I can get you in the National Guard." I ended up going to Lackland Air Force Base in San Antonio, Texas for basic training as an airman, then to Keesler Air Force Base in Biloxi, Mississippi for Radar Operators School. I became a "scope dope"—that was the name for radar operators.

You stood behind a Plexiglas wall and the radar operator would be on the radar machine looking at the plane, the blips, and he'd call signals and locations to you and you'd write it backward with a grease pen on the clear glass. I learned how to write and read backward and upside down, which came in handy over the years—being able to read someone else's memo across the table.

During the Cuban Missile Crisis in 1962, I got a call at First Insurance: "Grab your toothbrush and toilet kit and get your ass out to Kahuku." Up in the mountains there on the North Shore is a radar site in the hills right above Turtle Bay. We used to go there for military drills once a month, spend the whole weekend. We got there into the tunnel, with the Teletype coming across with the most extreme alerts. Soviet ships carrying missiles were sailing toward Cuba, and we were on duty as if the U.S. were going to war.

I was in the National Guard for three years but had to go all the way to Kahuku for drills, which was a pain at 4 o'clock in the morning. One time I fell asleep and sideswiped a telephone pole going out there because I had been out drag racing the night before.

In 1965, I heard the Dillingham Corporation was advertising for a community relations person. I applied and got the job. My boss, the head of PR and Advertising, was Norman Reyes, who before that had been anchor newscaster for KHON TV. He had a *great* voice. He was the man who broadcast around the world that Bataan had fallen in the early days of World War II. He was a Filipino lieutenant. His father had been a cabinet secretary to the president of the Philippines way back; his mother was a Jewish schoolteacher from Brooklyn.

Norman was captured by the Japanese, was forced on the Bataan Death March and ended up having to broadcast, under threat of death, propaganda from Tokyo Rose. He and I became close friends. Six months after I got to Dillingham, the advertising manager was fired and they put me in charge of advertising, which I knew nothing about other than looking through the window at Milici.

Meanwhile, I was getting tired of the hour-long drives to Kahuku. Norman Camara, who worked with me at First Insurance, was a captain in the Hawaii Army National Guard at Ft. Ruger, in the Public Information Detachment. He said, "Hey, I think I can get you transferred from the Air Guard to the Army Guard and I could use someone like you in public information." I said I'd love to. I was living in St. Louis Heights, and going to Ft. Ruger behind Diamond Head was way better than driving all the way out to Kahuku.

I never carried a rifle in my Army career (I made Spec. 5, the equivalent of buck sergeant), but I learned how to use a camera and write press releases. At the same time, I picked up the PR and press side in the Army National Guard and picked up the advertising side as ad manager for Dillingham.

Dillingham is a pretty remarkable story. The first part of the Dillingham corporate family was Oahu Railway & Land Company, which was founded in 1889 by Benjamin Franklin Dillingham. He had come to Hawaii in 1865 as a sailor, broke his leg while he was in port and never left town. With a franchise from King Kalakaua, Benjamin built a railroad that went from downtown out to Pearl Harbor in 1889, then eventually to Ewa and Wahiawa and up the Waianae Coast, along the North Shore and all the way to Kahuku. The railroad served sugar plantations that Dillingham had helped and provided access to developable land he had bought in west Oahu.

At first the idea was called "Dillingham's Folly." But he had the last laugh. The railroad worked for many years. Ironically, Dillingham's bank during his early years was the Bishop Bank, forerunner of First Hawaiian.

One of my first major projects at Dillingham was Ala Moana Center, Phase Two—the second half of Ala Moana Center. Most people today don't realize that that land used to be a swamp and a duck pond owned by Bishop Estate. The fact that it isn't a swamp any more owes a lot to the Dillinghams.

Ben and his son Walter borrowed $5,000 and built a dredge to start the Hawaiian Dredging & Construction Co. (Years later, the railroad and construction companies merged to create the Dillingham Corporation.) In 1912, Walter spent $25,000 to buy that swampy Ala Moana land from Bishop Estate. Over the years his company did a lot of dredging, including Pearl Harbor, Ala Moana Park and the Ala Wai Canal, using the ground-up coral they dredged up to fill their swampland at Ala Moana. I can remember it as a kid, just a mountain of coral piled high. No environmental impact statements were needed in those days, obviously.

It sat like that until the 1950s when Walter's son Lowell started thinking about using the land. He worked with Don Graham (head of Dillingham's development department) on a new concept—a "shopping center." Sears signed on as anchor tenant, and the open-air mall opened in 1959, just a few days before Hawaii became a state. The timing was perfect—Statehood, the growth of tourism, lots of parking for us locals.

> "When he was a teenager, my brother and a bunch of guys went hiking up behind Aina Haina. They got lost, and the police had to come and get them out of the mountains. The next day the paper had a story saying *'Policeman's Son Dods rescued from treacherous mountains.'* It was all the buzz at Saint Louis. Kind of embarrassing.
>
> "But being the good politician he was, Buster pointed to me and said, 'He's the one who got lost!' I never bothered to correct him."
>
> —*brother Bobby Dods*

Phase One ran from the old Sears to where the center stage and escalators are today. Phase Two in the 1960s went from there toward Waikiki down to the old J.C. Penney and Liberty House. They were working on Phase Two when I joined Dillingham, and we had to do a progress report monthly for Equitable Life Insurance Company, the lender who put up the money for it.

Dillingham Corporation was a huge success story here for a long time. But the old *kamaaina* never considered Dillingham to be part of the famous Big Five. (The Big Five, all with 19th-century roots in sugar, were Alexander & Baldwin, American Factors (later called Amfac), C. Brewer, Castle & Cooke, and Theo H. Davies—the financial and political powerhouses of the Territory of Hawaii.)

When I worked at Dillingham, I also did the advertising and marketing for the 1350 Ala Moana condo across from the shopping center, for the Arcadia retirement home and many other projects that Dillingham built in Waikiki and around the state. They were very big condominium and shopping center developers. They would develop the projects and then Hawaiian Dredging, the construction arm, would build them.

When Jack Burns was elected governor in 1962, the Dillinghams were Republican all the way. They and the whole business community were frightened of Burns. They thought because he was supported by the ILWU, he was communist-leaning in an anti-communist era.

Shortly after being elected, Burns called up Lowell Dillingham for an appointment and they wouldn't give him one. So one day Burns, as sitting governor, drove to Dillingham's headquarters, 1441 Ala Moana, went up to Lowell's office, and the secretary said: "I'm sorry, Mr. Dillingham isn't in and he's very busy with scheduled appointments all day." Burns said, "That's fine, I'll just wait here until he will see me."

And Governor Burns sat outside Lowell's office and waited and waited—I wasn't at Dillingham yet, but I've heard the story many times—it was legendary at Dillingham. After he waited for several hours, they finally did meet and eventually became close friends. It paid off later when the Community Chest—the forerunner of Aloha United Way—was in big trouble, failing in every way. Lowell Dillingham's most bitter enemy in Hawaii was Jack Hall, head of the Hawaii ILWU, which represented dockworkers and plantation workers. But Burns got Dillingham and Hall together and revived the Community Chest. Then the governor and Lowell became *really* good friends.

During the period I was at Dillingham, they were lobbying for putting condominiums on Magic Island off Ala Moana Park and on a second peninsula to be built on more reclaimed reef lands at the Kewalo Basin end of the park. They had a scale model of all these high-rise condominiums and they went to see Governor Burns at Washington Place late one night. I know because I was there as a kid who was in charge of getting the model to the meeting. I was just a fly on the wall.

The *quid pro quo* would be that Dillingham owned most of the Honolulu waterfront, all the piers, and would agree to sell that land to the State of Hawaii. In exchange, Dillingham would get several parcels of state land. That swap was announced by Burns in 1967. However, the key part of the swap was Burns' agreement to lobby for legislative approval for Dillingham to develop high-rises on a second peninsula to be built offshore at the ewa end Ala Moana Park.

Governor Burns, on the last night of the 1969 Legislature, pushed through a resolution that would have allowed that kind of offshore development at Ala Moana, a major controversy at the time. There was an issue about whether the measure legally passed before the Legislature adjourned at midnight, with Burns lurking in the wings in the Capitol basement ready to extend the session if he had to. After that session ended, there was a public uproar about the proposal: Local people felt their Ala Moana Beach was being taken away. The state was never able to deliver on Burns' promise, and the following year the Legislature repealed that development authorization, so Magic Island remains a park and the second peninsula never was built.

All these years later, Howard Hughes Corporation is sort of doing some of that same kind of development, but on the mauka side of Ala Moana Boulevard.

By the late 1960s, I had advanced at Dillingham and started to have ambitions to make something of myself. Dillingham was run by engineers, and I was never going to go much beyond where I was. One weekend I went to a barbeque at the home of Patt Patterson, an old PR guy in town. He told me that First National Bank of Hawaii was looking for a director of advertising and PR. I decided to apply.

Early in my career, we ran a cowboy-based advertising campaign with the slogan, "Take us for all we've got." We showed actor Andy Devine and a bunch of Hollywood cowboys actually riding up Bishop Street and entering the bank lobby. It was an expensive but short-lived campaign. Bellinger hated it. Somehow, however, I managed to coax him into wearing Western garb for this photo for our in-house employee newspaper. Left to right are Senior VP Harry Hutaff, Bellinger, Senior VP Hugh Pingree and me.

CHAPTER 3

Saying "Yes" to a Career in Banking

I didn't have to think too long before I decided to apply for the job at the bank, but first I did my homework. I asked newspaper guys I knew for their opinions about the bank. Even when I was a young kid at Dillingham, I knew it was important to be close to reporters. Local media people put on a roast called the Gridiron Show and I was involved. If you look at the old Gridiron programs, I'm listed as the "Executive Curtain Puller." I couldn't sing or dance, but I pulled the curtain.

So those days I was close to a lot of reporters. I enjoyed hanging out with them in my early days in PR. They were generally smart and serious about their work and fun to be around. But some were so bad. One in particular, a guy from the Mainland who worked here briefly decades ago, used to give me the yellow sheets that reporters would turn in to the City Desk. I would write the story and he'd turn it in to be printed in the paper just as I wrote it.

One night I invited some Gridiron Show people up to my bachelor apartment at 1717 Ala Wai for drinks. I always kept the curtains open because the view was beautiful, but they closed them. All of a sudden I smelled this strange odor. It was the first time in my life I'd ever seen pot. My dad was a cop and I had not been brought up that way. I thought I was going to lose my job, get arrested and thrown out of the building. Half the press in this town was smoking *pakalolo* in my apartment.

Despite that, I asked my reporter-friends about the bank's reputation, and they were very frank. The bank's PR guy was a retired Marine whose attitude toward the press was, "Now hear this! I'm making an announcement." All the reporters disliked the bank because of him.

My first job interview was with Larry Ronson, head of First National Bank's Marketing Division. We hit it off well, and he wanted me to meet Johnny Bellinger. He wasn't president yet but was already a power at the bank, though I didn't know that when I went to meet him. Mr. Bellinger was pretty proud of his bank.

The interview was going fairly well until he asked how I felt about the bank. Not realizing how powerful he was, I said, "Well, from my research, the bank's image stinks." He was taken aback. I explained to him that business reporters didn't feel he was receptive, they couldn't get comments out of the bank, and the bank had a lousy reputation among the media. Mr. Bellinger was surprised but asked me what I would do about it. I said, "One thing I would want to be able to do is pick my own advertising agency." That was very important because I needed to dramatically turn around the advertising and PR, to become more open, more cooperative, and let the public know what bankers really do. He said I could do that.

"Doyle Dane Bernbach, the worldwide advertising agency, bought Milici Valenti in 1972, but Ray Milici and Frank Valenti stayed on to run it until the early 1990s. After Frank died in 1993, DDB was shopping around, trying to sell the agency, without letting the local staff know. When we did find out, I went to see Walter to see if he could help me buy it to keep it in local hands. He said, 'If you're going to try it, I will help you.' He felt local guys could do it better and be more community-spirited.

"DDB thought they could sell the agency and the accounts; besides First Hawaiian, we also had Aloha Airlines, Hawaii Visitors Bureau and other key clients. Behind the scenes, Walt made sure DDB understood that he could take First Hawaiian's business wherever he wanted. In the end, with his help, I was able to buy the agency in 1994. I took a chance because I had Walter behind me. I felt if I had Walter behind me, how could I fail? That's why his picture is on the Hall of Fame wall in our office."

—*Nick Ng Pack, president & CEO, Milici Valenti Ng Pack*

Finally, with a little twinkle in his eye, Mr. Bellinger asked me how much I wanted. I asked for the stupendous sum of $800 a month, which I thought was really out of the park. My goal was to make $10,000 a year at some point of my life, which would have been $833.33 a month. To my surprise he said, "OK, when can you start?" I said, "Two weeks." He shook my hand and I thought I had the job.

I went back to Dillingham to give notice, and they told me, "Executives don't give two weeks' notice. You have to stay six months until you finish our annual report." All of a sudden I'm an executive, at $600 a month. I was young and felt I had to honor that obligation. I went back to see Mr. Bellinger to tell him I couldn't take the job. I didn't know a person had rights. He said, "You stick it out. Show them you're a bigger man and we'll keep the job open for you." That's what happened. I finished the annual report and came to the bank on December 23rd, the eve of Christmas Eve in 1968.

The company was in the process of changing its name to First Hawaiian Bank and becoming a state-chartered institution, so we had to get all these signs up at the branches, launch new ad campaigns. I came right in the middle of that change.

The thing I asked for when I accepted the job—pick my own advertising agency—was granted. I selected Milici Valenti, run by Ray Milici and Frank Valenti, based on my time as a window washer at First Insurance and watching them through the windows and later getting to know the people there. At the time it was one of the largest advertising accounts in Hawaii. It was a coup for them and a coup for me to be able to bring in my own team, and they still do the bank's advertising—today they're called Milici Valenti Ng Pack.

We went on an innovation spurt like nothing the local banking community had ever seen. We introduced Master Charge to Hawaii—it's called Master Card today. We improved it the next year by putting your picture on the back —the *photo card*, we called

Trying out an early ATM machine at a Mainland conference. People were a little afraid to use ATMs, but they eventually caught on.

> "We at First Hawaiian Bank believe deeply in the power of yes. We said yes in 1858 and became Hawaii's first kamaaina bank. And we haven't stopped saying yes yet. To banking innovations. To new conveniences. To you. There's no time like now for a bank that says yes."
>
> —1969 newspaper ad launching "The Bank That Says Yes."

it. It's more expensive to do, but I felt it would cut fraud, and time proved it. We had the lowest rate of fraud of any major bank in America. My theory has always been that if a thief steals a wallet, he looks through the cards and throws away the one with the picture because that's harder to use. To this day we still have the photo. That was one of my early marketing campaigns. Over the years, that has worked out very, very well for us. First Hawaiian has dramatically low fraud losses compared to the industry.

My first year we also invented the PayAnyDay loan, a revolutionary concept in 1969. At that time, you had block interest, so you had a fixed due date on loans. We had a genius named Don Jensen, vice president of Consumer Lending, who came up with a way of creating simple interest so you could pay any day of the month and your loan would be on time. If you paid earlier in the month, more would go toward your principal; later in the month, more would go to interest. In those days, car loans were either 36 months or 48; with PayAnyDay it could be 43, 47, whatever—all through programming. It became an instant hit in the community. We copyrighted and sold that name to other banks across the country. We made a lot of money on it over the years.

We introduced Hawaii's first ATM in 1972 and gave it a personality—we called it OTTO, for automatic teller—and won national awards for the OTTO media campaign in the Bank Marketing Association.

The Surf Check was another innovation that seems old hat today. Before that, all bank checks had a plain background. We had a TV commercial showing a surfer coming in on a big wave and it ended with a freeze frame. That freeze frame became the picture on the Surf Check. We did a lot of *firsts* in the country, including the first animated commercials in Hawaii's history. We had an animated character walking down the street, and stars and rainbows would come flying out.

The innovation I was most proud of was to be involved in creating the campaign that says, "The Bank That Says Yes!" Tom Baird from the Milici agency came up with it in 1969, and I worked with him to put the campaign together. The loan guys at the bank signed a petition to try to get me fired because they thought it was outrageous for a bank to claim to say "Yes." I was trying to create a philosophy and change the attitude of the bank, though it's obvious you can't always say "yes." (There are credit restrictions, for example.) The biggest problem any advertising or PR man or woman has is access to the top. In a lot of companies PR people are buried under layers of people, and ideas get watered down. If "The Bank That Says Yes" had gone through a committee before it got to Bellinger, the slogan would have been "Give Us the Possible Chance of Maybe Saying Yes." Yet, I sold Bellinger on the idea, and he overruled all the naysayers.

Early on in my banking career, we did a lot of things in marketing, which got me noticed by Bellinger. He became my biggest supporter. It wasn't long before I was reporting directly to him, and he kept promoting me. I came in as a non-officer as 1968 was coming to an end, as director of Marketing and PR. Within six months I became marketing officer, six months after that I became assistant vice president, and by the end of my second year I was vice president. I was senior vice president at the age of 32, and two years after that I was executive vice president and still just 34. I was only handling marketing and PR at that point.

The first thing I did outside of marketing was to take over the Economic Research Department, which was not really banking, but it helped me understand the economics of the community. It was run by a real classy guy, economist Dr. Tom Hitch. He was a senior VP, I was still just a VP, and he reported to me, which was a little awkward. I was a young Turk and he was the *dean of economists,* but he and I got along well.

In 1977 I set out to create the First Hawaiian Auto Show. All the car dealers fought me initially because they pretty much controlled the industry, so you couldn't buy or look at cars outside of their dealerships. At first I couldn't get the dealers to participate, but Bellinger backed me and I put my *cojones* on the line and announced the car show in a full-page newspaper ad even though it was all bluff—we didn't have dealers signed up yet.

I finally got one dealer, Alex Silan at Schuman Carriage, to go with me. Once we got the first one, Jimmy Pflueger came on board even though he was a little nervous. That first year we had half the dealers, and

"Back in 1973 when Walt was still in marketing, he helped me defuse a situation with our boss, Johnny Bellinger. I was at the Hilo Branch, and Mr. Bellinger wanted me to come back to Honolulu to be in charge of branch loans. In the tension of the moment, I foolishly said yes right away and the transfer was publicly announced. I caught heck from my wife, Jeanette, because she was a Hilo girl and our little boy was just starting to go to school there.

"I had second thoughts about leaving the Big Island, so I went to see Bill McKenzie, the old Scotsman who ran Hilo Electric Light Co. I said, 'Bill, I'm thinking of telling Mr. Bellinger I'm changing my mind and I'll probably be fired. Is there anything I can do at Hilo Electric?' He said, 'We have an opening for a No. 2 man.' I didn't know anything about electrical companies, but I had that in my back pocket and went back to Honolulu to see Johnny. Surprisingly he didn't throw me out the window or curse at me. He just said, 'All right, Hoag, we'll undo it.' And that was a problem because he had already named a replacement.

"Walter came over and talked to the press about how the bank said 'Yes' to me staying in Hilo because we have a big heart. By the time he finished his PR magic, there was an editorial in the Hilo paper praising the bank for 'putting human feelings and community concerns ahead of cold corporate considerations.'"

—*Jack Hoag, retired First Hawaiian Bank president*

over 100,000 people showed at Blaisdell Center. By the second year, we had every dealer. It remains a staple for the bank to this day, and we are now the No. 1 bank in auto lending.

At that point, Johnny hired Kennedy Randall from Bankers Trust in New York to run all lending at First Hawaiian. He and Johnny, over the years with the American Bankers Association, had become good friends. Randall would call on Hawaii, meeting with our bank, with Bank of Hawaii, with people like Chinn Ho. That's how he got known in this marketplace. He was the consummate New York corporate banker. He looked the part—a portly, silver-haired haole in starched white shirts, though he adapted to aloha shirts pretty quickly. He liked steak dinners, wine, cigars and entertaining CEOs of major corporations.

To him, consumer lending was a nuisance. I clearly remember asking him one day if he'd give me a shot at running the consumer lending part of the bank because it was neglected. I saw from the car show that, with the right products and right team, I could actually change market share. He said, "Help yourself." He gave me the consumer banking side, and I looked at that as an opportunity, kind of a hidden gem, in the bank.

First, I tried to tackle car loans. Nobody in the bank wanted the car business because we were doing so poorly at it. I remember we had 13 percent of the car market and Bank of Hawaii had 58 percent. I brought in some new people, and working together we created the Dealer Center, the first of its kind in Hawaii. It was a way to have a car salesman cut a deal with the consumer, then electronically, using a big phone that would work like a fax, transmit the loan application to First Hawaiian. This was long before the Internet. We would do a quick credit check on the buyer and turn it around in an hour or two. We ultimately got loan approval down to minutes. The money would go directly to the dealer, and the commission would go to the salesman. All of this was unheard of, and dealers, one by one, fell in love with it. Pretty soon, First Hawaiian became the dominant car lender among Hawaii banks, which we are to this day.

Also part of consumer lending was the credit card business, which was completely remaking the world of retailing. Fifty years ago, there weren't all-purpose credit cards. If people had any cards at all, and most people had none, the cards were issued by individual retailers—Sears, Liberty House, like that. It wasn't efficient. Then Bank of America, which was then based in California, created BankAmericard, which later became Visa. BankAmericard struggled at first, with a lot of delinquent accounts, but then it took hold. Federal laws prohibited banks from operating across state lines in most cases, so Bank of America couldn't expand its cards on its own. In the late 1960s, it started licensing the BankAmericard system to other banks across the country, including Bank of Hawaii.

Around the same time, other California banks set up a competing card system called Master Charge, and First Hawaiian picked up that brand. It was a very small market at the beginning, but its advantages became clear right away to both merchants and consumers. Before credit cards, merchants had to run their own in-house financing plans, which meant they were taking on credit risk, or they would accept your personal check to buy something. Merchants today criticize the commission they pay to banks for processing card transactions, but back then they lost tremendous amounts of money taking bad checks.

With a credit card, the bank would take all the risks of losses out of the merchant's hands in return for a commission. All of a sudden, the merchant didn't have to finance his customers. He said, "Whoa, I give up 2 percent and I get the $2,000 price of the refrigerator *now* instead of from the customer over two years. I'll take it." It took off, locally as well as nationally.

In addition, the consumer got an instant consumer loan rather than having to pay cash. If you were going to buy a $2,000 refrigerator and only had $300 in your checking account, you could charge it and pay it off over time without the hassle of loan documentation for either the consumer or the bank. Every time you put a regular consumer loan together, it cost the bank $50 to $200 in paperwork to create the loan documents, whereas credit cards were, in effect, instant electronic loans. If you didn't want to pay interest, you could pay it off in cash within 30 days and it would be free to you.

The startup for First Hawaiian was hard because Bank of Hawaii had been first in the market with BankAmericard, so we had trouble getting a critical mass of merchants to accept our Master Charge cards. It's like the chicken or the egg—the merchant says: "Why should I take your card when you don't have any customers?" And the customers were saying: "Why should I take your card when you don't have any merchants?"

Glenn Kaya, who was president of GEM stores in Hawaii at the time, saved us at the start. He was a close friend of Bellinger's and he did something unheard of. At that time, GEM was what Costco is today—the *big bear* in town among discount stores. Bellinger called me up one day and said, "See Glenn Kaya. He's going to cut us a special deal." Glenn announced that GEM stores would carry only Master Card, not BankAmericard, which was bigger at the time. And *that* was a breakthrough for our bank to have a big merchant who was carrying our card. Glenn took a lot of gas for that, especially from the competition. But he did it because of his

> "I first met Walt at a party Johnny Bellinger threw at the Willows for bank customers. I came out and there was this young kid—he had hair then—helping bring up the valet-parked cars so people wouldn't have to wait. He ran and got my car and, trying to impress him, I reached in my pocket and gave him $2, which he declined. Years later I told him, 'If I knew you were going to be chairman, I would have tipped you more.'"
>
> —*Glenn Kaya, former First Hawaiian Bank director*

love for Johnny. It's those personal relationships that build companies. He stuck it out there. Later, when we had gotten firmly into the market, he accepted BankAmericard again.

In the late 1970s, when Kennedy Randall got sick, I ended up taking over all of lending and increasingly taking on other responsibilities. By 1981, Johnny put me in charge of something called General Banking, which included all 46 branches. That was a big step up because I was responsible for all the loans in the branches, the operations, the deposits. Branches are the heart and soul of any community bank like First Hawaiian.

People sometimes think of the bank as the big building downtown, but your customers are all out at the branches. First Hawaiian Bank today has over $15 billion in deposits; less than $3 billion is in the downtown headquarters. Hawaii is really a small business community financially.

Philosophically, I felt that every branch manager was the president of the bank in his or her local community. They were the go-to people for community service work. These days, investment bankers on Wall Street are the bad guys. But community bankers always had a very good reputation, here and around the country. They'd head up the local Aloha United Way drives, the PTAs, local nonprofit boards. Community service like that was always part of the job description in *our* bank. Part of our DNA. We expected you to be a community leader, not just a community banker. It was easy to have it happen because, in a local neighborhood, people looked to the banker. A lot of it has to do with finance. They will want someone to help figure out the budget for the PTA or advice for building a local community swimming pool. Ultimately the banker would end up as treasurer of a lot of community organizations and some political campaigns. They became key players. I know nationally from traveling across the country as the American Bankers Association president that small-town bankers fill that role everywhere. They make the loans, do the mortgages and get kids off to college with student loans. The branches to this day are the heart and soul of First Hawaiian.

Lois Tojio has been running our Aina Haina branch *forever*, and she is Ms. Aina Haina. Any merchant, anybody who banks there, will tell you, "I don't make a

> "In 1981, I had worked on the Mainland for 10 years and was coming back. I had accepted a job in lending—which was my background—at Bank of Hawaii. Then a friend at First Hawaiian talked me into interviewing for an opening in marketing. I was surprised when Walt, who was head of all Retail Banking, took the time to talk to me. He was an executive with a human side, and I thought it would be fun to work for a company like that. So I gave notice to Bankoh without ever starting there.
>
> "Walt hired me because I was a local girl. I graduated from Roosevelt and UH and was coming home. He wants local people to succeed. Later, when I took over the bank's charitable foundation, he asked me to start using my middle name—Shiroma—so people would know I'm local."
>
> —Sharon Shiroma Brown, president, First Hawaiian Bank Foundation

move without talking to Lois." There are those kinds of bankers throughout Hawaii. Jack Hoag was one in Hilo and ultimately became bank president. Johnny Bellinger was a banker like that in Waimea, Kauai. We have a history of many of our community managers rising all the way to the top. Our current CEO, Bob Harrison, was manager of our Kapiolani Branch.

In those days everything was done out in the branches—counting the cash, proofing (sorting checks and typing in amounts on magnetic ink), key punching. All the back-of-the-shop functions were done by the branches. Over the years it became more centralized. The bank always had, to this day, lots of parking, good facilities and that caring, friendly aloha spirit.

Once I started moving up the ranks, I was able to argue for bringing a marketing, consumer-oriented focus to banking decisions. For example, in 1986, the other local banks dropped their savings interest rate to 5 percent and we kept it at 5.5 percent for a long time. That was one of the most important decisions I made in my banking career. First Hawaiian had always had a much smaller share of market than Bank of Hawaii in savings deposits. Under normal circumstances it would have taken forever to catch them even if we grew at a faster rate.

I made an emotional plea to the bank that this was a one-time opportunity to try to change market share, which is *very* hard to do. I said, "We are going to pay a price by paying a little more interest, but I think we can move accounts." The investment side of the bank fought me because clearly that was going to cost us money. As a marketing guy, I felt you rarely have this kind of window. Bellinger backed me and we fundamentally changed the deposit market share between the banks. People closed their accounts and brought them to us for half a percent. By keeping the interest rate at 5.5 percent for 18 months, we doubled the amount of passbook savings deposits to $471 million. Ultimately the rates evened out again, but in the meantime we had significantly moved market share from our major competitor.

As a result of that experience, when I became CEO I always insisted that there be somebody representing the consumer on those committees that set interest rates for deposits and certificates of deposit. Sure, you have to be profitable or you are not going to be in business, but you have to be sure that it is not purely a decision focusing on short-term profits. The investment side may win most of the arguments, but I always wanted somebody to represent the customer's side in those debates to say, "Hey, this is crossing the line with the customers."

> "In 2004, Walt set up a 10-day trip to Paris for me to meet everybody from the president of BNP Paribas on down. Walt said, 'I think it would be a good idea for your career.' It was awkward because I was still manager at the Kapiolani Branch, and in Paris it was like 'Why are you here?' Walter and Don Horner thought of it as a good way to get to know the BNP group."
>
> —*Bob Harrison, chairman & CEO, First Hawaiian Bank*

> "We used to rent Walt's house on the Kona Coast for several years. It was at the bottom of the real estate market and he said to me a half-dozen times: 'I don't even want to make any money on this house. It cost me a million and a half to buy the land and build it and I just want to get a million and a half out of it.' At that point the house was worth maybe $900,000.
>
> "We really liked the house. It was within walking distance of Mauna Lani Beach—a nice, safe beach for our small grandchildren. My wife Barbara said to me one day, 'Let's offer him a million and buy it.' And I said, 'If we offer him a million dollars after what he said to me, I'll lose a friend for life.' A little later Walt called me and said he was being foolish in wanting to get his money back, so he took $900,000 for it and had to take back some paper to sell it even at that price. I raced over to Oahu and told him Barbara and I were willing to pay more, but it was too late. I don't think I ever told Barbara the whole story."
>
> —Dick Rosenberg, retired chairman & CEO, Bank of America

That was the start of making marketing more central to the bank itself, and that voice is certainly heard now. In the old days, marketing wasn't considered really banking. At the time I became CEO, Dick Rosenberg, head of Bank of America, and I were the only two guys out of 10,000 bank CEOs who came up the marketing route. Most CEOs came up from either finance or loans, with a few from operations.

Rosenberg took a shine to me, we became friends, and then he pushed me for the Bank Marketing Association Board, a national board that catapulted me into visibility with banks around the country. Dick is one of my mentors and to this day a dear friend.

First Hawaiian was always on the cutting edge with computers. There was a great guy named George Hata who had gone to Mid-Pacific Institute. He'd been accepted to a lot of Mainland colleges and probably could have gone to Harvard, but his parents told him they couldn't afford it and there was no reason why he shouldn't just go to the University of Hawaii. He was a math guy who became the father of our computer system, started it from scratch with Bellinger. In the 1960s, all the state election tabulations were done from First National Bank's computer center on the sixth floor of our old headquarters at Bishop and King. There was a classic picture of Tom Gill and Jack Burns—bitter rivals—sitting on a bench on election night outside the bank computer room refusing to speak to each other while waiting for the election results to come in off our computers.

George, who had put all that together, later became ill, and I ended up having to run all the computer operations, too. That's the period I went through severe 24-hour headaches for one whole year. I couldn't figure out what was wrong—I thought I had cancer of the brain. I went to doctors everywhere. One day I went to a local doctor for a physical, and he said, "Look, I know you are going to be upset, but just try this." And he gave me a tranquilizer, and after 24 hours the headaches were gone after one year of 'round-the-clock pain. It was stress!

One of the causes of stress was my mentor and biggest supporter, my boss, Johnny Bellinger, a great mentor but a hard man to work for at times. Actually, it was only because of an odd sequence of events that Johnny *was* my boss. At the time I joined the bank in 1968, Johnny was executive vice president, the only one with that rank, and was in line to become president. In fact, he was named to the job two months after I was hired when his predecessor, Dan Dorman, became chairman and CEO.

But for a quirk of fate a year earlier, Johnny might never have gotten the top job. The man who preceded him as executive VP and who seemed to be next in line behind Dorman, was involved in a mysterious incident in his home in which he was assaulted. Following that, out of the blue the bank announced that the man had "elected early retirement" for health reasons.

Three weeks later, Johnny was promoted into the new retiree's executive VP slot, the only one who held that rank, and Johnny went on to get the top job in 1969. But for that odd series of events, Johnny wouldn't have been in a position to help me so much during my career, and I might never have become a CEO myself. To be sure, Johnny Bellinger was the key reason I had the chance to climb the ladder at First Hawaiian.

John D. Bellinger was at times a tyrant, but had a huge Hawaiian heart. He was critical to my career.

CHAPTER 4

Oh, Johnny!
The Bellinger Years

"You need a godfather in life, and Walt had one in Johnny Bellinger."
John K. (Jack) Tsui, retired First Hawaiian Bank president

"Johnny Bellinger was hard but fair. People would criticize him for yelling and screaming at people but, when he did yell at you, it was because you did something wrong. Once he got it off his chest, he was the kindest person around."
Howard Karr, retired First Hawaiian vice chairman & CFO

Every Christmas, John Bellinger—CEO of First Hawaiian from 1969 to 1989—would go around all the islands and tour the branches to wish everybody Merry Christmas and to inspect everything. A few of us would go with him. If there was a piece of Scotch tape on a counter, he'd notice it. We spent all this money taking every weed out of every flowerbed at all 60 branches, repainting, resanding, repolishing.

We went to one branch on Kauai, and Bellinger was proud of his friend, the manager, because he was a Kauai guy. Johnny asked how things were going, and the manager says, "Oh, the branch is great, except the lobby feels dark." We're all frightened to death. You never said something like that because Bellinger designed and supervised the building of every branch that came up in his era.

He looks up and all the lights are burned out in the ceiling, probably been out for years. He grabs the manager by the neck—the customers are right there, waiting in line. Johnny lifts this short AJA guy up off the floor and starts screaming at him. This guy's legs are just thrashing, and Bellinger says, "Change the lights, you stupid jerk!" The customers are howling. That was typical Bellinger. But then, he'd be fine the next day.

Johnny was a take-no-prisoners kind of guy, but very emotional, generous, with a big Hawaiian heart. If he loved you, he would do anything for you. But also, he was "My way or the highway!" His style was right for his time.

He blustered, threatened and yelled. Sometimes he'd fire people, only to take it back later. I got yelled at plenty of times. I never got fired, but I was tempted to quit more than once. I'd come home and tell my wife, Diane, "I got to leave." I'd count my pennies and say, "We can get by for this many months without the job." I learned a lot from him, too.

The first time I met him, I had never heard of him, but I soon realized he was pretty powerful. He was an executive vice president when he interviewed me for my first bank job, but within a few months he was promoted to president. His personality, which was larger than life, dominated First Hawaiian Bank until the day he died. The bank on the whole was a pretty casual place to work, but everybody called him "Mr. Bellinger."

I think Johnny was the first part-Hawaiian to be CEO of a major company in town. When he was at Roosevelt High School, he was an all-star track and football player. He was the only football player in Island history, probably to this day, who was an end who called plays. That tells you a lot about him. For the rest of his life, he never stopped calling the plays. He and his wife, Joan, were high school sweethearts. She was a song leader; he was the colonel in the ROTC.

Bellinger started at the bank as a $115-a-month teller right out of high school. When World War II came, he was drafted and worked on military payroll at the bank's office at Fort Shafter. After the war he came back and worked at the bank until he died—47 years. He was just a high school graduate from Kaimuki who worked his way up; very ambitious, aggressive, willing to work hard. His big break was becoming manager of a little branch in Waimea, Kauai. To the day he died, he had friends on Kauai based on this.

Bellinger went out of his way to give local kids a chance—including me. More than that, he made sure they had a better chance than everyone else. He was a one-man affirmative action program. To this day, if you take a look at senior management at First Hawaiian compared to our competitor, you'd be shocked. Of the top 15 management people at First Hawaiian, all but one or two are local.

Even after he had made it big, he was pretty much shunned by the Big Five because he wouldn't fall in line. He was *always* an outlier in that group. They couldn't control him because he was always independent and would march to his own drummer. They never liked that.

Even when they started the Hawaii Community Foundation, they didn't invite Bellinger. They asked the trust departments of the banks to ask their clients to be the start of the foundation and tried to get Bellinger to just go in and do it their way. He said no, and we were never part of it initially. When I became CEO, I said

> "Johnny was clear about his authority. 'You want me to run this bank, I run the bank. Don't tell me what to do.' That can lead to an imperial CEO where they can do anything they want and nobody has oversight. Johnny would never have survived in today's corporate world. He would go nuts. Neither would Bobby Pfeiffer or any of the old-time guys."
>
> —attorney Jeff Watanabe

the community needed to have one community foundation. I smoked the peace pipe with them and put it together.

Johnny was the first guy to push local Asians into membership at Waialae Country Club, mostly Americans of Japanese ancestry. To get them into Waialae, he had to fight some of the Big Five leaders. Johnny was chairman of the club's membership committee and was trying to put local people through. One of the Big Five's CEOs was president, and they froze all the local applications. Johnny said, "OK, two can play this game." The CEO had some WASP that he wanted to get into Waialae who had to go through the membership committee. Bellinger sat on it; he wouldn't let *any* names come out of the committee. Finally the Big Five man went to see Johnny and said, "Hey, I really want to get this guy in." Bellinger said, "Fine, we'll zip him right through as soon as you open up opportunities for locals as well." That's how more local guys got into Waialae.

One guy who had been turned down a couple times was Wally Fujiyama, the well-known attorney. Bellinger got Wally into Waialae later on, which kind of split the club in half because a lot of the lawyers who had been on the opposite side of legal cases with Wally hated him. Wally, later in life, said that Johnny Bellinger had kind of legitimized him. Bellinger put him on the bank board, too. Prior to that, Wally was a successful renegade but never had downtown respectability or credibility until Bellinger.

He had worked his way up the operations side, mostly focused on internal matters within the bank, and was very good at it. Until I got there, he hadn't had an external focus. He relied on me for a lot of external things. I think that was the first part of our relationship. I was able to translate the image of the bank into a positive one. "The Bank That Says Yes," which I put together, brought up

> "Both Mr. Bellinger and Walt were role models for me. Johnny operated more on instinct; Walt was more of a relationship person. Both of them loved the bank and its people. One way that Johnny tested people was screaming at them. I think he admired you if you stood your ground, and Walt would hold his ground in a very diplomatic way. Walt would protect his people. If Johnny was screaming about someone, Walt would step up and take the bullet. That's one reason the troops gravitated around him.

> "John's strong suit wasn't marketing. First Hawaiian had been No. 1 and slipped to No. 2 because Bank of Hawaii became a marketing bank where they actually picked up the phone to call and ask for business. We were still waiting for the phone to ring. Walt introduced the concept of marketing to First Hawaiian Bank.

> "I think Mr. Bellinger saw Walter as the future, someone who complemented him in marketing, public relations, branding, as well as banking in general. He did things Mr. Bellinger probably didn't want to do. Johnny did not want to talk to reporters."

—*Don Horner,*
retired chairman & CEO,
First Hawaiian Bank

> "The bank's financial results spoke a lot about John Bellinger's leadership. First Hawaiian was doing well, and he was the man in charge, so I respected his ability. The year he died was the 25th consecutive year of record earnings for First Hawaiian Bank. There was only one other bank in the United States that had a streak that long at the time."
>
> —Kit Smith, *former* Honolulu Advertiser *business editor*

Bellinger's prestige as well. That, and the fact I got him more involved in the community.

Also, we had a big age difference. I was never a threat to him where some of the other guys around his age early on might have been. I would tell him things that nobody else would because I was dumb enough at the time to give him honest opinions when he asked. Everyone else would not tell him anything other than, "Yes, Johnny." We developed a trust.

Within the bank, he was known for his terrible temper. About eight of us senior managers met in his office daily, and we formed an *incredible* bond of closeness because every day somebody was going to get his ass chewed in a violent manner. We'd think, *There but for the Grace of God go I!* Each of us would have sympathy for the guy being shot at, so we'd cover for each other. Besides myself, the others were Hugh Pingree, the president before me; Ken Bentley, who was our operations guy; chief financial officer Howard Karr; and George Hata, the computer man. Philip Ching, who ran Trust, regularly got chewed out. Later on, toward the end, Don Horner, who eventually succeeded me as CEO, was part of the group.

Johnny would lose his temper *badly*, but then later on he'd feel bad about it. He'd never say sorry but would find a way to make it up to his target. To give you an idea how dominant he was, if he called you, you'd better be in his office in 30 seconds. He had wired all the phones so it was a direct line, not a ringing but a *ding dong*, so the whole floor could hear. Secretaries would go running around, "Mr. Dods, Mr. Dods, Mr. Bellinger is trying to reach you!" *Every day*.

If you weren't in your office when he called, they'd find you and he'd want you, *right now*. I remember Don Daly, who was in charge of all the branch properties, went to the Mainland, and something went wrong with the sprinkler system at one branch. Bellinger called and got him as he got off the plane and said, "Get your ass back here!" He had to turn right around and get the next plane back.

Johnny loved his *poi*, had to have it every night at dinner. We were on Maui at dinner with customers one night, and Bellinger says to Roger MacArthur, bank manager for the island, "Where's my poi?" Roger said, "Johnny, don't worry. It's coming." A little while later he says, "Where's my poi?" Roger said, "Johnny, it's coming." I took Roger to the bathroom and said, "Roger, your whole career is on the line; find that poi NOW!" The poi went to some other banquet. Roger didn't get a raise for a while.

That was the bad side of him. The good side was he had a big heart. If somebody had personal problems, he'd be the first one there to help them, be with them, visit them in the hospital. We had a real good employee who was in the Army Reserve. He went for his annual training, and after receiving immunizations he became paralyzed. Johnny kept him on full pay for almost two years until he was able to come back to work in a wheelchair. Several times we had Neighbor Island employees who had family hospitalized in Honolulu. When they were released, Johnny had them flown home in the bank jet. There was a teller whose eyesight deteriorated due to diabetes; he moved her to a switchboard job with a specially modified work station so she could continue to work. Another employee couple had a son being treated on the Mainland for a life-threatening illness. Johnny gave them several months off with pay to be with their son.

So Johnny had that big, big heart to go with his short fuse. He was an interesting human being who had a lot of wonderful qualities.

He *loved* to play cribbage, and one of my smarter career moves was to say, "I don't know how to play cribbage." As a result I never got drawn into the card game. He'd play in the corporate dining room on the 19th floor of our old headquarters every day he wasn't having lunch with customers. He would force guys to come from like 11 o'clock until almost 2 o'clock. Then, they'd have to go back and scramble to get all their work done because he wasn't going to let them get away without doing their work.

He was a stickler for detail. I remember going into the Makiki branch with him right after it was built. We walked in the door—all polished, beautiful—and Bellinger says, "The teller counters are too high." The branch supervisor says, "Oh, Mr. Bellinger, I supervised this job and I guarantee you they are *exactly* correct." Bellinger says, "No, they're not." He grabbed the plans, measured the counters and they were off by six inches. When it came to branch specs, this guy knew his stuff.

Branch architecture was important to him. Look at Bank of Hawaii's branches and look at First Hawaiian's major branches. Ours are designed to community standards, all Hawaiian-looking or—if not—whatever fits in that particular community.

"Johnny Bellinger was a poker-playing buddy of my dad. One day my father took me to the bank. Johnny was taking us to meet someone else to sign some papers. We went past this desk that had files piled on top. It was a mess. Bellinger put out his arm and swept everything off the desk onto the floor, never even slowed down. I could never warm up to him after that."

—*Paul Mullin Ganley, longtime First Hawaiian board member*

"I had just started with the bank, maybe 25 years old, and was a loan representative at Moanalua Branch. One day, everybody above me is gone, and Bellinger comes storming into the branch, unannounced. He yells, 'Who the fuck is in charge here?' I looked up and it was... God. 'Did you see your parking lot?' He had been roaming around, pulls in to Moanalua Branch, finds windblown trash in the lot and he's fuming. He yells at me, 'If I have to do your job, I don't need you.' Then he jumps in his big black car and takes off, and I'm shaking. When the manager came back and I tell him, he just laughed at me and said, 'Don't worry about it.'

"But you know, every morning before we opened, I'm out there making sure the lot is clean from the night before. His message was he wanted our branches to always be in top shape. It was a real learning experience.

"Later, I saw a totally different side of him. I was manager at Hawaii Kai, and out of the blue he transfers me to Maui. My wife, Tiare, had just given birth to my son, and he would use the bank jet to fly us home to visit because we had no family on Maui. He had a very warm heart."

—Ray Ono, First Hawaiian Bank
vice chairman

Bank of Hawaii's look like pillboxes. It doesn't cost any more to have taste. That all started under Bellinger, and we continue that today.

One area he did not work on was succession planning. He truly felt he was going to be there forever. I knew of discussions with the board where he felt nobody was ready to take his place. In some ways he might have considered me as a successor, but he never felt I was ready to run the bank. There was never any kind of formalized succession planning at the other levels of the bank, either. People would rise up just based on the stress and having to jump in and handle things. That's why when he passed on and I took over suddenly, I vowed I'd never let that happen to the bank again. Early on, I identified people who could move up.

Well before he died, it turns out he had retired from the bank without anyone at the bank knowing except for the board. He retired to get all of his pension, and the next day became, under contract, the CEO. It was totally invisible to anybody else. He was convinced that he could not be replaced. Just a few months before he died, he announced that he had agreed to remain as chairman and CEO for an additional five years.

As it turned out, despite all those times I got yelled at, I was glad I stayed.

In 1979, Johnny named Hugh Pingree president of the bank, the No. 2 position. Hugh was a self-made man who had risen up through the ranks and knew how hard it was. He was a gentle giant of a man who still carried around shrapnel in his legs from World War II, but he never complained. Like Johnny, he was a high school graduate who started as a teller, but he was practically a banking genius who never forgot where he came from. He was a very good banker, but I guess Johnny realized he was not the right guy to run the bank down the road. Also, he and Pingree were about the same age, so I guess he was looking for the next generation.

Over the years, thanks to Johnny's support and encouragement, my areas of responsibility kept growing. When I ended up being executive vice president in 1976 at the age of 34, I might have been considered among the potential successors to Johnny a long way down the road.

Another person who had the potential for the top job was Jack Hoag. He had come to Hawaii as a Marine helicopter pilot and married a wonderful Hawaiian girl, Jeanette. Jack is a super, solid banker's banker who came up the traditional route. He started as a management trainee in the early 1960s and then ran our Hilo branch, which was one of our bigger branches at the time. Jack would have definitely been in there as a contender.

Others may have tried to see it as competition for the top job between the two of us, but we never did. But, within the bank, I suppose people might have speculated between Jack and me.

Finally, in 1984, Johnny called me in to say he was moving Pingree up to vice chairman and making me president. He wasn't great at explaining things, telling you why he was doing it. He just did things! And you accepted.

At the time, I was an executive vice president running General Banking, which included all the branches, plus Consumer Lending. When I was named president, I added Commercial, Corporate Lending, Real Estate and International. I had everything but Trust and Investments.

I was even responsible for data processing because George Hata, who was in charge of that area, was quite sick. He was a wonderful guy who was like David Ige—he got accepted into every Mainland college he applied to but went to UH because his parents couldn't afford it. He brought modern computer technology into First Hawaiian Bank.

> "Johnny really liked Walter's style and trusted his judgment, maybe because Johnny was a local boy, too. There was no point in directly confronting someone like Johnny, but Walter could have been a great diplomat; instead of trying to change Johnny 180 degrees, Walter was adept enough to get 90 degrees of what he wanted and come back later for the other 90. Walt would wait for the right moment and then slide in with his proposal."
>
> —*Jack Hoag, retired First Hawaiian Bank president*

When I became president, I was responsible for 70 or 80 percent of the bank. To become president at the age of 43 surprised a lot of people inside and outside the bank, I guess. While I wasn't nervous, I realized this was the dividing line of all the promotions, the one where you felt like, "This is for real." My whole career I always ran scared, always took jobs over my level, so by then I was used to doing it.

Of course, Bellinger was still there, still the dominant CEO. People knew he was still the boss. There was 18 years difference between us. I was born the year of Pearl Harbor, and that was the year he graduated from high school. That's how I always remembered the difference. That got me into trouble one night at a cocktail party

Johnny and Joan Bellinger.

because somebody asked his wife, Joan, what year she graduated from high school, and I said, "1941." She said, "Well, how would you know that?" I said, "That was the year I was born." She got ticked off at me at first, but she and I had that running joke for years.

Even as president, I had to do things very carefully. John was the right man at the right time because he got the operations of the bank down pat; we were solid and had a very good reputation with our government regulators. I felt as if the bank was slipping in terms of new technology, new techniques and marketing. There were things I wanted to do. I tried to grow my portfolio as best I could, but Bellinger was still running the place. More and more decisions would be made by me, but he would have the ultimate authority.

During all the years I worked for him, Johnny and I never had a conversation in which he told me that I was going to be next in line to succeed him. I guess the fact that I kept getting promoted quickly was sending a signal. He may have told others, but he never said to me, "You're going to be the guy."

The closest time was when I had just become president and we had an interview in Bellinger's office with Russ Lynch, the *Star-Bulletin* business writer. Russ asked him point-blank: "Can we assume your designated successor is Walter Dods?" Bellinger was a domineering guy. There was only one person in the room, and the oxygen was all taken out by him. You didn't discuss who was going to be this or that. I was on pins and needles that Russ *dared* ask Bellinger the question.

The room went silent! Bellinger is going to be here for another 50 years in his mind. He said, for the first time, something really humble, which blew me away, something like, "Well, if it's OK with Walter, yeah, you can quote me on that." Walking out of the room I was thinking, *Did he really say that?* Russ found out the same time I did.

> "Years ago, maybe 10 people showed up for bank annual meetings, which were over in 15 or 20 minutes. Johnny had the script, and at the end he asked, 'Are there any questions?' He fully expected none. A Japanese lady sitting in front raised her hand and said, 'Mr. Bellinger, why do you not have any women on your board of directors?' Mr. Bellinger said, 'There are none qualified.' I saw Walter's heart break. Fortunately, there were no media present. Obviously Walter corrected that when he became chairman of the board."
>
> —Don Horner

The collapse of Manoa Finance in 1983 thrust me into the limelight as I led an effort to rescue the savings of its depositors.

CHAPTER 5

Manoa Finance: Digging Out of a Deep Hole

"Many, many elderly people will now have a Merry Christmas!"
*Charles Klenske, trustee for bankrupt Manoa Finance, after thousands
of checks went to depositors five days before Christmas, 1985*

One of the biggest risks of my professional career was resolved not downtown on Bishop Street, strangely enough, but rather during a secret, late-night meeting at the state Capitol with two extremely unlikely allies.

It was 1985, the year before the ongoing savings and loan crisis exploded across the country, and a number of Hawaii industrial loan companies (popularly known as "thrifts") were in trouble. At least two were at the point of collapse. These weren't like regular banks, whose interest rates were regulated; they offered very high interest rates on deposits and used that money to make real estate loans and investments. Unlike banks, they were not insured by the FDIC and could not offer savings, checking accounts or credit cards. They were basically borrowing money from their customers and issuing "IOU" certificates without security.

A few of these companies were subsidiaries of a larger company—like Amfac Financial, which was bought by General Electric's GECC Financial Corp.—and were financially sound. But most were smaller, many of them owned by individuals or families. Many of the smallest ones were not the best managed and, because they were paying higher interest rates to their depositors, they had to raise more money for their lending.

Not only that, banks and savings and loans could only do traditional banking services; they couldn't actually engage in business. Thrifts could do pretty much what they wanted with the money they got from the depositors. The companies that got into trouble didn't limit themselves to quality loans. They actually took the money and invested in assets directly. One example that comes to mind was that Manoa Finance owned part of the Japanese Cultural and Community Center in San Francisco and some other California assets, both raw land and developed properties.

When the real estate market went sour in the 1980s, a lot of these operations got into trouble. There was the possibility of a serious run on the troubled companies and maybe even the good ones. Thousands of depositors stood to lose their life savings.

That's when I got involved, and it was one of the major defining moments of my career, and probably in my progress in the bank. But a little history here would help.

Back in the mid-'70s, First Hawaiian had wanted to get into the finance business, as an additional business either through acquisition or by starting our own company. But, boy, were the thrifts vehemently against it. They fought us at the Legislature tooth and nail. At that point, even though we were a large institution, we were pretty naïve as to how politically connected they were. Many of these small companies had state legislators as either their lawyers or their directors. They were very, very powerful. Powerful enough every year to smash the banks' finance company ambitions and make sure we never got into the business. But then an opportunity opened up:

A company called Hawaii Thrift & Loan got into trouble in 1975. The state was desperate to have somebody take it over—the state asked other thrift companies—but nobody would do it. At that point, banks weren't supposed to own thrift companies, but they were so desperate, the state government went as far as to go to New York, to Citicorp, and if it agreed to take it over, the state would either amend the laws or give an emergency exemption to let Citicorp come into Hawaii and, as a bank, own Hawaii Thrift & Loan. Even with that, Citicorp turned the state down. Everyone was frustrated. Finally, we were contacted to see if we could help.

Johnny Bellinger was in the Philippines at the time, and in his absence, I took the call. Some of the directors of Hawaii Thrift came to me, and we put a takeover plan together.

Sometimes you take risks in your career, and I took a big risk on this one. There was already a run starting on Hawaii Thrift & Loan—people starting to pull out their deposits in panic. A bank run is one of the most frightening financial things you'll ever want to see. We worked over that weekend, and we had a great lawyer named Fred Schutte, a partner in Cades Schutte and a Roosevelt High School local boy. We sat for hours in our bank lunchroom, and Schutte wrote out the entire agreement, without law books or outside consultants, in *longhand* on a yellow tablet. But it still had to be typed up and approved by boards. On Monday morning, we put officers of First Hawaiian Bank right there in the lobbies of Hawaii Thrift & Loan. They just stood there and said, "We are from First Hawaiian Bank and we are going to stand behind Hawaii Thrift & Loan." And we stopped the run!

Had we not done that, the company would have just disappeared, and all the people—the depositors and their money—would have been out of luck.

It was an unbelievable business risk because we didn't legally own the thrift at that point. We did have an agreement, but if it had fallen apart, we would have been exposed to hundreds of millions in losses. This was beyond gutsy.

(As a sidelight, Fred Schutte was a fabulous man. A few years later I recommended him to Governor Ariyoshi for appointment to the state Supreme Court. The governor loved him but he couldn't get it through the Senate. Fred was too solid a citizen, too honest, too good a guy to get through that.)

In any event, we were in the thrift business, but the industry as a whole was still in trouble. We were stable at Hawaii Thrift & Loan, Finance Factors was stable and

GECC Financial was OK. We were the three big dogs, and below us were all these companies that were really shaky yet had big political ties.

Still, they couldn't completely ignore the problems in their own industry. A sign of weakness was the 1976 failure of Pan American Financial. The thrift companies were able to lobby a bill called the Thrift Guaranty Corporation, which was supposed to be like a mini FDIC. The thrift companies would pay assessments every year into an insurance fund that supposedly would cover depositors up to $10,000 if the company failed. The legislation was patterned after thrift guarantee programs in some Mainland states and the FDIC. It was a pretty modest guarantee, but it allowed them to put a sticker on the door to give people confidence in their deposits at the thrift companies. If all that the depositors knew was the word "guarantee" and the sticker on the door, they probably had a sense of confidence that there was something behind that guarantee. Eventually, if the crisis hadn't happened when it did, it might have worked. It just happened that Thrift Guaranty Corporation hadn't been around long enough to build up its reserves.

I had envisioned this happening. I remember lobbying against the bill and meeting with Wayne Minami, who was then with the Department of Regulatory Agencies. I told him:

"Look, insurance is based on the law of large numbers. I know. I started in the insurance business. That means you have to have a large, diverse base to make insurance work. But when you take a small community like Hawaii and have insurance concentrated over just a few companies—many of which we already know are in trouble—and it was public knowledge that they have problems, this

> "We got a call on the Tuesday before Memorial Day 1975 asking if we would be interested in acquiring Hawaii Thrift & Loan, which was having financial troubles. We did the deal over a weekend. We had to keep it very quiet to avoid a run on HT&L.
>
> "On Thursday, Memorial Day eve, we went into their building on Kaheka Street after work because we didn't want anyone around to know we were there. We worked through Thursday night and into the weekend. Then on Sunday we all met at the bank discussing the amount we wanted to pay. I had run the due diligence and I suggested a price of $3 million to Mr. Bellinger, which we agreed to offer. Monday we made the announcement—if we had waited any longer than that there would have been a run. Some unions were starting to pull their money out. They had $70 million in deposits, and I think $15–20 million went out. First Hawaiian Bank people had to go out to the major customers of HT&L, and I think we recovered most of the money that had been withdrawn. We were able to save the deposits of a lot of people that would have been lost, including a lot of seniors."
>
> —Howard Karr, retired First Hawaiian Bank vice chairman & CFO

> "Theoretically, all those thrift companies could have survived. That was the big argument from their side. Manoa Finance and Great Hawaiian were saying, 'We have all these assets.' The only problem is they weren't liquid. They were probably solvent in a balance sheet sense because their assets at least equaled their liabilities, but they couldn't generate any cash from all their assets. If there were a run, they couldn't have raised the money."
>
> —Tom Huber, retired First Hawaiian Bank general counsel

insurance thing is going to fail on Day One. The insurance fund would go bankrupt pretty quickly because it couldn't work."

Well, we went around and around on this and finally I said to him, "At least put into the legislation that the thrifts have to have outside auditors look at their finances and then, like the FDIC, have the firms qualify for the insurance membership. They should have to prove they were credit-worthy.'

Finally, in the dark of night, after another of our long arguments over this, Wayne said to me: "Look, if I were to agree to that requirement, none of these finance companies would qualify!" In fairness to him, he was trying to cobble together a bill that would stabilize the industry, but, in effect, he acknowledged that the bill would have been moot. Nonetheless, the bill became law in 1977, and we all began to pay big insurance premiums.

In the first years after Thrift Guaranty was created, several of the smaller companies failed, and paying off the depositors depleted its reserve fund before it could be built up.

Meanwhile, the biggest of the small players were Manoa Finance, run by Hirotoshi Yamamoto, and Great Hawaiian Financial, run by Norman Inaba. Over time, they got caught up in the real estate slump. In February 1983 the state shut Manoa Finance down; it owed more in interest payments than it was collecting on its investments. When they went down, they left depositors with *tremendous* potential losses—around $45 million in the case of Manoa Finance alone.

Most of the Great Hawaiian and Manoa Finance depositors were older Americans of Japanese ancestry, and their life savings were at risk. The companies were shut down, and the depositors didn't know if they were going to get anything. There would be meetings, and these folks would show up, weeping; they had lost everything. A number of people, maybe 15 or 20, died while they waited to see if they would get their money back.

There was talk about the Thrift Guaranty fund eventually seizing Manoa Finance and Great Hawaiian, although there wasn't yet enough money to pay off their depositors. Tom Huber, a private attorney at the Cades Schutte law firm who later became my top counsel at First Hawaiian, was helping the state and Thrift Guaranty work out the problem. The state and Thrift Guaranty put together a plan providing that Thrift Guaranty would pay out as much as it could toward the insured, guaranteed portion of the deposits. Fairly quickly, that partial payment of $12.6 million went out in early 1983. While the depositors were glad to get it, the $12.6 million was only about one-third of the insured deposits. As a result of that payout, Thrift Guaranty acquired control over all the assets that remained at Manoa Finance and Great Hawaiian.

The state and Thrift Guaranty spent quite a while trying to figure out ways to ultimately realize cash from those assets and pay the depositors the rest of the guarantee. But the real estate crisis was still going on, so the properties weren't marketable at the time, and there was a lot of hand-wringing. The issue dragged on for a couple of years without being resolved. That's when I got involved, at the request of Donna Tanoue, the state banking supervisor.

Donna had searched and searched for a buyer of the assets and couldn't find anyone. She went to Governor Ariyoshi in 1985 and said, "We're at our wits' end." She had talked to me earlier about First Hawaiian buying them, but these were toxic dogs, and we didn't want anything to do with them. However, she came back and we had lunch in the upstairs dining room, and like a fool at the time, I said, "OK, I'll take this on as a public service, try to find a way to bail this thing out. Let me take a shot at it." There was some ego involved. I thought if I could solve something that nobody else could solve, it would be pretty cool. But I didn't know that so many people at the Legislature were intimately involved with these finance companies. If I had known that, I wouldn't have taken it on because it was gruesome.

Depositors at Manoa Finance stand at the door wondering if they will ever get their money back. Eventually, they did.

Also, politically, this was important. Most of the depositors were loyal Democratic voters, and it made sense to see what we could do. I was a strong Ariyoshi supporter and I had pretty deep relationships with the AJA community. My primary motivation was to help George and help the Japanese community. Both Donna and the governor were very appreciative. This was not easy for Ariyoshi because he and Inaba had been good, good friends. As a private attorney, George had done legal work for Inaba.

To be honest, a second motivation was definitely that our Hawaii Thrift & Loan subsidiary would have been paying assessments to Thrift Guaranty forever. That was secondary, but the ability to stop the assessments was very helpful to me to get owners of the other companies to come in and put real money up front.

The first thing I did was ask around for who was the best lawyer in the field. The name that kept popping up was Tom Huber from Cades Schutte, who had already been helping Thrift Guaranty. He agreed to be my alter ego on the project. There were at least 20 lawyers involved, representing Manoa Finance and Great Hawaiian and their bankruptcy trustees, the state, depositors and various mortgagees.

And they were all fighting each other.

I put together this plan—the press named it the Dods Plan—and I started pushing it around town in February 1985. I had these three-by-five cards and a big white board and five charts in an old leather case explaining the plan, and I would go around trying to sell it. I went to see the solvent thrift companies and told them, "We have to put money into it to stabilize the insurance fund." It simply didn't have enough money to take care of the depositors.

My idea was that the 11 remaining solvent companies would make loans totaling $21.2 million into Thrift Guaranty, and the state would loan the fund about $9.5 million more. That would allow repayment of the depositors right away and buy us time to take all the properties owned by Manoa Finance and Great Hawaiian and liquidate them in an orderly manner over time, rather than have a fire sale. Eventually the loans would be paid back.

I wanted to use all the money to pay the depositors, but Manoa Finance and Great Hawaiian had other creditors who weren't depositors; under bankruptcy law, when assets of a debtor are liquidated, they have to be shared with all creditors. People thought that depositors had priority over non-depositor creditors, but that wasn't the case. I crunched the numbers and found we were $9–10 million short of paying off the creditors. I thought the state had part of the responsibility and ought to take a role in solving it. So I developed my plan for the state to make up the difference and put up substantial money.

> "Walter understood the significance of the issue to our community. There were so many constituencies involved, but Walter took the bull by the horns. He was a real rock."
>
> —Donna Tanoue, former Hawaii banking commissioner, on efforts to help depositors of Manoa Finance and Great Hawaiian Financial

MANOA FINANCE: DIGGING OUT OF A DEEP HOLE

Many of the shell-shocked depositors of Manoa Finance were elderly Americans of Japanese ancestry, shown here at a meeting at Manoa Elementary School cafeteria.

There would be two loans; one from the other thrift companies together, and one from the state. Together, that would be enough money. The state and the companies would take mortgages on the assets to protect their interests in getting repaid. As part of the plan, the remaining thrifts would need to obtain FDIC insurance to protect their depositors. FDIC coverage had just been made available through legislation pushed through Congress by Sen. Dan Inouye. All of the remaining thrift companies qualified for FDIC insurance, and Thrift Guaranty's guarantee would no longer be needed.

If it worked, we thrift companies would no longer be required to pay assessments into the Thrift Guaranty fund. I had to convince both the state and the other companies to throw money at this, and it was not an easy sell.

Meanwhile, Bellinger was really pissed at me. He didn't want me to do it because it was taking up a lot of my time away from the bank. A couple of times he called me into his office and said, "You tried, but this thing isn't going anywhere. Get back to work." I begged him to let me keep going. I stupidly believed I could pull it off.

I did, but it was brutal.

To make a long story short, I got screwed by everybody. I didn't realize until I got to the Legislature how many legislators or legislative staff were connected to these small companies, and they were trying to kill everything I tried to do. I went into their offices and got this cold silence. I found out later that they were on the board or their chief of staff is a director or their lawyer is part-owner of one of these finance companies. It was horrible to realize how big the snake pit was, but we just kept at it.

At one point, they even got to Donna. They pressured her to not back the bailout. She came to me saying, "I may have to back out of this." I told her, "Listen, Donna. You asked me to get into this. We can solve this problem." To her credit, she slowly came back into it, but the pressure was so great on her that she was sadly considering backing out at the time.

Finally, the pressure on everybody was so great that they started buying in, one by one. Then I took my white board and started presenting this to the actual depositor groups, and they had some faith in me. Those meetings were very emotional. In the beginning, they were hostile, even to me, but they began to come around. To this day I have some unusual relationships with elderly Japanese. They come to me in shopping centers and they'll pull me aside and say to their children, "This is the man who saved your grandfather's money." That kind of thing happens to me to this day.

The rescue plan ran into huge political resistance from some in the Legislature, but constituents' flocked to community meetings and helped persuade legislators to pass the "Dods Plan," which eventually got depositors' money back.

We finally got this Thrift Guaranty bailout bill into a position where it could be passed, but we still had resistance. Two politicians whom I did not care for at the time—we had disagreements on business philosophy among other things—were major roadblocks: Senators Ben Cayetano and Neil Abercrombie, each of whom would later became governor. They both were skeptical about using taxpayer dollars to bail out businesses.

I met with them and some of the other senators in a Senate caucus room late at night. It was down in the basement, koa walls and koa furniture everywhere. They were hostile at first. It was like, "You bankers have to have some angle in here. You guys are just trying to make some money." Some of them tore me up trying to get their side of it in for the consumers. I fought right back. At one point, they said they would do this, but they would not let the banks off from paying their dues into the Thrift Guaranty Corp. I said, "Fine, then the banks aren't going to put up our share of the bailout."

It was a standoff.

I tried to tell them we weren't the ones who created the problem. They left me, went off and huddled and came back and accepted it. We shook hands, and by the end of a long night, we ended up having respect for each other coming out of that room. Ben and Neil made it happen. Ben was chair of Ways and Means at the time and was in a position to do something about it, while Neil was the yeller and screamer and defender of the Japanese, many of them from his district in Manoa. In the end, the tide turned when both senators stood up to the plate and pledged their support for the bailout bill even though Abercrombie was the only one of all 76 House and Senate members to vote against creation of Thrift Guaranty in the first place eight years earlier.

I know Neil made his work on behalf of the Manoa Finance creditors a core part of his political resume even though he had zero to do with coming up with the mechanism to solve it. Still, in all fairness, he and Ben did step up to the plate, and without them, it wouldn't have passed.

After a lot of hard work, the bailout bill passed, but we still needed a sign-off from Hirotoshi Yamamoto, the head of Manoa Finance. He wouldn't agree to it. We couldn't figure out how to get him to sign off. Then we learned that what Hirotoshi valued more than anything was his Waialae Country Club membership. He had lost pretty much everything, but he'd still go to Waialae a lot. So I finally took it on my own and invited him to meet me at Waialae for lunch, just the two of us. I said, "Look, all these elderly depositors are losing their life's savings because of you. We have to get this thing settled, and you won't sign the release for us to get this all settled. Here's what I'm going to do. I'm going to take your Waialae Country Club certificate away from you and you are going to lose your membership in Waialae."

"OK: I'll sign."

That's how we got this thing settled. After all the lawyers and everything, it was because I was going to confiscate his Waialae membership.

The deal was done. We worked hard to get the money back to those suffering depositors in time for Christmas that same year.

But there's always one more mini-crisis. The day of the closing, December 20, 1985, all the thrift companies were supposed to deposit their share of the $21.2 million loan to Thrift Guaranty into an escrow account at the bank so that, in the morning, we would know that all the money was on hand and we could close the mortgages and send out the checks to the depositors.

All the local offices did their part, depositing the funds to escrow. In the morning we discovered belatedly that the GECC Financial money had disappeared. Their treasurer's office in Connecticut had seen that balance in the night and just followed their

> "I remember a lot of meetings with Ben Cayetano, who was chair of the Senate Ways and Means Committee, to try to sell the Legislature on the idea of the state putting up money. One day, I was walking downtown, and Ben was out walking. We stopped to chat and right away got to the Dods Plan. He asked a technical question, and I said, 'Well, if we decide to do this then …" and he cut me off and said, '*We* decide.' By '*we*,' I meant the banks, the thrift companies *and* the Legislature, but he made it a point by saying, '*we*'— and pointed to himself—'*decide.*'"
>
> —Tom Huber

> "I've heard a thousand times about Walter being a marketing person. That's been a terrific asset for him, but people grossly underestimate him if they classify Walter as just a marketing person. That to me is an extremely minor part of what he does. I think he is a fabulous strategic thinker."
>
> —Bill Mills, Walt's investment partner

ordinary course and drew the balance back. The local management was extremely embarrassed and spent the morning scrambling to get the money back into escrow. We closed on time. It turned out to not be a big deal, but I was burned up about it. That might be the day I went bald.

When the closing session was held, checks to all the depositors had already been cut. They were in bankers' boxes sitting on hand trucks in a room downstairs at First Hawaiian, waiting to be put in the mail. It was about three hand trucks full. As a last step, they were going to deliver the checks to the post office. I wanted it all to be very public.

I pushed one of the carts, and Dave Hill from GECC grabbed one. I told my lawyer, Tom Huber, "Get him off of that!" because I was ticked at what GECC had done with its cash that morning. Somebody else volunteered to take it. TV cameras and newspaper photographers were there, following along as we rolled these hand trucks two blocks down Merchant Street to the post office. It was very satisfying.

In the end, the depositors got back 100 cents on the dollar of their insured money, and Manoa Finance depositors even got the full amount over and above the $10,000 insurance level. A total of 6,681 checks for $33.8 million went out to depositors of the two companies. The depositors lost interest payments, but they were damn happy to get their money back. It seemed as if it took forever, but it was less than three years, compared to the initial forecast of six years if the normal bankruptcy process had been used. Over time the full amount of the loans made by the other thrifts and the state were repaid by the sale of those properties. Huber gave me a set of those notes marked "paid in full," which was pretty gratifying.

Within the bank, there is no question in my mind that senior people from directors to Bellinger himself had their view about me changed from the "marketing guy" to somebody who could do something. I got laws changed, saved people's deposits, and we and the other thrifts no longer would have to pay $2 million a year into this Thrift Guaranty fund for ever and ever. It had a positive effect on the bank, but that's not why I did it.

I got involved for the challenge of it. Could I do what everybody else in town said could not be done? That became one of the turning points in my career, without question.

Despite the last-minute flap about the GECC Financial money on the day we closed, I had developed a special relationship with David Porteus, one of the top people in the local GECC operation. He was the son of Heb Porteus, whom I served with for so long on the bank's board and at Damon Estate. I bonded well with David.

When I first came up with my crazy scheme, it was not well received. In one meeting I pitched all the companies about putting up more money to get this bailout together. David said to me, "Dods, if you pull this off, I'll kiss your ass on Bishop Street." When we finally got the whole thing done, I said, "Well, Porteus, are you ready?"

He said, "How about I buy you lunch instead?"

A side note to Hawaii's crisis: The savings and loan debacle that began in the early 1980s but exploded a year after the Hawaii fiasco lasted for about a decade more. Nationwide, 747 institutions with a book value of more than $400 billion had to be closed. The American taxpayers' bill to clean up that mess was about $132 billion.

Although I was initially reluctant to get involved, I was honored to co-chair every one of George Ariyoshi's election campaigns for lieutenant governor and governor.

CHAPTER 6

Politics: Building a Community

Hawaii's modern political history can fairly be said to have begun in 1954. That's when Democrats, powered by ambitious returning World War II vets—mostly Japanese Americans—and muscled by politically canny labor unions, managed to win control of the Territorial Legislature, long dominated by Republicans and their influential friends in the downtown business community.

Historians like to call that the "Revolution of 1954," although the seeds of the turnover had been in the making for some time. I was a teenager at the time and had little interest in politics or much of anything other than cars and girls, to tell the truth.

That Democratic dominance, with a few detours here and there, carried on for about six decades, with one generation of Democrats moving in after another to take control at the state and federal levels and in most of the counties, as well.

I came of age in 1962, not long after the 1959 Admission Act that made Hawaii a state. Meanwhile, the Democrats were cementing their hold on political power at home and in Washington. Through work or social connections, I was drawn into a few early political campaigns at the most basic envelope-filling level. Forgettable stuff.

Today, I know I have a reputation as a political "insider" and mastermind of political campaigns, and I'll admit I enjoy that reputation. But if people think my approach is to align myself with the likely winner and then enjoy the benefits, that's anything but true. Over the years, I have joined up with candidates who looked more like likely losers than front-runners. Just as in my banking career, I went with my gut rather than what made the most sense at the time.

The best example is George Ariyoshi, whom I have been with ever since his first run for lieutenant governor in 1970. Over and over, including in his three campaigns for governor, the polls suggested George was going to lose. However, I believed there was something there that, if we could only "market" it and get the public to see Ariyoshi for who he was, we could win. Later, I was also involved in several Dan Inouye campaigns for the U.S. Senate, which always looked like a slam dunk until 1992 when a controversy involving charges of sexual impropriety almost derailed the effort. (More on that in Chapter 17.) Then, of course, there was my last campaign—really!—in 2014 for U.S. Rep. Colleen Hanabusa for the U.S. Senate, which, according to the vote count, we lost. Yet I will always insist we "won," considering the odds against us.

I have said many times over the years that I'm through with politics, but after that last campaign with Hanabusa, it's true. I might support people in the future, maybe write them a check or give informal advice, but I'm through running or chairing campaigns.

We thought we had a good shot with Colleen against Brian Schatz, the former lieutenant governor who had been appointed by Gov. Neil Abercrombie in 2012 to fill the U.S. Senate seat when Inouye died. Andy Winer, Schatz's chief of staff, created the aura of his boss being a major figure because he was a sitting U.S. senator, although he had served only briefly and as an appointee. Schatz's election record had not been that strong. He came in sixth in the special U.S. Congress election in 2006. He went on to become lieutenant governor in 2012 because there were seven people running, and he got in with 35 percent of the vote.

Schatz was clearly qualified as a senator, but I believe Colleen had the edge in authentic experience and leadership. In the state Senate, she became its first woman president. She hadn't been there for that long; she was 47 years old before she got into politics. Yet, she quickly moved up the ranks in the Senate and was well received during her two terms in the U.S. House. In the campaign, we were trying to show her experience, judgment, maturity, collegiality and also her independence. A key point for us: She wasn't a rubberstamp legislator. She actually read the legislation she had to deal with. She did her homework, aided by her experience as an attorney. But those are hard concepts to get across to people during a campaign.

Also, the Schatz campaign had a lot of union backing, such as the Hawaii Government Employees Association (HGEA). Almost always in politics it comes down to money and organization; they had a superior organization because of strong union backing. Of course, Colleen had some labor unions behind her, but the big-body union is the HGEA.

The Schatz campaign's field operation, not "field" as in holding signs on streets, but rather targeting specific voters, was very smart. They had extremely sophisticated polling to the point that they could find Caucasian pockets in non-Caucasian areas, zero in on those people and get them out to vote. Plus, the money overwhelmed us.

Having said all of that, if just the Hilo area, which Hanabusa won, had its normal voter turnout, we would have won. Political pundits keep talking about those two precincts in Puna that had delayed voting because of the hurricane that hit Hawaii Island that weekend, but the approaching storm kept turnout low in the whole Hilo area.

Still, I believe we could have dealt with all that, but we just couldn't compete with the money. In that election, the difference was $4 million between the two campaigns. The conservation group Climate Hawks and others such as the League of Conservation Voters put huge money into TV ads for Brian. MoveOn.org and other

> "Walter Dods will support you, but he would never tell you what to do. He'd never tell you to vote a certain way or call in the chits. He never told me the kind of candidate I should be. That's the big takeaway. Fundamentally, he is so local to the core. The one thing people don't appreciate is the fact that he has never lost his local roots."
>
> —former U.S. Rep. Colleen Hanabusa

progressive groups were in for a half-million, so overall there was a difference of about $4 million between the Schatz and Hanabusa campaigns. We came close. The final difference in the election was around 1,800 votes, a 900-vote swing. I'm certain we could have put in $4 million more and turned around those 900 folks we needed. However, there was simply too much money on the other side and with it the sophistication that money can buy—constant polling, targeted direct-mail pieces, get-out-the-vote efforts, paid staff and so on.

Losing was tough. It still hurts.

Back when I was active at First Hawaiian Bank, I often ran into a wall of opposition over my political work from many friends both inside and outside the bank. Yet I always felt that my political involvement was good for both the community and the bank.

> "In our campaign (against Brian Schatz), we would sit and meet. I'm such a lousy politician, so Walt was basically running the campaign. He was the one we all looked to for strategy. What we did not expect was the amount of money that came in (against us)."
>
> —Colleen Hanabusa

Over the years, I've come to believe you can't be a good banker unless you understand what matters to your customers and the community. One way to get there is to get involved in politics. Not that everyone, including me at first, always understood that! In fact, I had to be dragged kicking and screaming into my first real campaign. That was in 1970 when George Ariyoshi decided to run for lieutenant governor. Most people think he was handpicked by then-Gov. Jack Burns to be his lieutenant governor partner—handsome, AJA, and experienced in the Legislature. But it was actually the other way around; Ariyoshi decided he would run in the Democratic primary, and Burns had to be sold on the idea. So did I.

I was new at the bank, handling only marketing and public relations, and I turned George down when he first asked me to help out. However, my boss, Johnny Bellinger, pointed out to me—quite forcefully—that Ariyoshi was on our board of directors, and it would make good sense to help out. I started out on the campaign committee and, by the end of the primary campaign, I was co-chairman.

Basically, I ran the primary campaign because the other co-chairman was Larry Mehau, the Big Island rancher and former Honolulu cop. He did his special thing—rounding up troops for rallies, using his connections with Waikiki performers to provide entertainment at fundraisers. As far as I was concerned, we were equal. He wasn't involved in the day-to-day campaign. Ariyoshi named him co-chairman, but basically I ran the campaign. In the general election, the lieutenant governor's campaign was attached to Burns' effort because, in Hawaii, the governor and lieutenant governor nominees run on the same ticket. I was just a small-time player with the Ariyoshi campaign. Burns had the horses.

Still, I had an eye on everything, including watching the making of the televised campaign movie, *To Catch a Wave*, and working with some top people. Among them were Joe Napolitan, the legendary national Democratic political consultant, and Harry Muheim, who wrote, directed and produced *To Catch a Wave*, a powerful 30-minute campaign ad that ran over and over on prime-time TV. Muheim was a genius. He had written many television scripts for programs such as *Playhouse 90* and later moved into documentaries and political films. He had done commercials for everyone from Robert Kennedy and Hubert Humphrey to both governors Pat and Jerry Brown of California. Later, he worked on both the Jimmy Carter and Walter Mondale campaigns. So it was a thrill for me just to be in the room watching how he made this film. It was groundbreaking for Hawaii; Tom Coffman wrote about it in his book, *Catch a Wave*.

For his part, Napolitan had worked for everyone from Hubert Humphrey to former Philippines dictator Ferdinand Marcos, who lived in Hawaii after his exile. Napolitan was a real character. He would blow into town for three or four days of meetings, and his skill was to listen to what everyone had to say and then distill it back. He would ask the right questions and force everybody to come up with what they needed to be doing. Then, he would put out a memo telling us what to do before his next trip. He was a pretty cool guy. He also tended to have a "friend" in every port, which was fine with me.

That first Ariyoshi campaign in 1970 was my start in politics. I did the media strategy, wrote speeches, that side of the campaign. While I may have been incidentally involved in the grassroots side, it was really run by Jimmy Takushi, a longtime personal friend of Ariyoshi's and later a member of his cabinet, and later by Bob Oshiro, key organizer for the Burns campaign. George's old senatorial support group handled the grassroots in that first campaign. The problem was, a statewide race is a whole different ballgame from a state Senate district. They didn't have the expertise on strategy and media that I had from the nonpolitical things I'd done, so I just converted my business skills into running a campaign.

With U.S. Rep. Colleen Hanabusa, whose campaign for Senate I chaired in 2014.

One of the things I did over the course of several Ariyoshi campaigns in a dozen years was come up with slogans and themes, often based on market research. I did it instinctively. With "Quiet but Effective," I tried to make a positive out of the fact that George was indeed quiet and understated. "Integrity Is the Issue, Ariyoshi Is the Answer" is a slogan we used in a later campaign against Frank Fasi, which really pissed off the longtime mayor, who repeatedly (and unsuccessfully) ran for governor. There was one other: "Ariyoshi for Governor Because *Hawaii Is a Special Place*." That came from polling in which we asked voters what they thought about Hawaii, and it hit home.

Napolitan and local ad man Jack Seigle were *the* team for political campaigns in the day. They owned the franchise. In the end, they kind of drifted away. Later, when Ed Case was thinking about running for governor in 2002, they contacted me. They wanted to know if I were going to run, which I was considering. (More on that in Chapter 16.) Mostly, however, they just wanted excuses to come in, be put up in suites at the Royal Hawaiian and have a good time. Napolitan did end up working for Case's campaign briefly. Today, Joe has passed on and Jack has moved to Medellin, Colombia, where he has a new family.

Ariyoshi was effective mostly in small groups. He had an unbelievable amount of energy. He'd go from early in the morning until midnight, every day, so he was great at retail campaigning. His speaking ability, which was never spectacular, started off modestly but improved with time. If you ask me, he went on too often about building a future for our "children's children." To the rest of us it was like. . . "Please!" But he meant it! He didn't read prepared speeches that well in the beginning. We tried to do speech training and media coaching, how to handle press conferences and details like that. Over the years and the campaigns, he became much better, but he never really enjoyed that part of the job.

Early in that 1970 campaign, a lot of people believed that Governor Burns was finished and that Tom Gill, who was then lieutenant governor, would win the Democratic nomination for governor. But not George. He was convinced that Burns would win. He and Bob Oshiro were among the few believers. Burns brought in Oshiro, who was in the state House, to run his grassroots campaign, and Bob basically gave up his life, his job, everything, to go on this quest to get Burns reelected. During his third term, Burns got sick, Ariyoshi became acting governor, and Oshiro stayed with George all the way through his next three successful campaigns.

I clearly remember the November night in 1970 when the Burns-Ariyoshi ticket won, beating Republican Judge Sam King in every county. There was the usual big celebration at campaign headquarters, but the old-time Burns people had a smaller party at Washington Place that night, quietly, away from the media, and Burns' press

> "Right after I got elected lieutenant governor, Walt said, 'You need a strong person for PR advice.' He recommended Jack Kellner, a TV reporter and good friend of his. I told Walt I had already picked somebody—Diane Nosse, who had been Dan Inouye's press secretary. Walt wasn't happy. He said, 'You can't get a dumb broad involved.'
>
> "It turned out Diane was outside my office, and I asked my secretary, Ruby, to send her in. That was the first time she and Walt met. And of course, today she's Diane Dods."
>
> —*former governor George Ariyoshi*

"I was on the board of First Hawaiian Bank when I was organizing a run for lieutenant governor in 1970. I didn't really know Walter, but I knew he had media and communications experience and asked him to help. He turned me down at first. But then, (First Hawaiian President Johnny) Bellinger told him: 'You go and campaign for him.'
So he did.

"Walt was very important in the media part of my campaign, which I really needed at first. I had been in office since the 1950s, been Senate majority leader, but when they did a poll, they found I had 2.5 percent name recognition. He was an invaluable part of every one of my campaigns after that. He offered media advice and focused on campaign finances. I never got into debt in any of my campaigns."

—*George Ariyoshi*

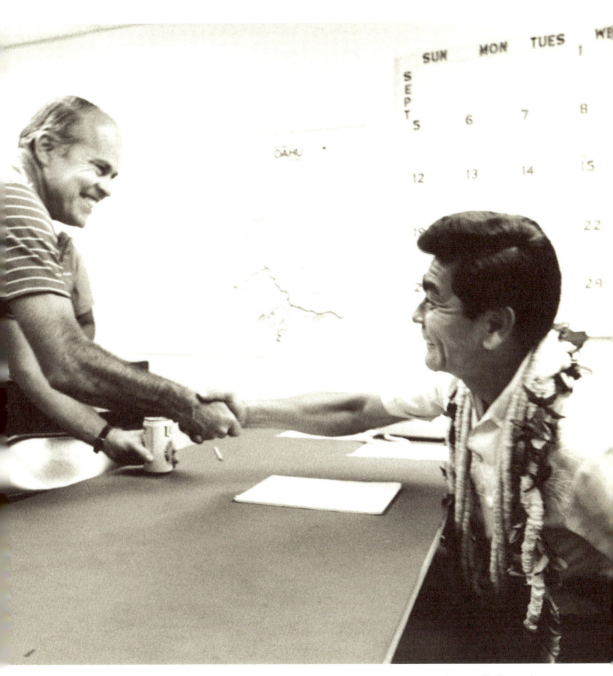

The governor and I were pretty happy after he secured re-election to a third term. He'll go down in history as the last three-term governor. Even before George left office, the 1978 Constitutional Convention imposed a two-term limit.

> "Being governor can be a lonely job. You have to have people on the outside to consult and seek advice from. When it came to issues involving the business community, Walter was the man. You have to have people you can trust, and Walter was the person I called. I don't think any other governor has had a person like that on his side."
>
> —George Ariyoshi

secretary, Don Horio, invited me to attend. I was still a young kid, just 29, but a witness to history. Governor Burns was there, and Ariyoshi, of course. Then all the old-timers, Oshiro and grassroots activists with nicknames like Dynamite (Tokuichi Takushi) and Crabby (Takumi Koyama). And of course, gruff-talking Dan Aoki, an aide to the governor and veteran of the all-AJA 442nd Regimental Combat Team who was kind of the top sergeant of the Burns campaign. Balloon was his nickname. They were just sitting around eating and having a beer, quietly celebrating and attacking each other in a friendly way. For me, that was a thrill.

As it worked out, we had three legs on almost all the campaigns. We had grassroots (Oshiro), media strategy (me) and the money guy—finance. That was mostly Frank Hata, whose family had the food company (Y. Hata & Co.) and, not incidentally, a pretty good computer system, which we were allowed to use. Frank was always complaining. He would raise the money, and then I would go and spend it or the grassroots side would spend it for meals and logistics. There was always a little tension between the fundraiser and the spenders, but it was a healthy tension. Each of us knew how important the other legs were, so none rose above the others in the three big races. We were truly co-equals.

George was a unique guy to work with. Once he got faith in me, which happened fairly quickly, he never questioned my judgment, never changed my ads, unlike some politicians who want to rewrite everything. George Ariyoshi's confidence was a blessing and a curse. A blessing because he never second-guessed our creative work. The curse was that his confidence put unbelievable pressure on me personally—being responsible for whether I was going to bomb out or not. I've worked on a lot of campaigns since then, and some politicians would rewrite or debate everything, even if they had no knowledge whatsoever of the subject. George never did that. The relationship got to the point where I would call George and say, "I want to show you an ad." He would say, "Do you like it?" I would tell him, "Yeah, I think this is the way to go." I would explain it to him and he would say, "Go." We had that level of trust.

After he became governor, George Ariyoshi and I would go months without seeing one another, and then I might see him every day for three weeks when there was a crisis. In 1982, there was a flap over the insecticide heptachlor, which was found on pineapple tops that had been used as cattle feed and, from there, got into the local milk supply. Thousands of gallons of milk had to be thrown away, and mothers worried about heptachlor getting into their breast milk. It became a big story, locally and nationally. It just seemed every time you opened a newspaper, heptachlor was on the front page. Ben Cayetano was in the Legislature then, and he had a special investigative committee. He would stir the pot every day.

I was trying to help put a cap on it. I finally told the governor, "George, the only way you are going to get on top of this is to replace George Yuen." Yuen, the state health director, was a nice guy, but he had been with the Honolulu Board of Water Supply his whole life before this job, and this was something quite different. It's like the episode decades later when Kauai's Gen. Eric Shinseki was running the Veterans' Administration for President Obama. Once the media is on you, no matter *what* you're trying to do, nothing works. But did you notice that the day Shinseki resigned, there was no more front-page crisis in the VA? The critics got their scalp, and now they moved on to the next thing.

Initially, Ariyoshi was hostile to my suggestion that Yuen had to go. Then, about a week later, he called me and said, "I thought about what you said, and I agree." I told the governor, "You have to get somebody who is universally respected, so when he says something, people will know he is telling the truth." I suggested Charlie Clark, who had been both city managing director and superintendent of the Department of Education. George said, "Yeah, I like Charlie." We approached Charlie, he agreed to take on the Health Department, and soon enough the thing just ended. Boom!

One thing about Ariyoshi, which I have not yet seen in any other politician to this day, is that George had no ego. Often, he didn't have his picture in the ads. If supporters would call him up to criticize the stuff I put out, he might tell me, just as feedback, but he never said, "Change it because I'm getting this reaction."

The 1974 election for governor was the first time since statehood that there was no sitting elected governor on the ballot, although Ariyoshi had been serving as acting governor for a year after Burns fell ill with colon cancer. The Democratic race

"If you take a look at Walter's career at the bank, I suspect that there is a relationship between the political success he had, primarily with George Ariyoshi, and his advancement at First Hawaiian.

"Walter always had people around him who understood data. Gary Caulfield was one; I'm sure there were others that would feed him data about attitudes, the status of polls, what the trends were. He also understood the impact the media could have on the electorate. He had all the relationships in the media, PR and government relations world because that's where he came from. Whoever had Walter had those relationships.

"I think Johnny Bellinger recognized the fact that Walter was taking a risk, because George was always behind, always the underdog. If it weren't for a Democratic closed primary, where he could always beat Frank Fasi, he probably wouldn't have been governor for as long as he was"

—*Jeff Watanabe, attorney and longtime friend*

was wide open. The other three candidates in the primary election were Honolulu Mayor Frank Fasi, former lieutenant governor Tom Gill and Senate President David McClung, a longshot. If Fasi and Gill split the haole vote, all we needed was Ariyoshi's core AJA vote to win. It was a perfect political equation for us. We figured the second time around maybe we could win one-on-one. But to get that 50 percent the first time around was not going to be easy. No Japanese American had ever been elected governor.

In fact, Peter Hart, who was *the* Democratic pollster nationally at the time, did a survey for us and concluded we couldn't win. We had a breakfast meeting at Washington Place, and Hart told Ariyoshi he should pull out, there's no way he can win. "Save your reputation and get out," Hart said. George was stoic; he would just sit there and let the rest of us talk. Hart said, "People say that you don't speak well, they don't know what you have accomplished. . ." and so forth. I said to Hart, "You just don't understand the locals. They respect people who don't take credit." That's the genesis of the "Quiet but Effective" campaign slogan we used. I feel a lot of people don't know how to interpret polls in Hawaii. You have to look for nuggets in the data, not necessarily the way a national pollster would look at results.

Hart had been brought in by campaign consultant Joe Napolitan. Joe would go into a new place and his famous line was, "When I go into meetings to test a message, they always say, 'You don't understand. In Hawaii things are different.' That's what they told me when I won an upset race in Philadelphia, in New York, in Chicago, in Manila, in Mexico City. . ." He would list 20 races where his candidate was behind and still won. He said, "Every place would tell me they were different. There is no difference. Don't tell me things are different in Hawaii because they are not."

I understood his point, because all campaigns are essentially alike. But I firmly believe that Hawaii is different; and Joe understood that there are nuances. And after all, Joe did help Ariyoshi win with a later campaign that used as a slogan "Hawaii Is a Special Place." In the end, Hart was wrong. Ariyoshi won with just over 36 percent of the Democratic primary vote in that '74 race and then went on to easily beat Republican Randy Crossley in the general for the first of his three terms as governor

While I enjoyed politics and campaigning, it wasn't always easy for me professionally. I remember one campaign, when polls showed Ariyoshi lagging, and Johnny

> "I doubt if there's one prominent politician or business person that I know that hasn't one time or another gone in and asked Walter for advice or asked him, 'Should I run for office?' What they're really saying is, 'Will you help me and run my campaign?' or 'Will you help give money?' I never heard him say no to anybody, or at least that he wouldn't talk to him, though he might tell them, 'No, I don't think it's the right time for you to run.' But they all go to him."
>
> —*fellow investor and longtime friend Bill Mills*

POLITICS: BUILDING A COMMUNITY

I emceed Ariyoshi's inaguration held at the Royal Bandstand on the grounds of Iolani Palace.

Bellinger didn't want me to get involved anymore because I had too senior a role in the bank. He felt my role could hurt with customers and hurt the bank. It came to a point where he was telling me, "You have to give it up." However, I said, "Well, I enjoyed the ride up with him, and I can't walk away now when he's in trouble. If you have to let me go, let me go." Johnny backed off. It wasn't a matter of being cocky or threatening. My heart just wouldn't allow me to desert George when things were tough.

What did I get out of it? I grew a lot from that political involvement. First of all, I met a lot of unbelievable people, a lifelong network of good friends who helped me personally, helped the bank, and helped the community. I grew in that job, and to this day when I talk to the bank's young trainees, I advise them, "If you want to be successful, go up several paths. You have to go up in your organization, but you also need to be heavily involved in the larger community. It can be charity work, it can be political work, whatever. I don't care which political party it is, in terms of managing the bank, but you have to be involved to know what is going on outside your company. The people you meet by doing good will help you do well. You don't do it because you think it is going to help your career. However, doing it *will help* your career. You have to do it with noble attitudes. Simply put, you derive your income from the community, so you should put some of your effort and drive back into the community."

Johnny Bellinger, Gov. George Ariyoshi and I at one of the early meetings of the Japan-Hawaii Economic Council. Johnny was the group's founding chairman on the Hawaii side (there was also a Japan chairman) in the early 1970s. I succeeded him as Hawaii chairman after his death.

CHAPTER 7

Japan Deal Could Have Killed Bank

I've always been involved with Japan, which is terribly important to the Hawaii economy. That's why I spent so much time and effort over the years as co-chairman of the Japan-Hawaii Economic Council, promoting business ties between Japan and Hawaii. However, an earlier adventure in Japan that happened under Johnny Bellinger could have been a disaster for First Hawaiian. It involves the *yakuza* (Japanese organized crime) as well as two of the richest men in Japan, Kenji Osano and Yasuo Takei. The final chapter of this complex story involved a dinner at a fancy Tokyo restaurant with Bellinger and Osano, a legendary Tokyo investor and developer whose Kyo-ya company still owns many of the major hotels in Waikiki.

Bellinger loved Japan. I did, too, and we started traveling there to meet with clients, Japanese companies doing business in Hawaii. He was convinced that one way to increase the bank's profits was to start a finance company subsidiary in Japan. Sort of a "Go West" philosophy.

In 1978, Johnny set up a subsidiary of our Hawaii Thrift & Loan company named Japan-Hawaii Finance Kabushiki Kaisha. The man hired to run it was Shigeru Kimura, the brother of Shunichi Kimura, the former Big Island mayor and judge. Shigeru had previously managed a small thrift company in Hilo.

These consumer finance operations in Japan are called *sarakin* or "salaryman" companies. ("Salaryman" roughly translates as a white-collar businessman.) In Johnny's mind, he sees Japanese borrowers—he was thinking of local Japanese people—as thrifty, hardworking folks who pay their bills.

These Japanese consumer finance companies were routinely charging 30 to 40 percent on unsecured loans, sometimes even up to 100 percent annual interest. You go there and get a short-term loan—the equivalent of a few hundred dollars at a time. Borrowers would have to pay a really high interest rate but wouldn't have the loan out for long and then pay it off when they got their bonuses.

Back in the 1970s, many of these companies were connected to the yakuza, Japanese crime syndicate types. Today, they are cleaned up and are respected financial institutions. Many of the survivors are now listed on the Tokyo stock exchange, very well regarded. They are still referred to as sarakin companies, but it's not the old pejorative term. They're not yakuza-connected today, but that wasn't true back when First Hawaiian tried to enter the sarakin business.

Then, Japanese banks were so strong that they had two laws concerning these finance companies. Our bank hadn't done enough homework on these rules. First, a sarakin company was not allowed to advertise. You could do posters in train stations but not radio, television or newspaper ads, which is critical to business. Second, the Japanese banks wouldn't share customer credit information with us. The heart and soul of being able to make a loan in America is the credit bureaus. Before we lend you money, we can check your credit record. We can find out whether you are a very bad creditor who never pays a bill or maybe you've already stuck five other banks. In Japan, they wouldn't share this information with us.

Kimura quickly opened a lot of branches, basically storefront operations. In short order we had 21 offices. Then, the loans started going bad in large numbers. We started taking massive loan losses because less-than-creditworthy customers were coming in, and we couldn't check their financial information before loaning them money. Back in Honolulu, we were seeing these delinquent credits come in to our weekly management meetings. At one point, we had exposure in Japan of bad debt equal to the total capital of First Hawaiian Bank.

This venture had gotten out of hand and was frightening, but nobody wanted to tell the emperor (Bellinger) he had no clothes. It could have done serious damage to the financial ability of First Hawaiian Bank to survive. That's how serious it had become.

Finally, in the early 1980s, Bellinger decided we needed to get out of the sarakin business. We had a representative office in Tokyo run by a man named Peter Onodera. He found a prospective buyer, a company already in the sarakin business called Aichi Corporation, run by Yasumichi "Mamushi" Morishita. Philip Ching at the time was special assistant to Johnny, who asked him to put the deal together. Phil hired Alan Goda, a private attorney in Honolulu with terrific ties in Japan, to represent the bank in negotiating the sale.

Johnny was anxious to complete the deal and get out of Japan. The problem, as it turned out, was that

---

"Philip Ching (Bellinger's administrative assistant) and I spent a lot of time in Tokyo negotiating with Aichi's lawyers. We stayed for a month at the Imperial Hotel.

"I asked some of my contacts in the Japanese financial industry and national police department about Aichi and found that this was not a company that First Hawaiian Bank should be dealing with. Mr. Morishita's nickname was 'Mamushi.' In Japan there is a very small, very quick, very venomous snake called mamushi, and there was a reason for the name. This was a very dangerous man.

"Some of the terms Aichi was insisting on I didn't think would be acceptable to the bank."

—attorney Alan Goda

Morishita had a reputation of being connected with the yakuza. That, plus the way the deal was structured, gave some people pause.

(Years later, in 1992, "Mamushi" Morishita's name came up in a U.S. Senate hearing on Asian organized crime. The chief investigator for the Senate committee testified that Morishita used members of a yakuza group to handle debt collection for his Aichi Company. He added that Morishita owned golf courses in California and Arizona and part of Christie's Auction House in New York. He had bought $80 million worth of art for his Tokyo gallery, including works by Van Gogh and Picasso. The Senate testimony claimed that at least 50 properties in Hawaii had been bought as fronts for yakuza money laundering, mostly in the mid-1980s.)

One of the biggest potential problems with the terms of our potential deal was that Aichi wanted a line of credit from us that was bigger than First Hawaiian Bank's entire net worth at the time ($135 million). It was absolutely clear that as soon as we signed that guarantee, Mr. Morishita would draw down that line of credit. There was no way we could take a loss of that magnitude. Both Phil and Alan recommended against completing the Aichi deal. But Johnny wouldn't budge.

Among those who were worried about the potential deal were me and Hugh Pingree. At the time I was president of the bank and Hugh, the previous president, was vice chairman. The two of us went to Alan Goda's office and asked him to come for a walk.

As the three of us strolled down Fort Street, we said to Alan, "You know we can't allow this deal with Aichi to happen." We were trying to figure out how to stop it. Alan decided, on his own, to write a confidential letter to Johnny outlining all the reasons the deal should be called off, including the huge line of credit and a lot of other issues.

Johnny was livid when he got the letter. I heard that the next day he called Bert Kobayashi Jr., a bank director and Alan's law partner, and screamed at Bert about Alan's letter. Bert didn't even know about it until then.

In the face of all this opposition, Johnny agreed to pull out of the Aichi deal, but he still had the problem of how to get rid of our Tokyo subsidiary and all those bad loans. Johnny must have lived under a lucky star. He made friends who really loved him, and one of those friends was Kenji Osano, one of the earliest Japanese investors in Hawaii. In about 1961 his company bought the now-closed Kyo-ya restaurant on the edge of Waikiki. Osano, a bald-headed, rather secretive guy, then picked up the Moana Hotel, the Princess Kaiulani, the Sheraton Waikiki, the Sheraton Maui and the Royal Hawaiian.

Osano took a real liking to Johnny, and so they had dinner one night at a Tokyo restaurant. By now Bellinger realized his Japan subsidiary was a situation that could have a bad impact on the First Hawaiian franchise in Hawaii.

Osano told Bellinger, "You have got to get out of this because these are sharks over here and this is not a business for a nice Hawaiian banker to be in." Bellinger was a proud guy but said, "I could use your help. I'm open to any suggestions." Osano had a follow-up dinner with the head of Takefuji Corporation, the largest finance company in Japan, a big one, and it saved the whole bank. Osano told Yasuo Takei, the Takefuji owner, "I've been your friend for many years and we've done many things together. This guy (Bellinger) is a friend of mine from Hawaii. Take his finance company over, buy it out, and merge it in with your operations"—in effect, for a dollar. He took it over, took all the liabilities as a personal favor to Osano. And we got out of that entire episode in 1984 with our skin and our pride intact. If it hadn't been for that, there could have been massive repercussions on First Hawaiian Bank.

Ironically, years later Takei—who had become Japan's second richest man, worth over $5 billion—retired under a cloud himself. He was convicted of ordering the wire-tapping of a journalist who had written articles criticizing his company. He apologized and retired before he died.

That was a valuable lesson for me: Know the markets you're in; don't do business where you don't speak the language; make sure you know what you are getting into. I followed that dictate ever since. That doesn't mean I don't go out of my home market but, if I do, I need to understand the markets I'm going into and the cultures, the laws, the unofficial customs and rules.

Despite getting out of the consumer lending business in Japan, we still wanted to do business with Japanese companies and individuals with ties to Hawaii. First Hawaiian continued to operate its representative office in Tokyo for a long time. During the heyday of Japanese investments, we picked up many great customers in Japan who had investments in Hawaii. Our office was there to take care of our Japanese clients and was very important to us over the years. We dominated the Japanese business in Hawaii. That office made sure we called on our customers constantly, took care of any problems they had, made any loans. It wasn't a Japanese branch like Bank of Hawaii's to do business in Japan, but an office *in* Japan to service the Japanese customers who had investments in Hawaii.

Johnny and I would go over a couple times a year, calling on customers. From the earliest days of the Japan-Hawaii Economic Council, Johnny was the chairman of the Hawaii side and, after his death, I was the second chairman. I remained JHEC chair until the council shut down after the turn of the century.

The genesis of the JHEC goes back to the early 1970s with Gov. Jack Burns, who wanted to get more business from Japan to Hawaii. He formed a delegation of business and government leaders to go out on a trade mission that was to be led by Lt. Gov. George Ariyoshi. Bellinger was vice chairman. The day before they were to leave, George's father took seriously ill, so he had to cancel, and John became head of the trade mission. Out of that group was formed the Japan-Hawaii Economic Council.

Being involved with the top level of business in Japan, you learn a lot about the culture. First of all, there's a hierarchical system. As you walk into the room, with the

Japanese, only their top guy speaks. On our side, whoever is the top person speaks. There was a protocol. You'd sit in a certain chair, and the guest had the best view. At the height of their investing overseas, there would always be an extremely expensive piece of art. In almost every single meeting, a Renoir or Monet would be featured in this guest room.

It was a very formal setting in Japan in the early years. However, after a while, because of the annual meetings of the JHEC, we broke through those barriers, and it got to a point where we could talk *almost* American style. Relationships were built, relationships that lasted 30–40 years. That amazed American bankers. I can even tell you stories where it amazed French bankers. It's like us from some Podunk bank in Hawaii walking into the office of the chairman of IBM or General Motors, but because there was this love for Hawaii, they treated us differently than they would treat a bank from Kansas.

We developed personal friendships with people like the heads of Sony, Suntory and Meiji Yasuda Insurance, one of the largest in the world. They came to my home, and we spent time in their homes, which is extremely rare—Japanese never take you to their homes; it's always restaurants or the office. It was a business built on trust and relationships.

The JHEC was really helpful over the years in forging business-to-business ties. We helped push through a visa waiver that made it easier for Japanese to travel to the U.S. There were times when Japanese tourists were victims of crimes in Hawaii, and JHEC lobbied the chief of police and enforcement agencies in Hawaii to get Japanese-speaking police officers and be more aggressive in policing.

One of the major JHEC accomplishments was on the behalf of the papaya industry. Local papayas

"At one meeting in Johnny's office, I got down on one knee and pleaded with him, 'Don't do the deal with Aichi.' I felt the deal could have sunk the bank. Eventually, he agreed not to sell to the guy, but he made me suffer in my annual reviews for two straight years because of the episode.

"I will never forget those two annual reviews. The first year Bellinger said, 'One of our very important directors, Wally Fujiyama, wants me to fire you.' Wally, the attorney and a director of the bank, was a close friend of both Bellinger and Onodera. He was a powerhouse, responsible for a lot of Japanese bank clients.

"I just lucked into an appropriate response. I said, 'Johnny, if you want to fire me over the Japan Hawaii deal, that's fine, or tell me and I will submit my resignation. However, if you are going to fire me because Wally Fujiyama wants me fired, who is running the bank?' I'm amazed I actually said that to Bellinger.

"He looked at me, 'No raise.' I didn't have a raise for two years. But he kept me as his administrative assistant, and I lasted 11 years in that job until Bellinger's untimely death."

—*Philip Ching, retired First Hawaiian Bank vice chairman*

> "Kenji Osano was the real power behind the sarakin industry. They called him *kaicho*—chairman. Takefuji Corporation, owned by Yasuo Takei, was the No. 1 sarakin company in Japan. Philip Ching and I had dinner with Mr. Osano several times at Mr. Takei's mansion. They would say, 'Kaicho is coming.' When Mr. Osano came in, everybody stood up."
>
> —Alan Goda

were banned in Japan because of the fruit fly, but also because a cartel in Japan didn't want them imported. JHEC broke through on an informal basis and was able to get the government to let papayas into Japan.

We also worked to educate Japanese investors on philanthropy and giving back to the community because that wasn't part of their culture. They didn't have many nonprofits, and we spent a lot of time talking to them about corporate social responsibility.

For a banker, the Japanese investment bubble in the late 1980s was fascinating to watch. It changed Hawaii in many ways. It upgraded our visitor facilities, such as hotels, but it was a crazy time. A lot of the Japanese were almost like *nouveau riche*. They would have a parking lot or some property in Tokyo that was worth $800,000, and three years later it's worth $10 million, and they would borrow against it and buy things. So *a lot* of these companies in Japan were flooding the U.S. with money, and Hawaii got a disproportionate share. Hawaii has always been capital short, but that period was crazy!

We would have young bankers come in who were 28 or 30 years old, which is rare for Japan, with lending authorities that were larger than our bank. They would commit $50 million to this project or that with very little underlying spreadsheet analysis or judgment. They were just competing against each other for deals and acquisitions. JHEC kept counseling them to get good local partners so they knew what they were doing. Through contacts on both sides, many private business deals came together where the Japanese would get partners from Hawaii. We would be informal advisers to help match suitable partners.

Investment analysts always asked me why First Hawaiian never got caught in that whole bubble and never took a hit when it burst. I would tell them about Ken Yee, a quiet, unassuming guy who was our bank's chief appraiser. During the bubble, the Japanese would say this piece of property in Kahala was worth $4 million. The tax appraisal would say maybe $2 million, and Ken Yee said it was worth a million. He was so conservative!

Because we would lend only a percentage of Ken Yee's appraisal amount, we lost out on a lot of big deals because borrowers wanted to borrow, say, $4 million, and we would loan them only $800,000. As a result of sticking with Yee's appraisals, we never got burned because we always had so much "over-collateral" that, even if we foreclosed and sold, we came out OK. We ought to erect a statue of Ken at the bank.

We never got caught up in the craziness. We knew those values weren't real. During this whole Japanese bubble, we saw a lot of greed and local "consultants" for these people who wanted in on the gravy. If you happened to own an old building, or a home in Kahala, and somebody wanted to pay a crazy price, it was good for you, but it wasn't good for the market.

One caveat to that rule was in the visitor industry, where a lot of the money went. The hotels built then with money from Tokyo have benefitted Hawaii greatly ever since. They never could have been built without the Japanese because a lot of them never penciled out at all. They couldn't be made profitable with the amount of debt to be paid down.

Several factors contributed to the Hawaii part of the bubble. One is proximity. Two, the fact that there were so many Japanese here made the investors comfortable. Early on, Hawaii was smart enough through our JHEC and government moves to target that market by having Japanese-language signs in all the hotels, Japanese menus. Also, even Hawaii's high prices looked cheap to them by Tokyo standards.

Greed was *everywhere* during the bubble. It was very hard for First Hawaiian to resist these outlandish loan requests and maintain our discipline while we were losing deals to other lenders, but we did, and our resistance paid off. Even Mainland banks came in to participate with the Japanese banks in lending money in Hawaii. For example, Dick Flamson was head of Security Pacific Bank, the fourth-largest bank in the country. They wanted to come to Hawaii to make some of these loans, and Johnny Bellinger said, "No, we're not going to do work with you. We live in Hawaii and we know what our values are." They continued to make a lot of those loans and got into big trouble. That bank went under and ultimately had to be sold.

That was a time when we became "The Bank That Says *No*." For example, in all the megahotel deals by local developer Chris Hemmeter (more on him in Chapter 20), we would turn them down or take a small first position with other investors behind us in line. The stars of the period were all those Hemmeter projects.

The existence of JHEC paid off after the 9/11 attacks when the flow of Japanese tourists went virtually to zero. My marketing background helped a lot, too. At the request of Gov. Ben Cayetano, I worked around the clock with Peter Schall of Hilton Hotels and Tony Vericella of the Hawaii Visitors & Convention Bureau to design a $20 million promotion and recovery strategy for Japan tourism.

The package included both advertising and working directly with the people in Japan. Unlike U.S. travel, which was mostly FIT—free independent travelers—the Japan side was heavily group tours, and the dominant travel agency was JTB. A very close friend to this day is Isao Matsuhashi, CEO of JTB. I had known him both as a banker and as the JHEC vice chairman on the Japan side. He and his wife became personal friends; we would vacation at their homes.

My JTB friend told me advertising is tricky because the real reason the Japanese were not coming was they felt that, to show proper respect to America for its losses, it would be inappropriate for them to come and have fun in the U.S. He told me we

"Once we had agreed to sell Japan-Hawaii Finance to Takefuji, we needed Federal Reserve approval. I had dealt with a Fed guy in San Francisco named Harry Green. I used to send him boxes of macadamia nuts, which made a huge difference in talking to Harry. He said, 'You know, Philip, it's a sarakin company. You are still on the hook for these lines of credit. What is your assurance that this is a reputable company—because the whole industry is full of very shady characters?' I told him, 'Harry, this company is head and shoulders above all the others; the people who run it are honorable. The head of the fifth largest insurance company in the world, Terumichi Tsuchida, assured me Takefuji is solid, run by honorable people.' I said, 'Harry, our alternative is to continue the losses, or sell to a less reputable firm.' Finally, Harry approved the deal and we were safe."

—*Philip Ching*

should bring our group to Japan and meet high government officials.

Tony, Peter and I put a group together to go to Tokyo, and we wanted to meet with Prime Minister Junichiro Koizumi, the man with the long, flowing, very un-Japanese hairdo who was an absolute rock star. You couldn't get in to see him even if you had God with you asking for an invitation.

The way we finally arranged to see Koizumi is that George Ariyoshi was a close friend of Yoshiaki Tsutsumi, one of the most powerful men in all of Japan and at one point the wealthiest man in the world. He owned the Mauna Kea Beach Resort and the Prince Hotels, and George was on his board. Tsutsumi got Koizumi to extricate himself from all these meetings to give us an audience.

Somebody high up in the Japanese Diet, their parliament, had made a speech that it would be very bad for Japanese people to travel to Hawaii while the United States was suffering. We asked the prime minister to get a message to the Diet that you would hurt the people in Hawaii even more if you took that position.

After we came back, JTB and other travel agencies got together to get the message out that the people of Hawaii need the people of Japan to get Island tourism healthy again. That was a successful mission.

After all my work in and with Japan over the years, it was gratifying to be given one of that country's highest honors, the Order of the Rising Sun, with Gold and Silver Star, in a ceremony at the Consulate General in Honolulu just before I retired as bank CEO. The medal was primarily for my 15 years as Hawaii chair of the Japan-Hawaii Economic Council. However, in presenting the award, Consul General Masatoshi Muto also mentioned I had come to the rescue of many elderly Japanese-American depositors by working out the Manoa Finance bailout. He was also kind enough to give me credit for helping to resolve financial trouble at the Japanese Cultural Center of Hawaii (JCCH).

One with hair, one not. I met with Japan's charismatic Prime Minister Junichiro Koizumi in the wake of 9/11. Our bank's ties with Japan were close.

The JCCH was in difficult straits in 2002. They owed four local banks (First Hawaiian, Bank of Hawaii, Central Pacific and City Bank) $9 million in principal and interest on a construction loan they had never paid off. They were on the verge of selling the building, but Colbert Matsumoto, CEO of Island Insurance Co., stepped up to the plate to organize a last-minute fundraising campaign

Besides the overdue bank loans, the JCCH owed $500,000 to Mrs. Yoshiko Morita, widow of Sony founder Akio Morita. They had asked her for a short-term, temporary loan, but it went on for years. She got more and more upset and was demanding her money back. The JCCH leaders were at their wit's end. It was awkward. The guy who had gotten the money from her, who was the target of all of her screaming, was Yoshiharu Satoh, CEO of Central Pacific Bank.

My Order of the Rising Sun medal from the Japanese government.

In 2004, when I was presented one of Japan's highest honors, the Order of the Rising Sun, with Gold and Silver Star, I had to get all dressed up in a morning coat (it was warm and uncomfortable) for the ceremony at the Consulate General in Honolulu. I was the third head of our bank to receive the Order of the Rising Sun, following bank founder Charles Reed Bishop and my predecessor, Johnny Bellinger. With me, left to right, are my son Trippy (Walter III), daughter Lauren, wife Diane and sons Chris and Peter.

When the deadline for possible foreclosure was only a week away, I met with Colbert at a Kaimuki restaurant. I really lit into him about how the center had been mismanaged, which was unfair because he wasn't the problem. He was the solution—a young guy trying to raise money to bail the center out—but he took the brunt of my wrath. At the end of our meeting, I told him we'd pay off Mrs. Morita, which was a relief to them because the situation was becoming an international problem. I agreed to make a $500,000 donation to JCCH from First Hawaiian Bank Foundation to pay her off and also to work quietly with the other banks to buy them more time. The banks backed off a bit, Colbert amazingly came up with the $9 million, and JCCH was saved.

Flash forward to a year later. Colbert and I and a couple of others were invited to Mrs. Morita's mansion in Kahala so she could thank me for getting her her money back. Instead, she started an angry tirade in Japanese. I didn't know a word she was saying, but I knew it was directed at my friend Yoshiharu Satoh, and I knew she was angry. Satoh-san's head sunk lower and lower as she berated him. When she finished dumping on him, she thanked us for coming and left the room. I went there expecting to be praised; instead, I watched my friend get chewed out. Win a few, lose a few.

Shortly after I became First Hawaiian's CEO following Johnny Bellinger's sudden death, I named my colleague Jack Hoag as president of the bank.

CHAPTER 8

A Sudden Death, a Coup Attempt

I was in Budapest in September 1989 with my wife, brother-in-law and sister-in-law. I had been in Europe for a MasterCard Board meeting and had added a little vacation. We were in Budapest in one of those cheap hotels—my wife is great on bargains—no phones in the room. Somebody came knocking to tell me there was a telephone call. Howard Karr, the bank's chief financial officer, had been trying to reach me. It was kind of a broken connection, but I *finally* got out of it that he was telling me Johnny Bellinger had passed away.

It was quite sudden. He worked that day, played golf, had dinner and drinks with his good friends, went to sleep and never woke up. That's the best way to go, but still he was only 66 and had just signed a contract to remain in his job at least another five years—probably longer. I was in shock. Even though Johnny was a tough boss, I cared a lot for him, and we were very close despite the day-to-day travails.

Changing our reservations to get from Budapest back to Hawaii was not easy at that point. It was a historic time to be there. Earlier that year, Hungary had taken down the barbed-wire fence along its border with Austria, one of the first signs that the Soviet bloc in Eastern Europe was crumbling. As we were going in, people were leaving Hungary for the first time, peacefully. When we got there, they were taking the communist red stars off the buildings. That was a pretty remarkable sight.

It took me about 30 hours to get home. I remember breaking down in the plane, just sobbing. When I got home, it was apparent that the management transition would not be completely smooth because of rumblings within the board of directors.

During his years as CEO, Johnny had been pretty hard on several of the members of the board. With Johnny gone, I suspected that this group would try to have more influence in the bank by limiting the authority of the CEO. When I landed, there were several messages asking me to meet with their clique, immediately. I told my wife, "I'm not meeting with anybody until we honor Johnny." The first thing I wanted to do was visit Joan Bellinger, Johnny's widow. I spent time with her and the family, helping them prepare for the services.

I was president already. According to the bylaws of the bank, if something happened to the chairman and CEO (Johnny), I would also fill those positions unless and until the board decided otherwise. These directors kept calling to meet with me, and I decided to put it all on the line. I knew instinctively that they wanted to split responsibilities and authority between me and them. I knew that a split of authority like that would not be healthy for the bank. I decided I was going to be my own man, even

> "When Bellinger died, there was a big play as to who would be his successor. Some of the directors wanted to play a more active role in running the bank as opposed to just promoting Walter. Under this scenario, Hebden Porteus, one of the directors, would have been either chairman of the board or CEO. Maybe they might have put in Hugh Pingree, who had previously been president and had just retired as vice chairman, as president.
>
> "Walter asked me to approach three directors to speak on his behalf—Rod McPhee, Bob Wo and Sherry Ing. I spoke to them one by one and told them, 'I have known Walter a long time; there is no question in my mind that the future of this bank needs to be in Walter's hands.'"
>
> —Phil Ching, retired First Hawaiian Bank vice chairman

though I wasn't the "confirmed" CEO yet, but I figured it was all or nothing for me. I didn't want to take the job if I had to take it in a compromised position. That was a risk, but I decided to go for it.

When I finally met with them, they told me that they wanted to elect one of their number as chairman of the board. In the back of their mind, some of them didn't feel I was ready to take over. I said "no," that I expected to have all the titles and positions that Johnny had. They were shocked! They didn't expect that from me. In the meantime I had also talked to many other directors who felt the same way I did.

Within a few days, it came to the vote at the board. In the end, the directors who had opposed me realized they didn't have the votes. The leader of their group made the motion that I should inherit all of Johnny's titles, and the board unanimously selected me as chairman and CEO of both the holding company and the bank.

Immediately after that, I called the leader of the group that had challenged me and said, "First, I think this is the right thing for the bank. Second, you folks *are* directors and deserve a major voice in this bank. You should be heard and respected. I am going to make sure you are inside the tent going forward." We struck a wonderful relationship and never crossed swords once after that. They were great directors who just wanted their voices heard, which was their right.

Key guys on the board in helping me get through that challenge were George Freitas, Bobby Pfeiffer, Glenn Kaya and Sheridan (Sherry) Ing.

George Freitas had been on the bank's board for close to 50 years. He was the founder of Pacific Construction, which built many of the buildings in Waikiki and downtown. He built Freitas Hall up at Saint Louis School, which was named after his father. He stood up and said, "Walter Dods has done a great job. He deserves a chance, and I'm going to support him."

At that point one of the other larger shareholders was Alexander & Baldwin Inc., which owned more than 5 percent of the First Hawaiian stock. Bobby Pfeiffer, head of A&B, was a McKinley High School graduate and he stood up for me as well.

John Bellinger died suddenly at age 66, setting up a transition struggle.

"Johnny Bellinger was autocratic, intuitive and competent. John was a complete CEO. He built a succession many years ago and put it in place. Much has been written in the newspapers about John Bellinger's succession. It is assumed that it would be Walter Dods. Anything else will shake the public perception of this bank, with consequences in the stock market.

"Walter has been trained and groomed by a proven success. Let him show us what he can do. It is time for a new wind at this bank. I nominate Walter Dods to be chairman and CEO of this bank."

—*Glenn Kaya, longtime First Hawaiian Bank director*

Glenn Kaya, a Leilehua High graduate, was another one who backed me. Glenn went from nothing to become president of GEM stores on the Mainland. He traveled to the Mainland weekly for years.

The fourth local boy was Sherry Ing, a guy who went from Molokai and Roosevelt High to MIT and Harvard and became one of the great civic and business leaders of Hawaii.

In Hawaii we don't care what college you went to; it's all about what high school you attended. We are proud of that! Self-made guys who went to public schools somehow really touch me, and to have them in my corner made a big difference. Those men, from Saint Louis, McKinley, Roosevelt and Leilehua high schools, came to my defense or I never would have had the CEO job under the conditions I wanted to have.

They had *seen* it, in the old days, how lots of local kids didn't have a chance. These were self-made men. They weren't spoon-fed through private schools. Although Saint Louis was a private school, to me it wasn't private in local eyes—it's a parochial school. They all came from the school of hard knocks. To have those guys behind me made all the difference in the world.

I wasn't necessarily ready for the top job at that moment because Johnny had been so dominant. But life happens. You either grow into the job or you die. I was pretty comfortable with the areas of the bank I was already running, but I didn't have the board relationships down, which is very important with a company. I was on the board but didn't socialize or spend a lot of time with other directors because Johnny didn't like that. I had not done the investments side of the bank, so there were some gaps in my knowledge. But I knew a lot more about the bank than anybody else around and anybody on the board.

After I got over that bump, board relations were good. We opened it up, had more communications with directors. They never gave me a hard time in all of our major decisions—acquisitions, building major facilities.

Within a few weeks after I won the battle and became chairman, president and CEO, I insisted that I give up the president's title. I asked Jack Hoag, my old friend, to be president. If I got hit by a truck the next day, I wanted somebody there. I had always respected Jack, who's a solid banker. We made good partners.

I had the job, but what could I do with it?

"When Johnny died, they had a special emergency meeting of some of the board. Walter was in Europe and couldn't get home for the meeting. Hugh Pingree had just retired as vice chairman, and I was in charge in Walt's absence, so I was at the meeting. There was talk about Walter not succeeding Johnny by a handful of the directors. They were saying we should wait and have a search instead of just promoting Walter.

"I wasn't on the board myself and I was in awe of these people, but I surprisingly spoke up and said, 'You know, we do have a succession plan, and Walter is in line to become the CEO.' I don't know if I was all that persuasive, but nothing came out of the meeting. I don't think there was a formal vote, just consensus that we should let this alone. Walter came back to town and shortly thereafter became chairman and CEO."

—*Jack Hoag, retired First Hawaiian Bank president*

Soon after I became CEO, our 1990 deal to acquire First Interstate Bank of Hawaii started First Hawaiian down the road that eventually made us Hawaii's largest bank. Presiding over the sign changes were Tony Guerrero, then head of branch operations and later a First Hawaiian vice chairman, and Harriet Aoki, First Interstate's president.

CHAPTER 9

We Were No. 2; We Had to Try Harder

At the age of 48, I inherited from Johnny Bellinger a bank that was very well-run and in solid financial shape. We had record earnings and a stock price that rose 67 percent in 1989. Yet in the local market we were way down in the No. 2 position, about half the size of Bank of Hawaii, with no prospects of getting to the top spot unless we changed the paradigm, which is not easy to do.

Change comes very hard to people. To change a culture, you are talking three to five years if everything works right. Just because a legendary boss walks out the door, or in our case when he dies suddenly, the culture doesn't change overnight. You can try to do it more quickly by being dictatorial, yelling and screaming, but you are not really changing the culture.

We had a good bank, but size matters in this business. We were $5 billion in assets; Bank of Hawaii was approaching $10 billion. In the normal course of things, they were pulling away from us. Let's say we each have 10 percent growth; for them it's a billion a year, while for us, it's $500 million. Growing organically to catch them would have taken us forever. We would have had to build new branches, requiring tremendous capital. You can grow at a normal pace with a few new branches each year. Even if we grew at 11 percent and they grew at 9 percent, it would still take 50 years for us to catch up. To make that leap, acquisitions were a better way to do it.

You don't want to be large just to be the largest, but my management team and I had a goal when I took over—to be No. 1 in quality, in service, in profitability and in return to our shareholders. For us to get in the game, we needed to do some deals.

In banking, the best mergers are bank-to-bank, in-city deals, because all you need from the bank you acquire are the branches. You don't need another accounting department, another data processing department, risk department, human resources department. You can cut overhead dramatically. Just keep the branches and you get loan growth, deposit growth and customer reach. That's the ideal. You are willing to pay a little more for an in-city merger because the efficiencies are so tremendous.

My first attempt was with First Federal Savings & Loan. Right after I took over as CEO, Wayne Jack, president of First Federal, called me and asked if First Hawaiian would be interested in acquiring them. I said, "Absolutely. But on one condition: I'm brand new and we have a lot on our plate. If you are talking about getting involved in a bidding contest with somebody else, we are not interested. If you are talking about negotiating an honest deal with a fair price, we are." He said, "The second is what I want. We will work together and do it."

> "I spent five years as president under Walt as CEO. It was almost like when the caterpillar becomes a butterfly. It really unleashed his vision for First Hawaiian Bank. The very first thing he did was make it clear to the staff at all levels that he wanted to share governance. Johnny was a top-down guy. Managers in the branches could not pick out the carpeting; Johnny had to pick it out. When Johnny was in charge, we only bought black cars with no radios. Johnny did very many wonderful things, but there was a lot of fear factor. Walter brought some levity into the system, changing from fear to collaboration."
>
> —Jack Hoag, retired First Hawaiian president and longtime board member

We went through the due-diligence process. For example, our people would go in and look at all their loan files and make sure they own the title to their properties. We'd bring in accounting experts who would look at their records. It's a lot of time and effort. You are taking your employees, who have full-time jobs, and then at night and weekends they are going through all of First Fed's books.

I should have seen the early sign of trouble, but I didn't. Wayne had a very good line: "You can only come during these hours to look at our files because we don't want our employees to know you are looking." That seemed logical, so we only went at certain times. This process took several months, and we struck a deal on a price, subject to approval of both boards.

This was my first deal that I'd be taking to the board as CEO. We were in the middle of our board meeting, and Wayne was supposedly simultaneously meeting with his board to approve the deal. I got a call that Wayne wanted to speak to me immediately. I figured their board was not going to approve it, so I asked our board to recess.

Heb Porteus and a couple of other directors came with me to my office, and I put Wayne on speaker phone, which he didn't know. He said, "We have had a last-minute hitch." I said, "What do you mean? We had everything settled." He said, "Out of the clear blue, we received another offer. We are in the middle of our board meeting and, if you up your offer, we can get the board to approve it right now." I can't remember the exact dollar figure he wanted, but it wasn't a significant number for the size of the deal.

I said, "Wayne, I guess you still don't know me. I wouldn't buy your company now for five dollars! You lied to me." I slammed the phone down and had to go back in and tell my board. I'm a brand-new CEO, but I wouldn't do it. The whole time he was dealing with us, they were also negotiating with Bank of Hawaii, which subsequently did buy First Fed. He was trying to get our price up. Years later, I talked to Howard Stephenson, who was Bank of Hawaii CEO at the time, and he said they didn't know we were bidding, either.

When First Fed fell through, there were very few other local acquisition opportunities, but one that intrigued me was the old American Security Bank, which had changed its name to First Interstate Bank of Hawaii. It was the state's fourth-largest bank, with assets over $855 million—about one-sixth the size of First Hawaiian.

American Security was founded in the 1930s by Chinese Americans, same as the Americans of Japanese ancestry had founded City Bank and Central Pacific Bank for their ethnic community.

American Security always had a Chinese CEO, but they decided they needed to broaden their customer base. The Chinese community is a terrific community with a certain amount of wealth but wasn't a large population. ASB brought in a CEO from the Mainland, Don McGregor. He had worked for First Interstate as one of his stops along the way. He got a franchise where the local bank got the rights to the First Interstate name and branding. They were able to create a nice little market for themselves but still needed more capital to grow. Ultimately they sold to William Simon, former secretary of the Treasury under Presidents Nixon and Ford, and his partner Gerald Parsky, who had been undersecretary of the Treasury. The two of them owned more than half the stock.

Right after we missed out on First Federal, Bill Simon called me to introduce himself, and we had a private lunch. He wanted to see if we were interested in buying Honfed Bank, a savings and loan here that he also owned with a few other investors. We weren't interested in Honfed, which was the largest S&L in Hawaii but basically just a mortgage company.

(As it turned out, Honfed was sold in 1992 for $165 million to my friend Dick Rosenberg and Bank of America, which tried to use it as a launching pad to expand into the Islands. But BofA had a lot of trouble operating in Hawaii. Five years later, they sold Honfed to American Savings for $96 million—a $69 million loss from what they paid for it originally.)

Anyway, back to my lunch with Bill Simon. After I expressed no interest in Honfed, I went on to say, "Would you have any interest in selling First Interstate to me?" He put

"In the 1990s, everybody was acquiring like mad. The number of banks in the country was shrinking and shrinking as acquisitions went forward. Everybody was feeling they didn't want to be left out. They didn't want to be the rabbit; they wanted to be the fox. That must have been part of Walt's consideration.

"Under securities law, the management of any company had to act in the best interest of the shareholders. There came to be a doctrine that you can't just say 'no' to a takeover bid. You had to construct a plan for the future of the corporation. You had to set up methodologies for decisions to acquire or addressing acquisition proposals or hostile takeovers. You had to have a rational basis always favoring the interest of the shareholders for doing whatever you did.

"The New York lawyers were constantly pushing Walt and the board to come up with their business plan. Walt's preference was to just say 'no.' He wanted to preserve First Hawaiian as free-standing."

—Tom Huber, *retired general counsel of First Hawaiian Bank*

on a surprised look, but he's an investment banker, so he said, "No, we want to keep it but, you know, there is a price on everything. Let me think about it." He or Parsky called me up a little later and said, "Yes, we can talk, but it wouldn't be cheap." I always felt that, when he initially called me, selling First Interstate might have been in the back of his mind, but he was clever enough to have me make the first move.

In February 1990, just four months after I became CEO, we agreed to buy First Interstate in a cash deal for about $140 million, which was a little over two times book value of their company. (Book value is the value of a company according to its balance sheet.) A price over two times book was the higher end of the range of bank deals those days, and I was criticized in the national *American Banker* newspaper for the price we paid.

However, we knew what we were paying for, and I felt the transaction was crucial to our growth. It was the catalyst for us starting to become a growing and dynamic bank. Within three years, bank mergers were going for two and a half, three, four times book.

We had hoped to complete the merger in nine months. Early on we were told by experts that it was going to be hard to raise the money to complete the deal, but that the regulatory process would be easy. It turned out to be the other way around.

First, we had to raise the money to pay for the deal, so we went out for our first-ever public offering of First Hawaiian stock. We were trying to raise $118 million in new capital in anticipation of the deal, which was not yet approved by regulators. I went out with some of our senior people to do what's called a "road show" to sell the stock.

To do a road show, you pick an investment banker, and we picked Merrill Lynch. I wanted to take the retail model, going to smaller cities to sell our stock rather than just to New York's big institutions. I didn't mind having institutional shareholders, but I didn't want them to be dominant because they were more short-term holders. We hopscotched around the Mainland on our bank jet—me, my CFO, Howard Karr, and the Merrill Lynch guys—meeting in different cities with people who buy big blocks of stock. They call them "one on one" meetings, but there's usually five or 10 guys—in those days almost all younger men, very few women—on the other side of the table. These young analysts had researched our company back to 1858, and

> "When First Hawaiian Inc. announced that it will buy First Interstate of Hawaii from William E. Simon's merchant banking firm for an estimated $140 million, some observers thought the young chief executive of the acquiring company, Walter Dods Jr., had been taken to the cleaners. Former Treasury Secretary Simon paid less than half that amount for (First Interstate) a year ago... Mr. Dods, however, bristles at the notion that he is overpaying, (and) the purchase may yet prove to be a good one for First Hawaiian."
>
> —American Banker
> *newspaper, February 9, 1990.*

they knew everything about us going in. We'd repeat our same pitch three or four times a day to different groups.

We had a good story to tell. We had just gotten named by *Business Week* as the "most solid bank in the United States." We would start our presentation with a graph showing 25 straight years of record earnings. What sold our stock was that fact and our minimal loan losses—about .05 percent of assets, less than one-tenth of one percent. One of the pitches we made was, "We have not had a single mortgage foreclosure in five years." In the banking business, that's unheard of.

That phenomenon has a lot to do both with the underwriting standards of our bank and with the culture of Hawaii. People in Hawaii, as a rule, honor their debts. That's both the Asian culture and our mixed local culture. Then and now, at First Hawaiian we know our customers. We are more comfortable making a stretch loan where the balance sheet might not be perfect but where we know the character of the borrowers so well that we know they'll find a way to pay us back. That has been our culture all along.

The very first road-show stop was at a company called Janus in Denver. We go through our presentation and, as we leave—and this is the Portuguese part of the story—this Janus guy says, "I'm very impressed. I will take 350,000." I thank him very much, walk out the door and tell the Merrill Lynch guy, "Hey, we got our first 350,000 dollars." He says, "You dumb shit, that's 350,000 shares!" The guy had bought 350,000 times the price per share—about $8 million! That's how naïve I was. Those guys never let me forget that story.

One of our last stops was at Fidelity, the granddaddy of them all, in Boston. They buy really big chunks, and they're one of the institutional holders I would feel comfortable holding our stock because they have the reputation for being a longer-term shareholder. We get into the meeting with six guys. Their top bank analyst, the one who decides what they are going to buy and what they are not going to buy, doesn't show up until near the end.

This is 1990—during the Japanese Bubble, where they are investing all over the world, especially in Hawaii. I'm sitting there with Karr, who is half-Japanese and half-German. I always told him he had the worst qualities of those two races sometimes when he got mad. This Fidelity guy walks into the room and says, "I don't want to hear all this shit. Just one question: When are the Japs going to take over Hawaii?" I'm sitting next to Howard, and I could see him getting ready to jump across the table

> "I worked as coordinator of the First Interstate acquisition. There was pressure to lay off people and get more financial gain from the deal, but Walt insisted on keeping all the First Interstate employees. He always wanted to look at it from the people point of view. Johnny Bellinger's style was more top-down. Walt wanted people to do things together. In implementing the First Interstate deal, we set up task forces from both companies to work out the details. Everybody got to have input."
>
> —Wesley Park, retired First Hawaiian board member

"Bank of America's venture into Hawaii was one of my big mistakes. We did it by buying Honfed, a savings and loan, in 1992, and it's always difficult to turn a savings and loan into a bank. The other hurdle is that Hawaii is kind of a closed community. Maybe if we had acquired First Hawaiian or Bank of Hawaii, we would have enough of a base of being part of the Islands. But what we acquired was an outsider to begin with—Honfed was owned by former Treasury Secretary Bill Simon—and when an outsider like BofA acquires the outsider, there's no possibility of success.

"In all honesty, it probably was going to be the first step that would lead to BofA acquiring one of the big banks. If you looked at the future, First Hawaiian would probably not have survived in the form it was in if BNP, a foreign bank, hadn't acquired it. And Bank of Hawaii came very close to not surviving. As a first step, our acquisition of Honfed would probably have been OK; as an end game, it was impossible.

"In the end, though, I never did approach either of the big Hawaii banks about acquiring them."

—Dick Rosenberg, retired chairman & CEO, Bank of America

and punch the Fidelity guy. I'm squeezing his knee as hard as I could to calm him down. We have millions at stake, and his face was turning colors, but I got him cooled off. We made the pitch and they did buy stock. When we looked back on it later, it was kind of funny. At the time, it wasn't.

I also wanted to raise $20 million of the total in Japan. I wanted geographic diversification, and we were really becoming the preferred bank for Japanese investors. I had a very close friend in Japan named Terumichi Tsuchida, CEO of Meiji Life Insurance, one of the largest life insurance companies in the world. He was also on a lot of Mitsubishi company boards. He was my vice chairman on the Japan-Hawaii Economic Council, and we became really close. He loved Hawaii. He would come to my home in Hawaii, which is rare, and I would visit him and his wife. He was also president of the sumo fan club for Jesse Kuhaulua—the famed sumo wrestler from Maui who became known as Takamiyama.

I asked Teru if he would set up a meeting with some large banks and insurance companies that could be potential buyers of our stock. We presented to all these Japanese executives, and after the meeting he pulled me aside and said, "How much are you trying to raise?" I told him, "Oh, $20 million would be terrific." He looks at me and says, "They are all my friends and they would be happy to buy, but I will take it all." Bang, that was it.

First Hawaiian was probably one of their best investments. When we sold it to BNP 10 years later, they made a lot of money, but they were devastated because they didn't want to sell. They loved to own a piece of Hawaii. That was a beautiful thing Teru did for me, which I never forgot.

When he passed on, I went to his services in Tokyo. I've never seen a funeral like that in my

Meeting in my office with good friend Terumichi Tsuchida, CEO of Meiji Life Insurance, and his wife Kazuko. They both loved Hawaii.

life, but in Japan it's common for a big CEO. They take over big hotel ballrooms like in the Hilton Hawaiian Village, and one whole wall—maybe 20 feet tall by 100 feet long—is covered by white chrysanthemums. The service is like a military operation with thousands of people lining up to pay their respects. You go up 50 at a time, in rows. The front row goes up, the family bows to you, and you bow to them. They never get out of line. You don't individually talk to them. You bow and move out and the next 50 come. I came up in that line and I bowed, and Teru's wife, Kazuko, broke every Japanese protocol. She walked out of the line and came across to hug me. That was the relationship we had. The Japanese were aghast—"Wow, this guy must be somebody!" I wasn't somebody; it's just that we were really good friends.

With extra help like that, we didn't have much trouble raising the cash to pay for First Interstate. We completed the offering in a month. However, getting approval from the banking regulators turned out to be harder than we had imagined. Shortly after we announced our deal, the U.S. Justice Department challenged it, contending that it would add to concentration in the local banking market. We couldn't understand why.

This same Justice Department sat quietly by while Bank of Hawaii acquired First Federal. Bank of Hawaii was larger than we were; First Federal was slightly larger than First Interstate of Hawaii. We didn't feel our deal created more market concentration; we felt it was an issue of long-term survival.

"It was difficult for a smaller institution like Pioneer Federal to compete. There were more and more regulations and a need for more capital.

"In late 1992, Gerry Czarnecki, who was running Honfed Bank, approached me about buying Pioneer, but they were owned by Bank of America, and I didn't want us to become part of a Mainland bank. Instead, a few months later, I started talking to Walter about merging with First Hawaiian. My main goal was to protect our Pioneer employees, and it worked out well—our employees kept their jobs, our Pioneer shareholders profited. Walt was a man of his word."

—*Lily Yao, retired chairman & CEO of Pioneer Federal and former First Hawaiian vice chairman*

WE WERE NO. 2; WE HAD TO TRY HARDER

After acquiring Pioneer Federal Savings in 1993, we kept it as a separate subsidiary until 1997, when we merged it into First Hawaiian Bank and the signs were changed.

Pioneer Federal CEO Lily Yao and I celebrate our merger by doing First Hawaiian's patented "High-Y."

> "Walter convened a strategic planning meeting in Waikiki with this well-known consultant who was recommending a major overhaul of our technology systems. He told us, 'You've got to change your people. They won't be able to adapt.' Walt says, 'We're an *ohana* company, and we retrain our people.' That part of Johnny Bellinger's legacy stayed on through Walter, through Don Horner, and on to Bob Harrison today—the idea that we are a local bank, a family bank."
>
> —Jack Hoag

I remember being so frustrated that our lawyers couldn't get us across the finish line that I went to see the famous Washington lobbyist Tommy Boggs, who had done work in Hawaii for Campbell Estate and Duty Free Shoppers. His father was Hale Boggs, the late House majority leader; his mother was Lindy Boggs, also a member of Congress from Louisiana, and his sister is Cokie Roberts, the National Public Radio journalist. Tommy got his top lawyer, who had these new theories on market concentration, and I paid him good bucks, but the theories never went anywhere.

In the end, though, despite the opposition from Justice, we got through the Federal Reserve Board of Governors in November 1990 on a 3-2 vote after agreeing to sell off four First Interstate branches on the Neighbor Islands. But for that one vote from the Fed, First Hawaiian could still be a very small bank operating only in Hawaii.

We thought, *Wow, we've got it!* But the Justice Department didn't give up. A month later, they sued us despite the Fed approval, which is pretty unusual. In the end, we settled with the government by agreeing to sell seven branches around the state, mostly on the Neighbor Islands.

We had raised the money, finally gotten the regulatory approvals and closed the deal in May 1991, after 16 months of battle. We offered everybody at First Interstate a place in our organization, which is pretty rare for in-market acquisitions. We were able to do that because, going into the merger, we froze all First Hawaiian Bank vacant positions, and I asked First Interstate to do the same. The goal was to have openings available so we didn't have to lay off anybody on either side. For example, although we would have one human resources department, we froze positions so when the time came we could put their people into our HR department. Real estate, we did the same thing. With natural attrition, that left a lot of vacancies that we could fill without overstaffing.

The only one who didn't want to come was the First Interstate CEO, Don McGregor. I told him I would find a role in the bank for him, which he appreciated, but he had a deal with the Simon group that gave him a big bonus, and he wanted to move back to the Mainland. By that point, Harriet Aoki had become president of First Interstate. I made Harriet president of our First Hawaiian Creditcorp subsidiary and head of strategic planning and government affairs for the bank. She had a great career with us for years.

Because of the no-layoffs goal, we didn't get all the cost synergies from the merger immediately, but we got them within 24 months. We also got tremendous morale and support because everybody had a job. Some of the First Interstate people became key leaders at First Hawaiian—Harriet Aoki; Donnie Yannell, longtime manager in Waikiki; Jim Wayman, who ran our Bank Properties Division and supervised the First Hawaiian Center project; and quite a few others.

We acquired a good group of people who fit our culture pretty well. We had a *luau* the first weekend with all the employees at our recreation center in Makaha, designed so our branch people would sit with their branch people, real estate people would sit with real estate, etc. We had adopters for adoptees for every area of the bank.

Keeping the First Interstate employees happy went a long way toward keeping their customers in the fold. You are buying two things—the employees and their customer relationships. We made a list of every major customer. At the top, I personally met them with the contact officer from First Interstate. And the next level down, our executive vice presidents would go. We got to every business customer at some level.

By combining First Interstate with First Hawaiian, we were able to have a platform large enough to compete against Bank of Hawaii, even though we were still a lot smaller. That merger was pivotal in First Hawaiian starting to catch up to the competition. The second big catalyst for growth happened about 18 months later, in early 1993, when we agreed to acquire Pioneer Federal Savings and Loan. The idea came up when Lily Yao, head of Pioneer, called me to see if we would be interested. We met soon after to discuss the idea.

As with the earlier First Interstate deal, we kept all 266 employees from Pioneer's staff. In this acquisition, we kept Pioneer up and running as a separate institution until we merged it into First Hawaiian in 1997. Their two senior officers, Lily Yao and

> "Back in the 1960s, our bank was among the first in Hawaii to have mainframe computers, but by the time Walt took over in 1989, we had been underinvesting and had gotten behind the curve. Walt sent a few of us to five different banks on the West Coast to see what they were doing. That led to investing more in technology and building KIC—our operations center in Kalihi—in the early 1990s.
>
> "When I joined the bank, we had $2 billion in assets and 2,400 employees; now it's $18 billion and 2,200 people. There is only one way that happened—technology."
>
> —Gary Caulfield, vice chairman & chief information officer, First Hawaiian Bank

Al Yamada, stayed with us for years. Lily became a vice chairman of First Hawaiian until she retired, and Al later succeeded Howard Karr as our chief financial officer.

The $87 million cash transaction was good for Pioneer stockholders, who saw their share value climb by more than 25 percent when the deal was announced. It was also a good price for us—1.4 times book value. These two acquisitions put us over $7 billion in assets for the first time, helping us to close the gap with Bank of Hawaii, which still was nearly twice our asset size.

Around the same time, we also rolled out what we called our "relationship strategy," created by Don Horner, who took over our retail banking side in the early 1990s. Don, who later succeeded me as CEO, is a very smart, strategic banker. He did a lot of research and documented what you know instinctively—the more relationships you have with the customers, the better chance you have to keep them. Instead of looking for new customers all the time, sell more products to the ones you already have. If somebody has just a CD account, get them into checking, credit card, a mortgage, a car loan, a trust that the bank handles.

Given the nuisance of having to change all those accounts, customers tend to stay with you. (You have to do something really bad to lose a customer with multiple accounts. If you get up to six, seven accounts, you'd have to blow up the guy's garage to lose the banking relationship.) Don, Tony Guerrero and their team put together a program so that, at a certain level of loans and deposits, you would have a private banker, a personal banker or a business banker assigned to you. You can contact him or her directly if something goes wrong. That relationship banking strategy has been the cornerstone of First Hawaiian's success in the market in the last 20 years.

Acquisitions weren't the only thing we were doing in my early years as CEO. In between the First Interstate and Pioneer deals, we decided to build a new high-tech operations center, which the bank badly needed.

When I first took over, we hired Ram Charan, a strategic business consultant who works for some of the biggest companies in the world. He helped us realize we were way behind the curve on electronics and data processing. Although we were a good operations bank, we needed to revolutionize that whole technology area. Ram said

First Hawaiian's KIC tech operations center in Kalihi.

something I will never forget: "Technology is the one area where you can go from last place to first overnight. Just buy the latest contraptions."

Now we made a major commitment to build KIC (Kamehameha Industrial Center), a $62 million, 215,000-square-foot operations center in Kalihi, and change our entire technological platform, in the middle of buying First Interstate and Pioneer.

I cannot describe how complicated it is to change computer systems. You saw what happened when Hawaiian Electric did it, when Hawaiian Telcom did it. Having your telephone not work is a problem. Having all your bank records not work, your checks not clearing, merchants unable to transfer deposits and payroll—that is a whole different level of grief. To convert all of that successfully is a big, big job. Ken Bentley, Gary Caulfield and a lot of other guys pulled that off.

We were doing that while trying to convert First Interstate to our systems, moving Pioneer over to our systems, all in a four-year period. We were transforming a sleepy, well-run bank into a major player, all within that short time. It was pretty heady stuff. Doing all this in the middle of the Japanese bubble starting to burst was a feat. Looking back on it, I wonder why I had the guts to do it. Any one of those could have killed our earnings and slowed us down for years. We said as a management team, "We'll take one on the chin for earnings now, and long term this thing will really drive us to be part of our goal to be No. 1."

Then we added to the to-do list by announcing plans to build a new headquarters downtown.

This implosion on January 9, 1994 took down the old bank headquarters, making room for construction of First Hawaiian Center.

CHAPTER 10

Reaching for the Downtown Sky

> *"Walter had a lot of kid come out in him when he was building this building, not that he was treating it frivolously or not seriously, but that he was passionately wrapped up in it."*
>
> Jack Myers, developer of First Hawaiian Center

I have done a lot of crazy things in my life, particularly when I was a hot-rodding kid. But one of the craziest was in 1996 when we were in the middle of putting up the new First Hawaiian Center downtown. From my perspective—and I know not everyone agrees with me—it is the finest building in Honolulu.

I would often visit the construction site, slap on a hard hat and see how things were going. My friends kidded me that I was behaving more like a construction foreman than a banker.

One of the things that had always fascinated me was the climbing crane. The crane climbs up as the building rises. When they get up high and the crew needs to extend the crane to get up higher, the wind has to be less than 10 or 12 miles an hour because, in effect, the workers take out all the bolts and jack up the top. For a few moments, there is nothing holding it together. It has to be balanced so they can add another section and then rebolt it in as the building goes up. Now, that really amazed me.

I asked the operator if I could go up and experience that. One day when they were almost near the top, I climbed up. I had to get into the building halfway and then climb up the ladder. There was a little bridge, just a little skeleton walkway that you had to go across to get into the crane and climb up. Now, remember this is the tallest building in Honolulu (429 feet), but the crane is higher than the building. I could see Molokai through the Kaimuki dip. We got up there and sat in the cab while they jacked it up and added a piece in. Ironically now, when I stand near the edge of the building, my knees shake and I have to move back. But at that point, it didn't bother me.

That Monday morning when Denny Watts, president of Fletcher Pacific Construction, found out they had allowed me in the cab, he threatened to fire the manager. He didn't feel it was the proper place for the CEO, who was paying the bills for the construction, to be up there. I had to go see Denny and tell him it wasn't the guy's fault. I had to pressure him. He was really upset about it.

I followed the building's progress carefully from step one.

This was my biggest project by far, at a cost of $200 million, but I had long been fascinated by the intricacies of architecture and construction. It all started with Dillingham Corporation when I was their advertising and PR guy. One of their subsidiaries was Hawaiian Dredging Construction Co., which built most of the major buildings around town, and their land department people were the creators of a lot of stuff, including Ala Moana Center. Another project was 1350 Ala Moana, which was designed by Minoru Yamasaki, out of Detroit, who designed the World Trade Center.

Because of my interest in construction and architecture, when it came time for our building, I wanted it done right.

There were a lot of intricate details involved. One was the thrill of going out to select all the building materials. Building developer Jack Myers and I had gone through a lot of misery—and money—getting through the building permit process and fighting the "historic" status of the old bank building, which we had planned to take down. So we were ready for something different and more productive. We went to France to select the French limestone that you see around the building. The quarry was outside Lyon. There are thousands of variations in the colors. They had shown us samples, but we wanted to make sure what we saw was representative of those samples. Seeing a six-inch sample is one thing, but it's another to see 10 feet, 12 feet, 20 feet and get the flavor of it. The architect selects the colors, pattern and material, but we wanted to go there and absolutely confirm it was right.

The building's "skin" is what you see when the project is completed. Blending the right stone, glass and metal components is an art led by the architect in collaboration with the client. Getting into the stone quarry in France was fun, to be sure, but it was also essential to make certain what we were buying was, in fact, what we expected for the finished product.

The most thrilling experience was in Italy. We stayed in Portofino, close to where the famous

---

"We were in France picking out stone for First Hawaiian Center and I wanted to take the entourage to a very special lunch. There were 10 or 12 of us, including our wives. I found this restaurant called Georges Blanc, one of the most famous food and wine places in all of France.

"It was a four-hour lunch—spectacular and memorable. Our group drank a lot of wine. Diane Dods doesn't drink a lot. As I recall, she managed to kick Walter under the table for drinking much more than he might on a more normal occasion. That was the only time I think I got a little bit in my cups with Walt during all the years I worked with him, but we were really celebrating.

"I remember thinking, *Boy—this is going to be like $4,000 plus.* The tab was actually $11,000, proving what a good sommelier can sell to an enthusiastic customer—me! "

—*Jack Myers*

Carrara marble is mined. If you look down on the First Hawaiian Center lobby and main branch floor, all of that marble you see came from this one cave that they have been mining for marble since nearly the time of Christ. On the way up into the mountains, our host pointed out a faint roadway used in ancient times to transport marble from the quarry to build St. Peter's Basilica. Carrara marble was used by Michelangelo to carve the statue *David*.

We were looking for a particular stone with streaks. We got to the site and went into a cave. The workers wouldn't look us in the eye. Their whole life, all they worry about and all they care about is the marble.

Once in a while, one of the workers gets killed. The marble is compressed in this cold mountain for centuries, and when they take it out, sometimes it explodes and breaks up. It's dangerous work. In the cave, they took a little bottle of water and squirted it onto the stone. When the water hit, it showed the veins in the rock for us to select.

It may seem that we went to a lot of trouble over these kinds of details, but I wanted it to be a first-class project. A bank wants to build something that will last for a long time. In the end, it doesn't cost that much more to have a super-high-quality project over a run-of-the-mill project. To me, good taste makes good sense. The difference between good architectural materials and run-of-the-mill stuff might be 10 percent. The difference in architectural fees between the greatest architect in the U.S. and an average architect is nominal. It is usually about the same percentage of the project cost. If you can get the best, go for the best. When you are going to build a bank, you're going to do it once in 50 years or more, so do it right. The value to the bank is more than just whether the economics made sense on paper. There's a value to the brand that can't be measured in dollars.

From the beginning, I knew this new building would be controversial. I didn't want an ordinary building, no question about it. I wanted a building that was forward-thinking, forward-looking. The building impacts what people think about the bank, overall. In fact, when we finished the building and moved in, we did some opinion research. It was the same bank as it was before we built the building, but the research showed that we were now considered the more modern bank, more progressive. Our reputation had actually changed, and the employees felt different. Some people say, "Oh that's just Dods' monument." I never felt that way.

We had had a small building on a block that could hold a lot more, and we had run out of room. We desperately needed the space, so there was no question there was economic sense for the building. The proof is in the pudding. You take a look at our

> Walter Dods' achievement in leasing out 80 percent of the planned First Hawaiian Center even before the building was announced "has no precedent in Hawaii. He might have broken some arms along the way, but whatever he did, he did a fantastic job."
>
> —*Steve Sofos of Sofos Realty Co., 1993*

YES! A MEMOIR OF MODERN HAWAII

"Architect Bill Pedersen from New York came to meet with us in the dining room of our old downtown headquarters and he drew out some ideas on a napkin for how the building might look. He wanted First Hawaiian Center to be street-friendly, so he proposed setting it back from King Street. On that napkin, he also came up with the idea of the prow leaning across Bishop Street toward Bank of Hawaii. He felt the aggressive prow would send a message to Bank of Hawaii."

—*Jim Wayman, retired First Hawaiian senior VP and building project manager*

major competitor today. Their operating expenses are a lot higher than ours because they have to rent space or buy and build all around town because they do not have enough space where they are. We took all of that into consideration. Over half this building is just for First Hawaiian people.

Plus, I wanted to do it right. This building is at Ground Zero. Bank founder Charles Reed Bishop lived right across the street, and there is just a lot of wonderful history, so I wanted to do something that was forward-looking, that would give the community the ability to say, "Hey, we are as good as anybody, and we can be as modern as anybody."

I didn't think we could do a historic-style building like A&B—which I deeply admire architecturally and as a building—in a highrise. People have tried to do highrises that look like old Hawaii, and they are flops.

I concluded we needed a cutting-edge building, something completely fresh. Toward that end, I was able to get the very best architects in the U.S. to bid. At the time there was a recession, so almost all the top architects bid on this project. Ordinarily we would not have had the opportunity to even talk to these people. We got the best of the best to build the building.

We still had the company plane in those days, and I took off on a cross-country trip with Jack Myers, project manager Jim Wayman from the bank and a couple of others to meet with many of the best architects in the business. That final list—it was about five—came out of a winnowing-down project that brought prospects down from 20 to 12 and then the final five. By that time, unfortunately, there were no local architectural firms on the list. But we insisted that a local architect be brought in to do all the local facilitation and participate and work on all aspects of the building.

That interviewing trip was amazing. It was virtually breakfast in New York, lunch in Chicago and dinner in LA. One of the strangest meetings was in Chicago. The architect we were to meet—I won't use his name—sent us up a winding staircase into a little tower into what was like a castle conference room. Then the architect came sweeping into the room, wearing a cape. I was impressed with his architecture but not the man. I knew within minutes he wasn't the one, but I said nothing at the time; we had other interviews to go.

In the end, we selected Bill Pedersen from Kohn Pedersen Fox Associates of New York. He didn't just talk about the building he envisioned, but also about its place in Honolulu, its relationship with the mountains and the ocean. His design was organic to the place where it would be built. In fact, the rough sketch he showed us ended up remarkably similar to what was finally built. I knew within five minutes that he was our man, but again I didn't say anything because we were not through with our interviews. Later on, Myers, the building's developer, put it well:

"We were all drinking the Kool-Aid even before we left. Here was a guy that had not really spent time in Honolulu who had picked up on the really germane point of things which would be important to those of us who were going to live with this when it was all done. He scored."

We got back from the trip on a Friday, met on Monday, and by then it was clear that KPF was the one.

Pedersen was among the first to argue that the building would work better if we could go up higher than the existing 350-foot limit for downtown Honolulu. A higher tower would mean more open space at ground level and a more interesting building design. Not more net floor space, but a taller, skinnier building. But going higher meant we had to convince the City to change the zoning for downtown—not an easy task. We lobbied hard, not just with the City but with many other interested groups. In the end, the Council agreed, and I have to give credit to then Council members Donna Mercado Kim and Gary Gill for seeing the merits of our argument.

The rezoning applies to the entire downtown area, but it will be a long time before anyone else attempts something this ambitious. There just aren't the opportunities.

But there was one other task before we could get going. To construct the building we wanted, we would have to consolidate the entire block. We owned a big chunk of it, but Finance Factors, HonFed Bank and the Magoon Estate owned other parcels. None was particularly interested in selling. HonFed sold first, and then Finance Factors came along, in a deal that gave them First Hawaiian stock. To seal that deal, we also had to give Finance Factors the old 1930s-era scale that had been in our branch lobby for years. The boss at Finance Factors, Wendell Pang, used it often to check his weight and wouldn't agree to sell his parcel unless they got to take the scale with them to their new headquarters. (We replaced it with a modern one in the new branch.)

The Magoon Estate originally insisted on taking a tiny share of our building in exchange for their land, and we cut out a portion of the new building for their offices. They, too, eventually sold their interest, so we ended up with 100 percent of the block.

Now we had the zoning, the land, a terrific development team and arguably one of the best architects in the country.

Around that time, I received a surprising call from then-Mayor Frank Fasi, who was always full of ideas. Fasi proposed a land swap: The City would take over our recently consolidated block for a park and in exchange he would give us Block J, which was the last major remaining parcel mauka of downtown in the old Kukui Redevelopment Project. First Hawaiian could develop its new center there in conjunction with some kind of international center. I listened carefully but didn't want

> "Walter wanted to build a new headquarters, but to make it work he had to lease a lot of the space to others. For our ad agency, the rent at First Hawaiian Center was substantial, but we knew the business we got from the bank would help offset the higher rent. It was like taking money from the right pocket to the left. Before constructing the building, First Hawaiian was the No. 2 bank, but the building was part of his vision, and now it's far and away No. 1."
>
> —Nick Ng Pack, president & CEO, Milici Valenti Ng Pack

to get involved in another government hassle. Frank hung up and never mentioned the idea again. Today, the site is a car dealership and a condominium.

I started out believing our project would include saving the old Damon Building in one form or another. At the start we asked Myers—who was with us until the end—to conduct a study on what could be done with the property. That study, completed in 1990, assumed that restoration and retention of the Damon Building would be a goal of any redevelopment. But the more we looked into it, the clearer it became that this wouldn't be an option. Our space and design needs dictated something completely new.

While I knew I wanted to build something new and different, I also knew there were those who had a lot of affection for the old First Hawaiian building. Before we went ahead, we explored 37 different options, many of which included retaining the old Damon Building. One option was to dismantle that building, build parking underneath and then put it back up again. But that didn't really work. In the first place, the Damon Building wasn't a particularly good example of American Federal bank architecture for its time. Plus, it wasn't in good condition. In the end, it just didn't make economic or creative or architectural sense, and one by one we abandoned those ideas. That didn't stop people from fighting us.

I even had opposition from within my own management team. They were worried about the financial risk of taking on a project of this magnitude. But my thinking was if it impacted the bottom line by 2 to 3 percent or less, then it would be worth doing for future generations. And that's how it worked out.

I felt then and I feel today that the old building was not worth saving, particularly when you consider our space and growth needs. That old building was on no historic register; in fact, it hadn't been historic at all until we tried to take it down. I didn't expect that. I expected positive community reaction to the building. So the opposition came as a big surprise to me, it really did. And, basically, it was a small but vocal group, as always. Even Historic Hawaii didn't come out against us.

But the opponents had a weapon. They found an obscure federal law—Section 106 of the National Historic Preservation Act—that was created because some bank in North or South Carolina tore down an old building, and the National Preservation folks went wild. I didn't even know about that law; that was a surprise and a setback. We were stuck in federal bureaucracy and facing, of all things, an architectural review by the Federal Deposit Insurance Corp.

"After Walt first became CEO in 1989, he wanted to spruce up the 18th floor, which was the executive floor of our old headquarters at Bishop and King. We spent all this money renovating the 18th and the dining room. Then in '91 he started talking about knocking down the old building and putting up a new structure, and I'm thinking, *Jesus Christ, we just spent several million dollars in renovation costs that I'm now going to have to write off. Why didn't you tell me this before?* But I kept it to myself."

—Howard Karr, retired First Hawaiian Bank vice chairman & CFO

After First Hawaiian Bank announced plans in 1992 to develop a new headquarters on its Bishop-King Street block, a controversy erupted over whether to demolish the 1925 Damon Building that housed its Main Branch.

Eventually, we won before the FDIC and in related court battles and were still able to finish on time and on budget through herculean efforts by everybody. We had gone through a long, tough legal year and spent about a million dollars in legal fees.

We prevailed with the FDIC in September of 1993 and were ready to go ahead. But our determined opponents sought a restraining order on historic preservation and environmental grounds. That case quickly found its way to the 9th Circuit Court of Appeals in San Francisco, where they were unsuccessful.

We wasted no time in going ahead with the demolition of the Damon Building. The wrecking balls from Cleveland Wrecking went to work under floodlights less than two hours after that happy call from our lawyer in San Francisco. We weren't about to take any chances.

That left the office tower to deal with. Here, we took a different approach. Dynamite!

"The Damon Building is a rare example of American Federal bank architecture."

—Christopher Damon Haig, *great-grandson of Samuel M. Damon, for whom the building was named*

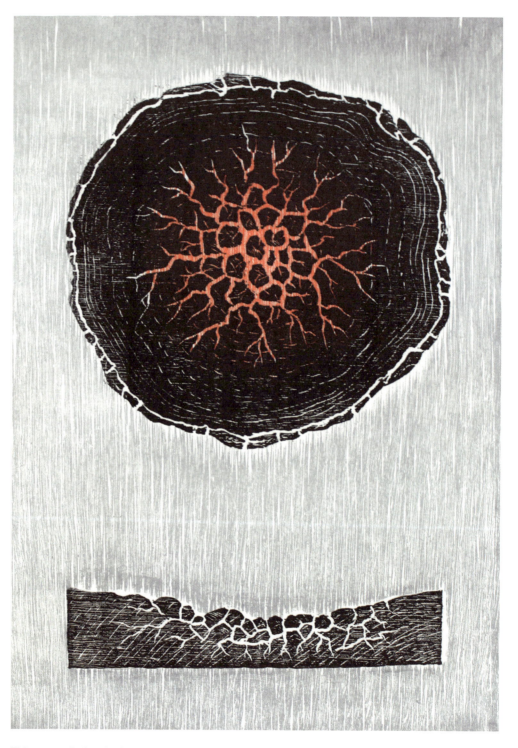

This artwork, *Implosion*, is one of a set of prints the bank commissioned by Hiroki Morinoue to mark key steps in the construction of First Hawaiian Center. The other prints are titled *Groundbreaking, Topping Off* and *Dedication*.

I got a kick out of putting in some of the dynamite sticks as we got ready for the implosion of First Hawaiian's old high-rise headquarters on January 9, 1994.

The process of blowing up a building is truly fascinating. Some of our people were a little nervous, but we had hired experienced Mainland demolition experts to handle the job. They blow up buildings all over the country. There were two companies involved: Controlled Demolition Inc. and Cleveland Wrecking. And here, once again, I did something that some people said was pretty stupid. I went into the old building and watched as they drilled the holes into the concrete and then put sticks of dynamite into them. Jim Wayman and I went down one day, and they let me put the dynamite sticks into holes. We posed for photos holding the dynamite sticks like big cigars. People were really upset that I did that!

On Sunday, January 9, 1994, the old office tower came down.

We chose a Sunday because the demo would cause the least disruption to business in downtown. My daughter Lauren was supposed to press the button. At first, she didn't push hard enough and nothing happened. I can tell you there were some stricken faces for a moment. But then she pressed harder, and with a roar, the building was down! Dust rolled up Bishop Street and covered the police cars there to keep the crowds away. It was exhilarating. But I must admit,

"While the Damon Building may be the last of its kind in Hawaii, there were hundreds much like it built across the Mainland in the first part of this century and plenty remain."

—Honolulu Advertiser *editorial*

"The demolition of such a pivotal resource would constitute a substantial loss to Hawaii's architectural heritage... as the last example of the neoclassical, turn-of-the-century style of bank architecture in the state."

—*John C. Harper, chairman, federal Council on Historic Preservation*

"While the S.M. Damon Building was no doubt very grand upon its completion, it has never impressed me as being anything other than an older, obsolete building. The S.M. Damon Building is not worthy of saving."

—*David Haig, Christopher's brother and a trustee of the S.M. Damon Estate*

years later, I had a slightly different feel about the whole experience when I watched, with sadness, the fall of the World Trade Center on 9/11.

Then with the building down and the rubble cleaned up, we had another challenge. How do we build this damn thing?

We knew there was a big underwater stream running almost directly down Bishop Street, from the mountains to the harbor. The building was designed to handle that. That part of the construction was fascinating. Seiko, the same folks who make the Seiko watch, had perfected a drilling procedure used in Japan where there are a lot of varied, lousy surface conditions and no space. It is a special kind of drill. Practically every highrise downtown has pile driving, and it goes "Boom! Boom! Boom!" for months. This building had zero piles, which was unique. This system dug up the dirt and created a Seiko soil mix wall with a mixture of powdered Bentonite clay (a very expansive clay), cement and water. The mix created a solid wall around the property so the water could be pumped around this wall.

Then you build your retaining wall for the parking lot and you dig down five stories and you have this little temporary wall. Then you build your concrete up and pour slabs and then, over time, the wall dissipates and just falls apart after the building is built.

I don't think that had ever been done in Honolulu.

And then we did something that I know had never been done in Hawaii's history, and I don't think it has been done since. We had rock anchors to help hold the building down. We had what is known as a floating slab, meaning there are no piles underneath. You pour the slab at the bottom, which was one of the largest pours in the history of Hawaii and probably still is, and then they drilled holes all through this slab. I don't know how many holes, but hundreds, and through those holes they dropped steel cables down 60 to 100 feet, through the water, through the slush to the bedrock of earth way down. The rock anchors were held in the ground with a water-activated expanding grout.

The parking garage is five stories down. I remember once you got to the water table, the cost was $45,000 an inch going down farther. An inch! But, it all gets recaptured in the cost of the parking.

So, you have a slab that is floating, with cables that are embedded in the rock. The cables are not stiff, and what happens is the water keeps pumping all around the sides of the building and continues on as it passes this site. When the building gets to the top, like a boat, there is now enough weight to hold the slab in place, and then they turned off the pumps and the water

> "Walt and I went to the construction site most days. One day, it was late afternoon, we weren't paying attention to the time, and we worked our way back down the building and found everybody was gone and the place was locked up. We had to climb up and over the perimeter fence to get out."
>
> —Jim Wayman

REACHING FOR THE DOWNTOWN SKY

The finished product, newest and tallest building in downtown Honolulu.

Our main branch lobby stairs lead up to a second-floor art gallery.

does whatever it does. Some people thought that when we turned off the pumps the building would pop up like a cork, but it didn't.

We had just about finished the building when the American Bankers Association came to town in October 1996 for its annual meeting. Because I was about to become ABA president, I wanted to have an event at the building to celebrate its completion and welcome the other bankers. It would be the first event in the building. In fact, that day they were still putting in the trees and the landscaping.

We took over the entire ground floor and held a big dinner in our new main branch (shown at left), which is a pretty remarkable space—marble floors and a 40-foot-high prismatic art glass wall. To this day it was the nicest formal dinner in the history of Hawaii, I think.

The Bankers Club dining room on the 30th floor was still unfinished—just raw cement—but we had the cocktail party up there anyway. We had wheelbarrows with ice and beer, very rustic. But the view was sensational—360 degrees from the Koolau Mountains past Diamond Head and Waikiki all around the coastline to the Waianae range. We hoisted a rented grand piano up to the top floor so my 12-year-old daughter, Lauren, could play during the cocktail hour.

Then all 140 guests took the glass elevators down to our main branch on the ground floor for dinner, an only-in-Hawaii menu—Waimea House Salad served *puolo* style (inside a ti leaf bag wrapped in beautiful woven *haku* flowers), sorbet served in a carved ice bowl, mahi mahi and all topped off with island coconut cake. Federal Reserve Chairman Alan Greenspan was my guest at my table along with Ricki Helfer, chair of the FDIC.

It was a miracle the dinner even happened. Like Murphy's Law says, "Anything that can go wrong, will go wrong." That day of all days, there was an underground gas line explosion downtown that blew off some manhole covers and left the Bankers Club kitchen stoves without gas to cook. They had to bring in portable grills and gas stoves. But Executive Chef Mel Arellano and his staff amazingly pulled it off. By the time we capped off dinner with a *keiki hula halau* walking down the big marble staircase and dancing their way through the tables, I was on Cloud Nine. And to add to that special week, I was sworn in as president of the ABA.

I doubt that the guests that night realized that they were in a very unusual structure. In effect, it floats on those rock anchors. It's alive. If you are out on the 30th-floor "prow" overlooking Bishop Street on a super windy day, you can get seasick; you can feel the movement so much.

I still get a little dizzy out there.

We put together this "Two Jacks" invitation to an event honoring the changing of the guard at First Hawaiian in 1994. Jack Tsui (top) became president, succeeding the retiring Jack Hoag (bottom).

CHAPTER 11

Two Jacks: Shock on Bishop Street

"The reaction inside First Hawaiian to hiring Jack Tsui was total shock. There were a lot of senior guys who thought they were going to be the next president."

Sharon Shiroma Brown, First Hawaiian Bank senior VP

First Hawaiian Bank and Bank of Hawaii face one another across Bishop Street in downtown Honolulu. Because the two of us are such intense competitors, rarely does a top executive of one bank jump across Bishop to the other. On the one occasion it happened during my career, it started with a secret late-night meeting in my garage in Makiki—a clandestine contact that later produced front-page news.

First Hawaiian has long prided itself on promoting from within, but sometimes there are skills needed elsewhere, and over the years we have brought in people for key positions. However, there aren't many examples. G. Harry Hutaff had been hired from Bank of California in the 1960s to become our controller. Also back in the 1970s, we didn't have a really good senior corporate lending officer, and Johnny brought in Kennedy Randall, who had great international contacts and the national corporate contacts that we as a bank didn't have.

For the most part, however, we filled top slots in-house. For example, I replaced Johnny, and when I became CEO, the first thing I did was promote Jack Hoag to be my No. 2 as president. We had a really great partnership for five years. We never had a cross word the whole time.

Jack had come to Hawaii as a hell-raising Marine helicopter pilot and a real party guy. There's a story he tells of himself about showing off his piloting skills for a buddy, a major, one day. He was sliding through the tall grass taking off, and his helicopter hit the stump of a tree and flipped upside down, spinning on its blades. They had a really close call.

Jack met his wife in the Islands and stayed here as a bank trainee when he got out of the military. One night when they were quite young, he and Jeanette were driving home on Likelike Highway, and a driver crossed the median strip and hit them head-on, almost killing both of them. They were in the hospital for a long time, and Jeannette to this day has never 100 percent recovered from her injuries.

> "I had known Walt socially and as a business acquaintance. 'Doc' Buyers, who was on the First Hawaiian board, acted as a matchmaker and brought us together. I was going to leave Bank of Hawaii anyway. They had made their choice for the top job there, and it wasn't me. I would have gone back to the Mainland, but I wanted to stay in Hawaii. And moving to FHB worked out well for me."
>
> —*John K. (Jack) Tsui, former Bank of Hawaii vice chairman, later president of First Hawaiian*

Jack made a pledge to her that, if they survived, he would convert to her Mormon faith, which he did. He became a very active Mormon, president of the Honolulu Stake at one point. During all the time I've known him, he was an active Mormon, a good leader and very principled.

Jack is nine years older than me, so I always figured he would retire first. Even though he was older, he was my succession plan. I was confident that, if I were hit by a bus, he could take over First Hawaiian without missing a beat. My plan was that, before he retired, the two of us would select his successor within the bank and groom him or her. But, in early 1994, he came to see me to tell me his church wanted him to retire early and run the Mormons' landowning arm in the Islands, Hawaii Reserves, Inc. It was a mission that he wanted to do, and I completely supported him.

So, now what do I do about a successor-in-waiting? I had already identified Don Horner as an up-and-coming star in the bank, somebody who could ultimately move up to the top rung. He was still pretty young—43 at the time—and I had thought I had several years to give Don a lot of other experiences.

When Jack suddenly changed that timeline, there was a gap, and I didn't feel it would be right to move Don up to president right away. There was nothing against Don; it was just early in the process of moving him around, giving him the opportunity to handle every increasing responsibility I knew a mature, seasoned executive should have.

I had been president for five years when Bellinger died, and even I didn't have enough training. He had held things close to the chest, so when I took over, I got baptized by fire. I wasn't ready, but when it happens, it happens whether you are ready or not. Either you are going to do it or someone else is.

As it turned out, an unorthodox opportunity to solve my successor problem opened up across Bishop Street. Just before Jack sprang his news on me, a four-year internal leadership competition had finally played itself out at Bank of Hawaii. In 1989, the year Johnny died and I took over on our side of Bishop Street, Bank of Hawaii's CEO, Howard Stephenson, had picked my old friend Larry Johnson to become Bankoh's president.

That same year, Bankoh also named three new vice chairmen, with the implicit message that one of them would eventually become Johnson's successor after Larry moved up to the top spot. The three contenders were Jack Tsui, who was in charge of corporate lending; Tom Kappock, head of Bankoh's retail banking; and Richard Dahl, chief financial officer and youngest of the three contenders.

The three of them stayed in place until December 1993, when Bank of Hawaii announced that Stephenson would retire the next summer and, as expected, be succeeded by Larry Johnson. At the same time, Johnson selected the 42-year-old Dahl to succeed him as president. That left Tsui and Kappock as odd men out at the same time I was looking for a successor to Jack Hoag.

I had a conversation one day with J.W.A. (Doc) Buyers, head of C. Brewer & Co. and a director of First Hawaiian. As a director, he was aware that Hoag was retiring and also aware of the Bank of Hawaii management picture. Tsui used to call on C. Brewer when he was a national corporate calling officer for Bank of New York. He told me I ought to consider approaching Jack, who might be interested in a change. I had known Jack as a superb banker, with a background unlike anybody else on the local scene. Before he joined Bank of Hawaii in 1984, he held top positions at Bank of New York, Philadelphia International Bank and Philadelphia Bank. He knows more about corporate lending—dealing with major national and international companies—than anyone I've known, and I've known a lot of prominent bankers.

There had been a tradition for years that Bank of Hawaii didn't poach executives from First Hawaiian and vice versa. At lower levels, branch managers might have gone back and forth; at senior levels, it was unheard of.

Yet I realized that Jack would probably not stay long at Bank of Hawaii after being passed over. I also knew that, with his East Coast background, he was culturally quite different from the typical banker at First Hawaiian. Before I approached him, I weighed whether he could fit in with our culture and came to the conclusion that our culture needed improvement. We were good at certain things with a very good caring culture, but not as sophisticated as I thought the bank should be in national corporate lending and other major loans. Jack Tsui was very, very strong in these areas.

I had Doc Buyers make the first approach to see if Jack would take a call from me. All Doc did was say, "Would you be willing to chat with Walt?" After doing that, Doc gave me Jack's private phone number (I could hardly call his Bank of Hawaii office). I called Jack and said, "This town is really small, and this one is explosive in the community. We can't talk at a hotel or restaurant or anywhere public." We agreed to meet at my home in Makiki late at night.

> "The departure of Bank of Hawaii vice chairman Tsui, described by many as a top corporate or 'wholesale' banker, is not entirely a surprise. Last December a younger executive, Richard Dahl, 42, was named as Bankoh's next president, thus apparently shutting out Tsui from ever rising to the No. 1 slot."
>
> —The Honolulu Advertiser
> *front-page story, June 30, 1994*

I put my car out on the street and left the garage door open. He drove into the garage, and I closed the door behind him. We went into my study and talked until the wee hours of the next morning—probably five hours or so. We discussed the opportunity to be president of our bank, the culture difference, and the internal problems that might ensue from an outsider coming in as president. And, of course, whether we could work with each other.

I had been told by people who know that Bank of Hawaii didn't want to lose Jack Tsui even after he was passed over. When the topic came up of whether he might move to First Hawaiian, they said, "Not to worry. That would never happen because Walter Dods and Jack Tsui could never get along." That was their analysis of the risk of losing Tsui.

I couldn't open up the circle very wide. I talked to just a few key people on my board executive committee and told them that I wanted to hire Jack. The town is so small; directors have social friends and connections, and both Tsui and I were very well-connected, too. There was too much potential for leaks. Even Doc Buyers only knew that he had passed off an introduction; he never knew whether it had progressed until we made the decision.

For me, the fact that Jack Tsui was three years older than me was important. It was a perfect solution for me. I was bringing in an extremely competent banker in an area where we needed some help on wholesale corporate lending, national lending. I've never been afraid of bringing in somebody smarter than I am, and that's how much respect I have for Jack's banking abilities. Yet, I didn't feel his hire would be a threat to the future leadership of the bank because clearly, if my health maintained and I continued to do my job, he wouldn't be replacing me because of our age difference. The decision would buy time for Tsui and me to work together and groom the next president coming along.

Hiring Jack Tsui was going to be a shock to the business community, and when it was announced, it was on the front page of the morning paper. However, I knew the big challenge for me was to manage the internal shock within the bank. Once I had the executive committee bless it, but before I went to the full board, I told my senior group of managers, and there was absolute shock in the room. We had been a tight-knit group and had never gone outside for a major hire since I

> "Jack Tsui was hired to help us in an area where First Hawaiian always had weakness—the corporate lending side of the business. We were a very strong retail bank, but not necessarily a strong wholesale bank. Jack brought more discipline and structure to wholesale lending. He added another 'club' to the bag and added an important earnings driver."
>
> —Don Horner, *retired chairman & CEO, First Hawaiian Bank*

In 1994, former top Bank of Hawaii executive Jack Tsui agreed to move across Bishop Street and become president of First Hawaiian. We wore "Yes" tuxedos at the party welcoming him.

> "When Walt hired Jack Tsui, it was like, 'What did you just say?' First Hawaiian and Bank of Hawaii is like high school rivals Iolani and Punahou. Eh, those guys across the street, to hell with them! Jack was the enemy. Now all of a sudden, he is going to be president of our bank!
>
> "Prior to Tsui, our president was Jack Hoag, whom everybody loved because he was a homegrown guy who came from the system. Now, a switch to a New York corporate type. Walter had to communicate why this was a good idea. His message was, 'We will continue to be a Hawaii bank, but we are going to need folks like Jack Tsui, a real high-end corporate lender who was an anomaly in this market.' We really didn't have someone with that kind of big bank lending background and network.
>
> "We just trusted Walter so much, a trust that evolved over time. Not just when he hired Jack Tsui."
>
> —Ray Ono, First Hawaiian Bank vice chairman

took over. Also, we and Bank of Hawaii were tough competitors.

Each person took it differently, but the one who surprised me the most was Tony Guerrero, an executive vice president who ran branch operations. I expected him to take it pretty easy, but he was such a competitive guy. He said, "You tell me to go through a wall for you and I will, but now you're asking me to embrace the enemy." It was like a sacrilege to him, the ultimate betrayal. He took it pretty hard initially, but he and Jack became good friends.

The guy who was most affected was Don Horner. I told Tsui one of his primary responsibilities was to get Don ready, give him more experience in major national corporate lending and other areas where Don hadn't yet had much exposure. When I announced Tsui's hiring, Don supported it 100 percent. He understood. At the same time we dropped the bombshell of Tsui's hiring, we also promoted Don to vice chairman of retail banking, a signal he would be next in line. I'm sure Don looked at it as a minor detour in the road. We spent time right away letting him know how we felt about him and continued to give him additional responsibilities. He understood it was part of the grooming process. Obviously, it worked out quite well; he succeeded me as chairman and CEO when I retired in 2004 and did a great job in his own right.

The move was equally stunning to those who worked across Bishop Street. The day it was to be announced, Jack Tsui called about 30 people who worked for him directly or indirectly into a conference room at Bank of Hawaii to tell them he had resigned and was becoming president of First Hawaiian Bank. One of those in the room was Bob Fujioka, a senior VP at Bankoh. Bob told me when Jack made his announcement he burst out laughing. He thought Jack was joking.

A year or so after Jack left, Bob (now a First Hawaiian vice chairman) was one of three key bankers who were concerned with Bank of Hawaii's strategic direction who spoke with Don Horner and eventually moved across the street as well. The others were Bob Harrison (now CEO of First Hawaiian) and Lance Mizumoto (president of Central Pacific Bank). The two Bobs—Harrison and Fujioka—were great additions to our First Hawaiian team. I doubt they would have moved if I hadn't hired Jack. He had mentored them earlier in his career and they wanted to join him. We didn't actively recruit them; they approached us.

In Tsui, I had the luxury of a seasoned executive who was older, who wouldn't disrupt the long-term succession plan of the bank and yet could provide us leadership in the interim until Don was ready to move up. Don handled it well, and it gave him more and more responsibilities. He was truly ready when his time came.

One of my senior managers said to me, "We need to First Hawaiianize Jack Tsui." I said to him, and I remember it to this day, "Yes, to a point, but we also need to Jack Tsui-ize First Hawaiian Bank." It was a very important point to make. To me, we had become very set in our ways, proud of our culture, but we needed to break out and be more competitive and do more deals.

When Jack came on, all the lending functions reported to him, and although we are both strong personalities, we got along very well. Despite all the predictions to the contrary, we knew our places, our respective skills. We might beef a little in private, but not often.

I respect that he's a New York banker with great banking skills on a national level. He brought a lot of sophistication and expertise to the bank. He's not a local banker. He was a little bit of a bull in a china shop, in our own shop. I knew he could break glass. I knew there would be times when I would have to

"There was shock and disbelief among those of us working at Bank of Hawaii when Jack Tsui moved to First Hawaiian. Once it was decided he wasn't going to become next in line after CEO Larry Johnson, the feeling was Jack might go back to the East Coast where he had so many contacts. It was a shock that he literally 'moved across the street.'

"Before Jack, that kind of move between banks never happened. Even Jack seemed like a one-off deal, but then, in 1996, Bob Fujioka (now FHB vice chairman), Lance Mizumoto (now Central Pacific Bank president) and I moved—a flood of three. We knew each other very well and were talking. Hiring Jack told us First Hawaiian is going to focus on commercial lending, business lending, which hadn't been the case before. Also, I'm not an Asia guy, and Bankoh's emphasis at the time was banking in the Asia-Pacific region. Lance and I quit the same day. Bob came a couple weeks later.

"Because it's such a small town, negotiating our move had to be discreet. Surprisingly, midafternoon at the Vineyard Zippy's is a real quiet place. So we met there with Don Horner and Tony Guerrero from First Hawaiian. It's next to downtown, but nobody downtown goes there."

—Bob Harrison, chairman & CEO, First Hawaiian Bank

come in and repair the broken glass, but I also knew that some of the glass needed breaking. I developed a skill over the years of having selective hearing.

One of the great lessons of leadership is to allow a certain amount of unhappiness when you do change because change is hard. People are uncomfortable with change, and I knew we needed changes in the corporate lending area, real estate, wholesale and international lending.

When it occasionally got to a level where I thought my intervention was required, we'd have private chats. I'd say, "Hey, maybe you're pushing this guy just a little too hard. Maybe we need to find a way to smooth this over a little bit." When we'd have these midcourse corrections, we'd work it out. When we left the room, nothing was ever festering, and it really shocked the community because people didn't believe it could work. They gave it six months. Jack stayed eight years until he retired and was a damn good banker. He's still on the First Hawaiian board.

TWO JACKS: SHOCK ON BISHOP STREET

As ABA president, I often had to preside over conference calls at 3 a.m. Hawaii time. I wasn't always able to stay awake.

Dick Adair cartoon, reprinted with permission of *Honolulu Star-Advertiser*.

CHAPTER 12

Ssshhh! ABA President Asleep on Sofa

I'm proud to have been the only Hawaii banker to serve as president of the American Bankers Association, but it's not a job I campaigned for. Instead, I was drafted for it in a hotel dining room in West Virginia.

In the early 1990s, I was on the board of the ABA, which was as far as I'd ever thought I'd go in the industry association. I formed a lot of deep relationships with other bankers on the board. The ABA had a tradition of rotating the presidency among small, midsize and large banks. They decided to change the bylaws so that there would be a first vice president who would be on track to be president-elect for a year, then president.

This bylaw change happened at an ABA board meeting at the Greenbrier, a great spa resort in the Allegheny Mountains of West Virginia that has been in business since the 1700s. I had ducked out of a session so I could have a meal with my wife, Diane. A bunch of the board guys came looking for me and finally found us in the grill. I was a little sheepish because I had skipped the meeting. They wanted to meet with me right away.

It turns out the board had to pick somebody from within their ranks to fill the new position. It was a time in the cycle for a president from a midsized bank like First Hawaiian. I just happened to be sitting in the right place at the right time and was drafted into the job. They formed a consensus and came after me. The lesson is: Be careful if you leave a meeting because those who stay will pile work on you.

I had been First Hawaiian CEO for almost five years and still had a lot on my plate—we were integrating two banks we had acquired, plus building our new downtown headquarters. Obviously it would be a big sacrifice of time and effort for me to take the ABA job. However, I thought the networking could help the bank. Maybe in the back of my mind was the thought that someday we'd want to expand outside Hawaii and it'd be nice to have these connections.

I had to decide before we left Greenbrier. Diane and I talked about it. I wouldn't have done it if she had said no. We knew it was going to entail a lot more travel and entertainment but decided to take it on. I hadn't sought it but agreed to do it. With the passage of time, I moved into the top job.

Given my roots in marketing, I guess it's not surprising that my major effort during my ABA term of office in 1997 was to try to enhance the image of the banking industry as a whole.

It was one of those cycles in which banking images were lousy. A national Harris Poll ranking the prestige of various professions put doctors at the top and bankers next to last—tied with journalists and above only labor union leaders at the bottom of the list. Bankers were seen by the public as the coldhearted bureaucrats depicted by Hollywood film directors. This was 10 years before the 2007 financial crisis that caused the Great Recession made a further mess, with good reason, of the image of banking, especially Wall Street bankers.

Banks around the country were spending $750 million a year for ads, each one making the case for one bank. No one was making the case for banking as an industry. I thought it was time to do both. I said it right off the bat, in my presidential acceptance speech:

> "It's time for us, as an industry, to make a case. Our image is hurting. I don't ever expect banks to be loved like puppy dogs or McDonald's (remember, this was 1996). But a realistic goal is to give Americans a better appreciation for the role banks play in our economy. Our research shows that young people don't have a good understanding of what banks are, and some don't feel they have a need for banks."

I made the pitch to the ABA board, and they all wrote checks. One who was supportive was L.M. (Bud) Baker, who was running Wachovia Bank in North Carolina, one of the great banks in America. He stood up and said, "How much do you want?" I gave him a number, and he said, "You got it." That's how it started around the table. We raised enough for a $1 million campaign.

Working with Interpublic Group's McCann Erickson Worldwide, we came up with a set of "test" ads that ran largely on CNN. The *Wall Street Journal* reported that one ad, titled "Dweeby Gerald," showed a nerdy 8-year-old wearing suspenders and taped-together glasses and being teased by his playmates, who plastered a "kick me" sign to his back. Undaunted, Gerald treks to the bank each week to invest his savings. We next see Gerald at 35, with a beautiful woman on his arm, sailing off on his yacht named *Kick Me*, as the announcer intones: "From mutual funds to annuities, CDs to securities, nothing works like money in the bank."

Another, dubbed "Fuddy Duddies," showed a bunch of stodgy bankers around a big wooden desk. A series of high-tech images follow, and in the final shot, the bankers appear again, only now shown from underneath the table. One of them is wearing jogging shoes, another has swim fins and a third has on in-line skates. I guess that last image came from me, because I was into skating at the time along with my daughter. The point of all this was that bankers are human, and fun. I still think the campaign was cute and worthwhile, but then the next ABA president came in and had a different goal for his year, so it died. The campaign had no long-term effect because every bank had its own challenges, its own problems and its own advertising budget.

One issue that was *thrust* upon me, which left me with a difficult decision to make, was the credit unions. Politically, credit unions are very popular, but the banking industry was concerned—and is to this day—about their expansion beyond their original rules and purpose. The original intent of credit unions was good. You get a band of people, almost like a local *tanomoshi*. (Tanomoshi are informal credit and loan associations popular among Japanese immigrants to save money and help one another. Members contribute the same amount periodically, and payments rotate among members until all members have been paid.) Under the original credit union rules, the people involved had to have a *common bond*; membership might be limited to employees of the Department of Education or Hawaiian Telcom, for example. I have no problem with that approach.

But then that concept became broadened beyond recognition, and the "common bond" became stretched way too far; it might be something like the entire island of Oahu. The problem from banks' point of view is that credit unions don't pay taxes; banks do. That saves the credit union industry hundreds of millions of dollars in tax subsidy, which affects the rates they can offer customers. If they don't pay taxes, they can offer more in a savings account and charge less for a car loan. When you have a nonprofit helping its own company employees, that's one thing, but when they start competing against the banks more broadly, it's not a level playing field. How does a company that pays its share of taxes compete against a company that doesn't?

As the leader of the industry, I was responsible for representing the ABA's point of view on Capitol Hill. It didn't take me 30 seconds to figure out it was an uphill challenge. We were never going to win. I walked into the Senate Office Building, and one complete side was the Senate Federal Credit Union. It had an office equal to the size of Dan Inouye's.

Taking that stand hurt our bank locally since a lot of credit unions pulled their business out of First Hawaiian while I was ABA president because I was obligated to represent the national banking point of view. That hurt our bank for years. But, when you take on a major responsibility, you take on the good and the bad with it.

Early in my ABA term, there was also a public flap over a White House meeting I attended as ABA president, which included President Clinton, as well as banking and financial regulators. The media and critics like Ralph Nader argued that it was a

> "One of Walter's significant achievements was becoming president of the American Bankers Association. It was wonderful for me to see the only other ex-marketer CEO rise to run the ABA. It's fundamentally a lobbying organization; that's why banks pay dues to ABA. I attribute Walt's rise in ABA not only to his banking background but also his political background."
>
> —Dick Rosenberg, retired chairman & CEO, Bank of America

special-interest meeting behind closed doors held to help Clinton's re-election campaign in 1996.

That meeting wasn't something the bankers put together; the White House invited us. They invited large, midsized and small banks. There was ethnic representation, and male and female. It really was a cross section of banks. We were invited to discuss "banking issues." In the room in addition to Clinton were the comptroller of the currency, secretary of the Treasury and Vice President Al Gore. We discussed only banking industry issues. Never was a single second spent on any political issues.

A month or two later I got a call from the ABA saying, "The *Washington Post* is looking for you; CBS is trying to get a quote." The media were calling the meeting "Coffeegate" as if there were some super-secret political conspiracy to raise funds for Clinton. When we were called by the White House, we actually thought we were going in there for a spanking. But it was just a general industry discussion. I was never asked for any money.

The mood was friendly. Clinton went around the room asking everybody to express their opinion on some issue. As ABA president, I had a list of issues the association wanted me to bring up. When my turn came, I covered those issues—I can't remember now what they were.

Bill Clinton and me at the White House "Coffeegate" meeting. In the middle is Eugene Ludwig, then Comptroller of the Currency.

"Walt played a significant role in the democratization of U.S. commercial banking. Historically, if you got to the top of a larger bank in the era when Walt and I grew up in banking, you almost certainly were male, white, Republican, Episcopalian or something near that, Ivy League—likely Harvard Business School. And you were a commercial lender who made loans to business, especially big businesses. Nobody paid attention to retail banking—focusing on consumers for deposits, loans, credit cards. Retail banking was one of the ways you got deposits to make loans, but what mattered was commercial loans and nice lunches in formal dining rooms.

"Walt was different. He was educated at a state school. He was a Democrat. He was a retail banker and marketer, not a commercial lender. He was married to a Japanese-Korean.

"But he played in the big leagues of the industry over the 30-plus years I've known him. We served together on the board of MasterCard and on the prestigious Financial Advisory Council, made up of one banker from each of the 12 Federal Reserve districts that advise the Fed on banking. And, of course, he was president of the American Bankers Association.

"Walt was part of the first generation that helped the banking industry begin to change very slowly. Now the executive ranks are full of people who are retail bankers, not commercial bankers. You see more women—not a lot, but a few. More minorities.

"Walt helped bring that change, and he did it in a very Hawaiian way. He's not confrontational, not an in-your-face table pounder. He did it in an enormously likable, gracious way through the industry associations and leadership groups that he participated in. Walt was very generous with his time to our industry. Taking on the ABA presidency and having to travel all over the country from Hawaii was a big deal."

—*Larry Fish, retired chairman & CEO of Citizens Bank*

Everything you ever heard or read about Clinton was true. He walks up to you, shakes your hand, looks you in the eye, puts one hand on your shoulder and says, "Walter, I've heard so much about you." You think you're the only person in the room. He was very, very impressive and intimidating. By the time I got back to Honolulu a few days later, I had a letter from the White House with a picture of Clinton and me and a note from him describing what I said in the meeting: "I really appreciated your comments on so and so. I'll certainly keep that in mind." A short letter, but highly personalized and on-point. There was a woman in the back corner who had been writing everything down. I thought that was very slick.

The media flap was much ado about nothing. Because of Watergate, you have this *gate* fetish in D.C. It hit the headlines for one or two days and then died because there really wasn't a story there.

The ABA presidency was a real hassle for somebody from Hawaii because of the time difference with Washington. I learned the intensity of jetlag. During my year in office, I traveled 277,000 miles to speak to bankers from nearly half the states. Those were the years First Hawaiian had its own corporate jet, so the flights were not uncomfortable, but the travel still took its toll. I remember getting up in strange hotel rooms, bumping into dressers and walls in the dark. I started leaving on a nightlight in hotel bathrooms.

I could get in trouble without even leaving home. We were living up on Tantalus in Makiki and our ABA Executive Committee conference calls would be at 9 a.m. Eastern time. Depending on the time of the year, it was either 3 or 4 a.m. for me. I didn't want to wake my wife or kids, so I would tiptoe into the living room to take the calls. I would be lying on the couch with the phone to my ear. Half the time someone would be screaming at me, "Walt, are you still there?" I'd be sound asleep on the sofa in the dark.

But it was worth it. I made a lot of tremendous friends in my industry through that experience. I always knew that would be an extra bonus. When you are way out in the Pacific, we are all competitors in the market, so you can't go to somebody next door for advice or to learn the latest technology. By making friends with people at similar-size banks around the country, I could call them up and get inside, detailed strategic information on issues that were very helpful to First Hawaiian.

Despite the negatives, I learned about best practices in operations and technology, charge cards, corporate lending, international lending. When I had a problem, I could pick up the phone and call people. It

Dick Adair cartoon.
"I hate ties."

In my final speech as head of the ABA, I celebrated by tearing off my white shirt, coat and tie to get back to my comfortable *aloha* attire.

was awesome. When you have a regulator challenging you on some product, some friend at a Mainland bank would refer you to their top product development specialist or a research institute that could fill you in on the latest trends and rules. As long as we were in a noncompetitive market area, I was able to get a lot of insight from other bankers.

One other thing I learned during my ABA term was how much I hate ties. I remember seeing a quote once from TV journalist Linda Ellerbee: "If men can run the world, why can't they stop wearing neckties? How intelligent is it to start the day by tying a little noose around your neck?"

We long ago figured that out in Hawaii, but as ABA president, you can't show up in Washington or Chicago in an aloha shirt and board shorts, so I spent most of 1997 wearing a suit and tie at speaking podiums or cocktail parties or board meetings.

I had a little fun with that notion in my final speech as ABA president at their convention in Boston in October 1997. At the tail end of my remarks, I took off my coat, tie and white shirt, one by one, dropped them on the floor and left the stage wearing my favorite aloha shirt, which I had on underneath. It was an eye-opening year, and I learned a lot and made friends who helped First Hawaiian, but I sure was happy when my term ended.

After the closing of our merger agreement with Bank of the West in 1998, their CEO Don McGrath and I rang the bell of the New York Stock Exchange to celebrate the listing of our new BancWest Corporation stock.

CHAPTER 13

Project Rainbow: Getting in Bed with the French

It had been gnawing at me for a while that First Hawaiian had year after year of record earnings, but our stock was languishing after the crash of the Japanese bubble in Hawaii in the early '90s. Even though we were listed in national publications as one of the best banks in the U.S., our stock didn't match our performance because of the sluggish Hawaii economy.

What do you do when you are in a market where you are performing well and your shareholders are not being rewarded because of the economy? The obvious answer is: diversify out of Hawaii. Easy to say; hard to do.

Our major competitor, Bank of Hawaii, had tried to diversify, but I didn't agree with the way they did it. They had gone to Asia and the South Pacific. I felt that a Hawaii bank couldn't succeed in Asia competing with the largest banks in the world—JP Morgan, Sumitomo Bank, Hongkong and Shanghai Banking Corporation (HSBC). I couldn't see any competitive advantage for a small Hawaii bank to do that. In the South Pacific, other than Guam and Saipan, which had U.S.-type laws and U.S. currency, the other islands have different kinds of rules, different currencies, different customs. Individually, each was quite small. It was very hard to make an economic case. And, in the end, that strategy failed.

Even Allan Landon, who later joined Bank of Hawaii and became its CEO, said Bankoh had become "America's smallest international bank and least efficient bank" before Mike O'Neill came on board in 2000 and pulled them out of Asia and the small Pacific island markets.

We had to break out of Hawaii, but not to Asia. I thought West Coast United States would be a better fit for First Hawaiian, but I felt it would be better not to be in California or a major metropolitan area where you face the biggest competition. Thanks to my extracurricular activities with the American Bankers Association, I was able to put together a transaction that changed the face of First Hawaiian.

When I was on track to be president of the ABA, Gerry Cameron, CEO of US Bank in Portland, was on the ABA board with me. We got to be friends, and one day we were having a drink and he tells me, "I'm buying West One, largest bank in Idaho, and the Justice Department is forcing me to sell branches for antitrust reasons. I have 30 branches and $700 million in deposits I have to get rid of. Would you be interested?" I said, "Absolutely." He says, "Wells Fargo, Bank of America and all the big players are going to be bidding, but you don't have to be the highest bidder. If you can just be competitive, I'll give you serious consideration because I don't want to sell to my competitors. It will hurt me financially in other ways, and that would more than justify the difference in the price."

We bid and came in third or fourth, but we got those branches. That was our real breakout to the Mainland. I never would have gotten that deal without being in the ABA leadership. This is one example of the benefits of getting into industry organizations. The networking and friendships will benefit you in ways you can't even dream of. We got almost $700 million in deposits for a purchase price of $38 million. From the time I became CEO in 1989 until completion of the Pacific One deal, we had increased the size of our company by 55 percent.

I couldn't make the Mainland properties into First Hawaiian branches because of laws limiting interstate banking. I had to create a bank in the Pacific Northwest within six months in order to buy those branches. We called it Pacific One Bank, and its formation might be an interesting lesson for my government friends.

I went to see the banking commissioner in Oregon and told him, "We need to get a bank charter within six months." The guy kind of hemmed and hawed and said, "Well, we are really busy right now and. . ." I thought, *Here it comes. He's going to kill the deal.* He said, "Would two months be OK?" I was flabbergasted. Later I went back to thank him and said, "I didn't expect you to do it. What caused this pro-business attitude?" He said, "We bureaucrats were always anti-business until we had a severe recession. Companies and jobs were leaving Oregon. We civil servants, not the Legislature or the governor, got together as a group and said, 'Hey, we need to start servicing the constituents, the small businesses. If we treat them well, maybe we will be able to keep jobs and grow.' So, we changed our attitude and cooperated."

We got those US Bank branches and deposits in June 1996, and also had to buy a small bank in Washington State called American National Bank to get a banking license there.

Not everything went well with Pacific One. On the day of closing, the seller gave us all the wrong computer tapes, so we were rejecting withdrawals and not approving deposits for thousands of customers on the first day. If your checking account deposit doesn't show up even though you know you put the money in the bank, it's a horrendous problem.

We had to fly 20 or 30 young First Hawaiian employees up to Portland. We took the boardroom over and dropped telephone lines down from the ceiling and had these kids working around the clock manually sorting all of this out. It never became public, fortunately.

We worked hard to keep the customers. We had little receptions in the branches with cookies and punch. We personally called on our larger customers; it's the old 80/20 rule—20 percent of your customers have 80 percent of the deposits. And the best thing that happened by far was all the employees stayed in the branches, so U.S. Bancorp customers knew the tellers and the branch managers. It helps when people see Sally who has always taken care of you is still there and Ralph, the old manager, is there.

My philosophy always was, "Don't slash and burn!" Banks always have a certain number of openings, so you find ways to keep everybody and through attrition get down to the level you need. Every deal we ever did, from Hawaii Thrift & Loan to First Interstate Bank to Pioneer, was never slash and burn, which is a typical Mainland way of doing deals.

I knew we would be successful with Pacific One, but I didn't realize how important that was for the ultimate deal that came later. That foothold in the Northwest drew the attention of Don McGrath, who ran Bank of the West in San Francisco and who later became my partner. However, Bank of the West wasn't the only merger target we considered. I had known Harris Simmons, CEO of Zions Bank in Salt Lake City, and thought Zions and First Hawaiian would be a good combination. We met secretly to discuss a transaction. I had just been to a retreat for our top sales people in the bank at Whistler resort, north of Vancouver, British Columbia. On my first ski run, a kid on a runaway snowboard hit me full on and fractured my ankle. They put on a portable cast, which I wore to a meeting the next day with Harris in my apartment in San Francisco. However, nothing came of our discussion.

At that point, some banks were in trouble in Japan. They were being pressed to sell their successful subsidiaries in California to recapitalize the parent companies. One was Sumitomo Bank of California, which was about our size. I tried to get meetings with them as well. Another was Bank of California, which wouldn't talk initially. My friend Teru Tsuchida was head of Meiji Life Insurance Co., part of the Mitsubishi group in Japan. He arranged for a meeting, and I did talk with Bank of California when I was

---

"In the Pacific One Bank deal, we had a lot of problems with the lawyers from the sellers, US Bank. They made life miserable. When you are putting together the wording to close any deal, there's a lot of standard boilerplate, the parts of a document that nobody wants to read. One of the documents they asked for was totally unstandard, very favorable to them. I was putting up a storm at the closing and they complained to Walt, who called me and said, 'What is this?' I started to explain, and he said, 'Sign it, do it!'

"Even the lawyer for the other side said later, 'I really felt sorry for you. We kind of pulled your chain and undercut you.' Walt properly had his eye focused on getting this deal done. Like they say, that's why he's a pay grade higher. In the end, we got the deal."

—Tom Huber, retired general counsel, First Hawaiian Bank

In our first foray to the Mainland, we created an entity called Pacific One Bank. I was astounded at how quickly Oregon regulators approved our charter.

thinking of expanding to the West Coast. There was a historical tie between our banks. After Bernice Pauahi Bishop died, Charles Reed Bishop—founder of First Hawaiian—left Hawaii heartbroken, moved to San Francisco and became a director for Bank of California. But they weren't interested. Eventually, they merged with Union Bank of California and are now called UnionBank on the West Coast. They're owned today by Bank of Tokyo-Mitsubishi UFJ.

The next year I went to a banking conference at the Biltmore Hotel in Phoenix. One of the other bankers was McGrath. His Bank of the West dates back to the 1870s, almost as old as First Hawaiian. It was originally Farmers National Gold Bank and then First National Bank of San Jose. After the savings and loan crisis in the 1980s, they grew by buying one troubled S&L after another in northern California and changed their name to Bank of the West. At the time Don and I met in Phoenix, his bank had been wholly owned since 1980 by Banque Nationale de Paris (BNP), the giant French bank. We struck up a friendship, and I gave him a ride back to California on the First Hawaiian Bank jet. Nothing happened right away, but we had made contact.

Why we approached First Hawaiian

"In 1997, the question was what our parent company, BNP, was going to do with Bank of the West. We had done several acquisitions but were still way too small to build brand awareness in a market dominated by Bank of America and Wells Fargo. BNP—this is before they became BNP Paribas—was having its own struggles at home. They were fighting for their life with major competitors—Credit Lyonnais, Paribas and Societe Generale. They didn't have a lot of capital, and there was even some discussion about whether they might sell Bank of the West to raise capital for use in France.

"I talked with Herb Lurie, head of Financial Institutions mergers and acquisitions at Merrill Lynch, about alternatives to BNP selling. We thought if we did a merger of equals with another bank about the same size, BNP could stay in U.S. retail banking with a bigger organization and could grow using its stock as the currency to make acquisitions.

"I met in our boardroom in San Francisco for a strategic discussion with BNP's CEO, Michel Pebereau, to show him various U.S. banks that might be merger alternatives. All the medium-sized banks on the Mainland had stock prices that were on fire; any deal would have been very expensive. First Hawaiian was a high-quality bank, but their stock price was low because of the perception that it would have trouble growing. They had so much market share in Hawaii that antitrust law blocked more acquisitions there. Also, their low stock price made it harder for Walt to do Mainland stock acquisitions. The quality vs. price ratio—high-quality bank, low stock price—added up to a possible deal at an attractive price with great potential for the stock to go up.

"I told Pebereau that First Hawaiian was our merger recommendation. There was dead silence. He chain-smoked cigars, and the room was covered in smoke. He gently put his cigar down, blew smoke out of his mouth and said, 'But Don, do you like the beach?'

"He approved an approach, so I called Walter in February 1998 to chat about a merger. I flew to Honolulu, and we were going to dinner at the Kahala Mandarin Hotel when we ran into Gen. Fred Weyand. Fred was on the Damon Estate board with Walt and also a director of First Hawaiian. Walt introduced me as his old friend from Mainland banking, but the general smelled a rat right away. Walt and I talked over dinner at Hoku's about what our companies might look like together. That started things off."

—Don McGrath, *retired chairman and CEO of Bank of the West and BancWest Corporation*

> "In our merger, the numbers made it clear that First Hawaiian was bigger and more profitable and would have the majority share of our combined company. But how big a majority? It was a matter of who owns what share—a paper rather than a cash transaction. Walter gave me a price and said, 'I'm not moving.' BNP said the same thing. Their numbers weren't even close. Walt proposed to give 38–39 percent control of the combined banks to BNP; they wanted 49 percent. We put the issue aside for a while and worked on other details. In the end, we agreed on 45 percent for the BNP side of the combined companies."
>
> —Don McGrath

In early 1998, I got a call from him saying, "Why don't we talk about seeing if there is any possibility of a combination of First Hawaiian and Bank of the West?" We met for dinner at Hoku's Restaurant at what was then called the Kahala Mandarin Hotel. The theory he pitched to me, which I totally agreed with, was that Bank of the West was able to grow during the S&L crisis by using cash from its French parent to buy sick savings and loans. Once that era had passed, however, they couldn't grow because other banks would make acquisitions with stock, not cash. That's what banks at that time wanted when they sold out. Exchanging stock for stock was tax free, and usually a stock is valued at higher than book value, so you are getting a multiple value on your stock. On the other hand, First Hawaiian had stock to use as currency to make acquisitions. However, after my First Interstate and Pioneer deals, we couldn't expand in Hawaii any more for antitrust reasons. The Feds wouldn't let us buy anything local.

Over the years, investment bankers had brought us Mainland deals to look at, but nothing really had appealed to us prior to this one. Don McGrath is a strategic thinker, a really smart finance guy. He had already done a pro forma spreadsheet on what our combined company would look like, just using publicly available numbers. It looked pretty good. He and I met several times to start fleshing it out. The biggest delicacy of the matter was BNP. It was a big worldwide bank, but they would go from a 100 percent owner of Bank of the West to less than 50 percent of our combined company.

After that first dinner at Hoku's, "Project Rainbow" began. It's customary in investment banking to pick code names to designate deals being worked on and the companies negotiating them. In Project Rainbow, Bank of the West was "Citrus" and First Hawaiian Bank was "Surf." One advantage is if any paperwork got leaked or lost, it wouldn't have actual company names in there, but the names they picked were pretty obvious. For example, I was just involved in selling Mid Pac Petroleum to Par Petroleum Corp., and the investment banker's name for the project was "Project Bogey."

I thought Bank of the West was a marriage made in heaven for us. We would still be majority owner and keep local management. I believed it would give our shareholders a long-term pop on the stock price because I thought we would eventually sell our 55 percent interest to BNP, though it wasn't part of the original deal.

Without a deal like this, First Hawaiian would be stagnant. We had hit our limit for local growth and were still a weak second to our major competitor. Of course, we didn't know that Bank of Hawaii would have a kind of implosion years later and have to shrink the size of its bank dramatically. Bank of Hawaii was a $15 billion bank at the time, and we were $7 billion in assets. When they had their problems later, they shrunk their bank by more than one-third, to below $10 billion. They got rid of non-Hawaii assets to clean up the bank, causing a dramatic change in our comparative size.

We went through negotiations about the split—how much would go to First Hawaiian shareholders and how much to BNP. On a mathematical basis based on comparative size, we would have gotten 57 percent and BNP 43. They pushed for 45, a little more than the mathematical split. I finally was convinced that, while I might give up a little bit now, I would get it back in the second round if BNP bid for the whole company. The value of our franchise was so good that I had no doubt we would get the price that we wanted for it eventually. Also, I felt the cost savings from combining the two banks would give us more in earnings. Our 55 percent would be worth way more than 100 percent of what we currently had. I told our guys, "We might take one or two percentage points less going in, but our shareholders are going to be well rewarded coming out." On that basis, we put the deal together.

Once we agreed on general terms, we went through the process called "due diligence," the single most important part of any deal. You have representations from the other side and their public documents, but you really don't know what you don't know until you get in and look under the hood. In this case, we sent a group of senior managers up to the Mainland to meet with the Bank of the West team at the Claremont Hotel in Berkeley. For example, our mortgage loan people would look at their mortgage documents. Any loan over a certain size, we would look at the application, underwriting, payment history. We would send an army of people to look at certain loans, and they would do the same with ours. We would look at legal files, pending lawsuits, bank examinations and capital structures. Technology people would look at their IT versus ours. Then, you get a list of questions and go back and do a second round.

One night, four of us were at dinner—myself, McGrath, and the two CFOs, Howard Karr and Doug Grigsby. McGrath challenged Howard on some numbers. Howard got upset and said, "I've never missed a number in my life. These numbers are good, and if you don't believe it, you have my resignation on day one." McGrath kind of backed down. They were still cynical because the First Hawaiian numbers were so good they were hard to believe. But, as history has shown, they were not only good then, they have stayed good to this day. In the end, everything looked good from both sides, and we moved ahead.

Of course, even with all the due diligence in the world, there are always risks in a deal of this magnitude that completely changes the look of your company. There's a risk that the chemistry doesn't work, that there's factions, or somebody comes in and says, "This is how we do things in Paris, and this is the way you are going to start doing things in Hawaii. You are going to start having formal dinners and stop eating poi." Operationally, could you get the cost savings you thought you could? Any time you do a merger, if you don't get cost savings, it really doesn't make a lot of sense to do it.

Finally, BNP wouldn't agree until they saw me personally. McGrath and I flew to Paris for dinner, then right back on one continuous loop. We arrived in Paris after a red-eye flight, freshened up and went to a little private dining room in their corporate headquarters, a famous 19th-century building called Maison Dorée. It was a formal setting with French food. I didn't know which fork and which knife to use, so I watched what everybody else did. This was the first time I had met anybody from BNP. There were five of us at dinner—Don and I, BNP Chairman Michel Pebereau and a couple of others from BNP. I speak zero French, and I told McGrath to tell them it was way too late in my life to learn a new language. Fortunately, they all spoke English.

After dinner, we got a few hours' sleep, then got on the next plane and flew back. That was a tough trip. I was wiped out for a week after. We had laid all the groundwork—due diligence work, looking through files, looking at loans—by the time we flew to Paris, yet in the end they wanted to make sure I wasn't—literally—some crazy Hawaiian.

We talked about how we operated and what our philosophies were and, right from day one, I made a strong pitch for keeping local control. I told them about companies that had come into Hawaii and tried to say, "This is how we do it in L.A. or New York." If you want to buy a bank and lose market share and lose your value, do that. Or you can let us run it. We've been setting records for years and will continue to do that. I'll never forget what Pebereau told me: "We are in 80 countries around the world, and whenever we came in and insisted on our management, we lost market share. When we had good local management, we gained market share."

The French became believers because we had people with high integrity and good character. We don't have rotating executives in Hawaii because people tend to stay. Not only executives, but lots of long-time employees 40 years and more. The more

> "People have asked whether we considered a merger with Bank of Hawaii instead. Bank of Hawaii was pursuing a 'Grand Pacific Strategy,' which I couldn't see working. An expansion strategy that put you in every rock in the Pacific, most of them separate countries with separate languages, didn't make a lot of sense to me. In the end it didn't work."
>
> —Don McGrath

What the fuck do we do now?

"Don McGrath and I were getting on a flight to Honolulu to sign the Bank of the West merger agreement with First Hawaiian. As I entered the SFO terminal, I could hear my boss, Don, the Bank of the West CEO, yelling into his phone down the concourse. Although the deal terms had already been finalized and approved by our parent company, BNP, and by First Hawaiian's board, Laurent Treca, a BNP senior executive, was insisting on a last-minute change.

"A standstill clause in the agreement prohibited BNP, without prior approval of the BancWest board, from acquiring more than the 45 percent interest they would own when the deal closed. In other words, BNP could not take 'creeping control' by going into the market and purchasing another 6 percent of the shares to reach 51 percent control. BNP wanted to delete that clause; Don knew Walter Dods would never agree. The heated conversation was left unresolved.

"When we arrived in Honolulu, Don called Treca and was told that our authorization to close the transaction had been withdrawn until we could resolve the issue. We also learned that word of the pending deal was beginning to leak when we took a call from an investment banker in New York attempting to talk us into taking a look at Bank of Hawaii instead. That conversation didn't last long.

"At Walt's office, Don explained to Walt that we were having a problem with BNP and would need 24 hours to fix it. Walt offered Don and me a conference room to talk in private. We closed the door and Don said, 'What the fuck do we do now?'

"What we did was head over to the Halekulani Hotel, where we worked out of Don's suite for the next 24 hours. We sent and received faxes all night trying to resolve the problem. Don will say that I emptied the liquor cabinet, but it really was a joint effort.

"We worked with Bank of the West's outside lawyers in San Francisco as well as our investment banker and BNP's outside lawyers and investment banker, all in New York. Despite the 12-hour time difference between Honolulu and Paris, we put together a joint letter to BNP outlining why the change they wanted would never be accepted and, in fact, Walt's fiduciary responsibility to his shareholders would preclude him from agreeing. The two investment banks and both sets of attorneys signed the letter, probably a historical precedent. As a result of the letter, BNP approved the original deal. We all lived happily ever after, but it was a very exciting 24 hours."

—Doug Grigsby, retired CFO, Bank of the West

When we announced the Bank of the West deal in the First Hawaiian boardroom, Don McGrath and I drank a toast with guava and orange juice.

they got to know us, the more Bank of the West and the French respected and liked our bank.

There was still a lot of ticklish fine-tuning before we could sign off on the deal. One of them was governance—how the board would operate with one side owning 55 percent and the other 45. It ended up being eleven First Hawaiian directors and nine representing Bank of the West and BNP. As the lawyers from each side haggled over language, McGrath and I would always be the court of last resort. The lawyers might get to a roadblock, and Don and I would get involved and find a way to get it done. Sometimes lawyers are more interested in showing they are smarter than the other lawyer and can screw up a deal. Bank of the West had an attorney named Rod Peck, who is still on their board today. He's very, very detailed on dotting i's and crossing t's. I tease him about it now. Investment bankers representing each side sometimes do the same. The egos get involved, but Don and I kept a close hold on that.

One time in our conference room we had the telephone on the table on speaker phone for 30 hours straight. We would go out of the room, lie down and take a little nap and come in shifts, and they would be arguing on points hour after hour.

After we had agreed on everything, we scheduled meetings of the two boards to vote, and then planned to announce the deal to the press. Right before that moment, Don arrived in Honolulu to sign and told me, "Somebody in France says we can't do the deal." Don, to his credit, fought through the problem. Right down to the last second, we didn't know whether we had an agreement. The whole thing could have fallen apart, easily. It's not a deal until it's done.

We announced the $1 billion deal to the public with a press conference on May 28, 1998 in our boardroom on the 30th floor of First Hawaiian Center. The room, which has a beautiful view of Waikiki and Diamond Head, was decked with banners of both banks and flags representing the places where we operated—Hawaii, Guam, Saipan, California, Oregon, Washington and Idaho. Don and I wore identical aloha shirts and toasted the deal with Hawaii guava juice and California orange juice. (It was too early in the day for wine.)

Because it was such a big change for our company, we made sure to quickly notify all Hawaii's political leaders in Congress, at the state Capitol and county governments. We made personal calls to all of First Hawaiian's top customers to assure them that nothing would change in their relationship with our bank. We knew our competitors would try to take advantage of the change by stealing customers away.

We had a reception for about 300 of our officers that evening at First Hawaiian Center, too. We didn't want our employees to worry.

Ordinarily, the long-term incentive plan for our senior managers would have paid out $9 million in bonuses after the change in the corporate situation. For each top executive, it would represent a bonus of 28 percent of salary. That didn't seem fair since our situation hadn't changed as a practical matter. I asked them to voluntarily agree to waive those windfall bonuses; all agreed to do so.

The deal gave us more geographic diversity and supported our strategy of expansion in Western states. To reflect our new regional focus, we changed the name of our holding company from First Hawaiian Inc. to BancWest.

We immediately set to work to shrink costs, eliminating several hundred jobs (mostly by attrition) in the two banks by combining back-office functions. For example, First Hawaiian began issuing Bank of the West's credit cards and servicing its residential mortgages; they started handling our Mainland consumer loans.

We also started growing BancWest within a matter of months by buying Sierra West Bank, which had $900 million in assets and branches in the Reno-Tahoe area. We then acquired United California Bank, the largest Los Angeles-based bank, for $2.4 billion in 2002. Other acquisitions included Union Safe Deposit Bank in California's Central Valley and Community First Bank in Fargo, N.D., both in 2004, and Commercial Federal Bank of Omaha, in 2005. Today, BancWest Corporation operates nearly 800 branches in

> "Walter was a great communicator. When we were merging with Bank of the West, and then later with BNP, it was really important how he communicated to us about what was happening, why we were doing this. Within the banking industry, there were a lot of acquisitions going on. He saw it as an opportunity for us to be proactive and find the right partner rather than be acquired. We believed in him, we trusted him."
>
> —*Ray Ono, First Hawaiian Bank vice chairman*

> "Walter did a magnificent job. First Hawaiian had 55 percent of the directors, Bank of the West had 45 percent. He was just a little Saint Louis grad in Hawaii dealing with one of the largest banks in the world. And not only dealing on even terms, he was getting 55 percent of the deal. A very good negotiator. BNP didn't realize what a gem they were getting, I don't think."
>
> —Jack Hoag, retired First Hawaiian Bank president

Hawaii, Guam, Saipan and 19 Western and Midwestern states. BancWest has assets of nearly $90 billion (Bank of Hawaii, in comparison, has about $15 billion in total assets).

The timing was terrific because economic expansion in the Western states in the early 21st century ran well ahead of the national average. The areas we were in were among the highest-growth states and, finally, Hawaii began rebounding as well.

Some bank mergers around the nation had troubles delivering, but ours didn't. Why? From the start, while we improved efficiency, we avoided slashing staff to the point that service suffered and both banks had a common vision.

One of the unique clauses in the contract merging First Hawaiian and Bank of the West was the "Standstill Agreement." It said that BNP could never own more than 45 percent, unless they bought 100 percent. In other words, they couldn't do "creeping control" where they got to 46, 47 and then 51 percent, and they might pay a really small amount for the incremental shares even though the shares gave them majority control. It had to be—"Stay at 45 or make an offer for *all* of the other 55 percent." BNP could never do a hostile transaction, and they could never do a public transaction. They would have to come confidentially to me and make a proposal for all of the other 55 percent.

We wanted that in there to protect our shareholders. And that clause tying BNP's hands was crucial, as you'll see in the next chapter.

Bank of the West deal at a Glance

First Hawaiian shareholders owned 55 percent of the combined company. Banque Nationale de Paris (BNP) received 25.9 million shares of First Hawaiian, Inc., and owned 45 percent. Based on First Hawaiian's stock price at the time, the merger was valued at more than $1 billion, the largest stock deal in history by a Hawaii company.

Walter Dods Jr. continued to run First Hawaiian and serve as chairman and CEO of the new company. Don McGrath continued to run Bank of the West and be president and chief operating officer of the new company, which was renamed BancWest Corporation and headquartered in Honolulu.

First Hawaiian had $8 billion in assets, including its Pacific One Bank subsidiary in Oregon; Bank of the West was $6 billion. First Hawaiian had higher net income. Combined, the deal created a $14 billion company, about evenly divided between Hawaii and the West Coast.

Unlike the earlier First Interstate acquisition, this one went smoothly. Announced in May 1998, approved by the Federal Reserve in September, completed November 1, 1998, with the new BancWest stock listed on the New York Stock Exchange.

Dick Adair cartoon, reprinted with permission of *Honolulu Star-Advertiser*

CHAPTER 14

Bidding in Barcelona: Selling a Bank on a Napkin

"At the time of our merger with First Hawaiian in 1998, I never expected BNP to try to buy the whole 100 percent of our combined company, BancWest. But, by 2001, circumstances had changed dramatically. BNP had become a much larger and healthier bank following its merger with Paribas and the change in name to BNP Paribas.

"Everybody likes a winner, and the 1998 BancWest merger had worked well. Our company was growing dramatically, the stock was doing well, and BNP Paribas liked the future potential, too. Walter did a great job. He got a good price for selling."

Don McGrath, retired chairman and CEO of Bank of the West and BancWest Corporation

Our First Hawaiian partnership with BNP Paribas was about two years old when I was invited to their annual global executive session in Barcelona, Spain, in February 2001, along with leaders of BNPP operations in about 80 countries. Pierre Mariani, BNP's head of International Retail Banking, asked me to meet with him and a few of their top people at our hotel. At that point, they already owned 45 percent of BancWest, First Hawaiian Bank's parent company, following our merger in 1998.

Pierre asked me if we would consider an offer from them to buy the rest of the BancWest stock; he needed our permission to make the offer under the terms of our original deal. I wasn't totally surprised that they approached me. When we did our merger with Bank of the West in 1998, in the back of my mind I suspected that someday BNP intended to buy all of BancWest Corporation, not remain as a minority shareholder forever. However, the offer came a little earlier than I anticipated.

Our original 1998 deal had a provision that blocked BNP from attempting a hostile takeover on us for a period of four years. They could not publicly try to buy us; they could only come to the CEO—me—or the board's Executive Committee with an offer for *all* the rest of the stock. They couldn't just take "creeping control" by buying a little here, a little there to get to 51 percent ownership. I had the right to turn them down without even taking the matter to our board of directors. Their ownership was capped at 45 percent under this standstill clause.

> "If you are in Paris watching the stock price of BancWest going up and up and up, that creates all the reason you need to pick up the phone and make the call to buy the rest of the bank."
>
> —David Winton, bank analyst for Keefe Bruyette & Woods Inc., New York

BancWest started doing very well immediately after our 1998 merger. We started buying other banks on the Mainland. Because we owned 55 percent of the stock and BNP owned 45, as we grew and became more successful, the remaining 55 percent became more expensive. The French decided they didn't want to wait for the expiration of the standstill agreement. They said, "We know we have a contract with you, but would you consider waiving those restrictions?" I said, "Yes, if it's in the best interest of the shareholders, of course I would. But, it would have to be a compelling offer." They are sitting there—Pierre with three guys from their investment banking negotiating team—and Pierre said, "Tell us what a compelling offer would be."

I went back to my room alone and took out my BancWest balance sheet information and used paper napkins and a felt pen to do some rough calculations. I wish I had kept those napkins! By the time I finished, they were all smeared with felt pen ink. I calculated what price per share and what dollar amount it would take for me to approach my board with their offer. What would be the number? The net worth of First Hawaiian Bank at that point was almost $800 million. I said I would consider it for $2.5 billion cash. That's three times book value, a pretty rich number.

Even though I was in Spain by myself, I was under no pressure to sell, so I could pick a good number for our shareholders. I knew the potential for the future profitability of First Hawaiian and Bank of the West was wonderful. We had already gotten synergies by combining the back-shop functions of the two banks. I tried to pick a number that was at the upper end of possible, but not so stupid that it would not only be rejected but also turn BNP off on the organization. It was a fine line to walk, but I had pretty good instincts. I knew what banks had been selling for. The French were a little surprised at the amount. They gulped and said, "Well, we'll have to think about that."

Don McGrath was also at the Barcelona conference but wasn't involved in this smaller meeting because of his long ties to BNP going back well before our 1998 merger. I told him what had happened in the meeting with Pierre, that $2.5 billion is going to be the number. He was pretty surprised.

About six weeks later, in March 2001, Pierre asked to meet me in San Francisco privately. We had further negotiations, just the two of us, over pasta and wine (French wine, as I recall) at Allegro, a little restaurant in San Francisco a block from my apartment on Russian Hill. We started working out the details, including the price.

It was a time when BNP had been incredibly active in acquisitions in France. In 1999, they had tried to do a double hostile takeover of two other major French banks—one was Paribas, the other Societe Generale. Michel Pebereau was acting out of self-preservation. Societe Generale, one of their major competitors, had announced that they were going to buy Paribas. BNP was about the same size, but if Soc Gen had gotten Paribas, then BNP would be the smaller player. Michel had done something unheard of in France's business history: trying a double hostile. He almost ended up getting them both. He acquired Paribas but lost the vote of Societe Generale shareholders. But in getting Paribas, he created the largest bank in the Eurozone. That's when they changed the name from Banque Nationale de Paris to BNP Paribas.

Pierre and I negotiated over the exact price during the rest of March and April. My original price on that Barcelona napkin, $2.5 billion, worked out to $35 a share, well above what BancWest stock was trading at the time on the New York Stock Exchange. The stock had hit an all-time high of $27.25 on January 29, 2001, nearly double the price of a year earlier. The fast rise in the stock may have triggered their request to meet with me in Barcelona; they didn't want the price to go too much higher before locking in a deal.

Anyway, their response to my original offer was $32 a share. I told them that wouldn't be "compelling" enough. They stuck with that price for a while. We countered with an offer of $37, even higher than my original suggested price. In the end, after all the dancing around different amounts, that original number I wrote on the napkin never changed, which is remarkable.

During that period, we had to create the proper legal mechanism to evaluate the offer. We set up a separate committee of independent BancWest directors representing the First Hawaiian side of the shareholder base, the 55 percent shareholders. That group of outside directors, not including me, hired their own investment banker and their own lawyers to examine the transaction. What an investment banker does is render a "fairness

"First Hawaiian's deal with BNP Paribas was a very smart deal for Walt to make. When you're playing tennis, you either want to be up at the net or at the very back. You don't want to be in the middle, and both First Hawaiian and Bank of Hawaii by themselves are in the middle-size range for banks. Bank of Hawaii has done a great job in surviving independently after some rough moments, but my view of the world, and it's true maybe everywhere except at the Bank of Hawaii, is that you have to be either a very small community bank or a very big bank.

"Walt's deal with BNP was a sensible, strategic move—and the way he did it tactically was equally as good. For all practical purposes, BNP doesn't exist in Hawaii. I'm sure Walt had a great deal to do with keeping BNP in the background, and I suspect it took a good deal of arm wrestling with the people in Paris. It's a tribute to Walt that BNP didn't put French expatriates on the First Hawaiian staff and also a tribute to First Hawaiian. Thanks to Walter's political skills, BNP was persuaded that they didn't want to screw up a good thing."

—*Dick Rosenberg, retired chairman & CEO, Bank of America*

> "Can you imagine a deal to sell a local bank to the French where the French never even appeared here publicly? Walt was able to say, 'No big change; we're still a local bank.'
>
> "It was a good deal for the shareholders and for officers who had a lot of stock options. They made money. The only problem is when you do a big transaction like that, the senior guys have what they call 'Change in Control Agreements.' That's usually a big part of motivating executives to do a deal like that because, if they lose their job, they get paid a big chunk of money.
>
> "But the way Walter did it, nobody lost their job. Change in Controls usually have what they call a 'double trigger.' Not only does it have to be a change in control of the company, but either your job has to be lost or they substantially change your responsibility. From a governing standpoint, when the bank was sold, it didn't trigger any change of control. You had senior guys going to Walter and saying, 'Walt, please fire me. Please, throw me out the door.' It was an unusual transaction that Walter did. It was real genius."
>
> —*Jeff Watanabe, attorney and longtime friend*

opinion." They charged us $5 million basically to say whether this was a fair transaction for the shareholders. Our investment banker, Goldman Sachs, was hired to protect the board, to be sure the board was acting in the best interest of its shareholders so that the shareholders would not come back at you and say, "Why did you sell it so cheap? It's worth $10 billion." Somehow, amazingly, they ended up saying $2.5 billion/$35 per share was fair.

Finally, on May 7, 2001, BNP Paribas announced its offer publicly. During that day, Goldman Sachs in New York did a "market check." They called around to other banks that might theoretically be interested in making an offer better than BNP's price, but nobody did. That evening, the 11 non-BNP directors of BancWest voted to approve the sale of the company.

Was it a good price or not? The best local proxy for the value of banks would be Bank of Hawaii. First Hawaiian was no longer a public company, so we didn't have a stock value, but Bank of Hawaii did. At the time we announced the deal, First Hawaiian's size was about $7.5 billion in assets. BNP Paribas paid $2.5 billion.

Now, 14 years later, Bank of Hawaii was about $15 billion in assets as of June 30, 2015—twice the size First Hawaiian was when we did the BNP deal in 2001—and Bankoh's market capitalization on that same date was $2.9 billion. (Market capitalization is a measure of how the stock market computes a company's total value; it is calculated by multiplying the share price by the number of shares outstanding—in effect, what the market says the entire company is worth.) Those numbers tell you we got a fantastic deal. If you took that $2.5 billion we received in 2001 dollars and invested it in something that returned you just 3 percent a year, it would be worth almost $4 billion today. That was for a bank half the size of what

Bank of Hawaii is today. The test of time has shown that our deal was a damn good one for our shareholders.

That $2.5 billion price worked out to $35 a share for BancWest stockholders. At the time the proposed deal was announced, a share of stock was trading at $24.98, so the deal produced an instant profit of 40 percent. The extra $5 million that BNP Paribas donated to the First Hawaiian Bank Foundation as part of the agreement enabled us to continue to be Hawaii's largest corporate donor to charity to this day. Eventually, the shareholder vote was 98 percent in favor of the offer—pretty unprecedented. They knew it was a terrific deal.

The deal was also good for shareholders within the First Hawaiian ohana. Many employees had bought stock over the years, and they profited. Also, senior managers (including myself) received incentive stock options each year that could be exercised over time. All those options could immediately be exercised when the company was sold, triggering a payout of $42 million for several dozen managers. Senior managers also were part of a benefit program called the "long-term incentive plan," which paid out another $8.9 million because the change in corporate control triggered an immediate, maximum payout.

We took care of our shareholders, we took care of our employees at all levels, who kept their jobs, which would not have happened if we were bought out in a hostile takeover.

The deals were also good for Hawaii as a whole. Our state has always been capital short, and during traumatic shocks to the economy, we've seen the importance of banks that have really solid parents that could stand behind them. In the years since our transaction, two major banks in Hawaii (not First Hawaiian) have had challenges. For a time, banking regulators put two banks under MOUs, Memorandums of Understanding, which restricted certain practices, restricted loans and credit. To have a bank like First Hawaiian backed by a trillion-dollar bank when the world went through the Great Recession was a wonderful thing for the people of Hawaii to have. First Hawaiian could rely on a much larger bank to inject capital if needed and also help line up major loans.

We took care of our community and—in all the years since the original deal in 1998—First Hawaiian

> "When BNP made a bid for all our stock in 2001, I chaired a five-man board committee that negotiated the final price. We finally landed at $35 a share, a 40 percent premium over the BancWest stock price. If I had been a guru with a crystal ball, I might have said, 'Walt, let's keep this thing.' But I didn't. At the time it seemed like the right thing to do. Walter said in one of our meetings, 'One of my goals is to make all my guys around me millionaires.' And he did make a lot of millionaires, including guys who were not really in the upper ranks but who had a lot of stock options."
>
> —*Jack Hoag, retired First Hawaiian Bank president and longtime director*

YES! A MEMOIR OF MODERN HAWAII

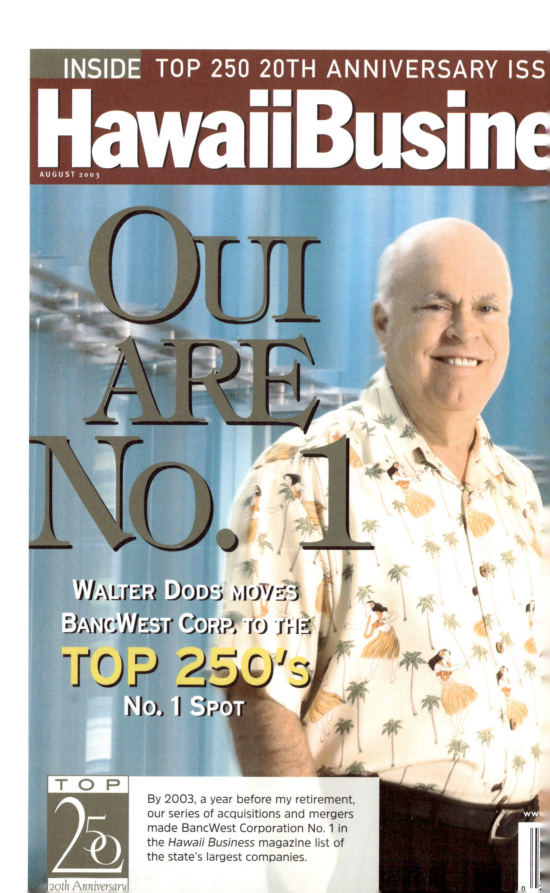

INSIDE TOP 250 20TH ANNIVERSARY ISS

HawaiiBusine

AUGUST 2003

Oui Are No. 1

WALTER DODS MOVES BANCWEST CORP. TO THE TOP 250's No. 1 SPOT

TOP 250 20th Anniversary

By 2003, a year before my retirement, our series of acquisitions and mergers made BancWest Corporation No. 1 in the *Hawaii Business* magazine list of the state's largest companies.

"When I was running Citizens Bank, we were owned by Royal Bank of Scotland, so I know about having a foreign owner. Walt was very good at keeping First Hawaiian independent after the acquisition by BNP Paribas. I think a small-business owner in Kailua is not aware that First Hawaiian is owned by BNP because Walt and his successors have done a great job of keeping the feel of the bank very local.

"As long as First Hawaiian continues to do well and Walt is around, I suspect it will stay that way. It's always easier to keep your owner at bay if the financial results are good, and Walt and his successors have produced great results. First Hawaiian has been a great investment for BNP Paribas, and Walt negotiated a terrific price for the shareholders."

—*Larry Fish, retired chairman & CEO of Citizens Bank, one of the largest U.S. banks*

> "We have had a great deal of confidence in the people of BancWest and in Walter Dods, Don McGrath and the management team. BancWest has an impressive record of growth, profitability and customer service, and we'll continue to count on its management team to further develop the bank's network."
>
> —*Michel Pebereau, BNP Paribas chairman & CEO, announcing its plan to buy BancWest in 2001*

is still a 100 percent locally managed bank. That is almost unprecedented. We have never had a single French executive sent from Paris to First Hawaiian. We had a couple of BNP Paribas representatives on the board, but never one in our Hawaii offices.

As you know, in most transactions, the buyer says, "Management will remain unchanged," and 99 percent of the time it's bullshit. The day the deal closes, everybody is out the door. In our case, I had told Michel Pebereau that we'd do a good job if he left us alone to manage it. I told him, "I give you my word that, if you folks deliver from your side, we will deliver from our side." To this day, it has worked that way.

When BNP Paribas approached me in 2001 about the total buyout, they said, "If we do the transaction, we want to keep the same management team in place." They said they would give me a contract to do it. I said, "We can talk about contracts later because I'm not looking to enrich myself, I'm looking to enrich the shareholders." Eventually, I did sign a contract to remain as chairman and CEO of both BancWest Corporation and First Hawaiian for three years. Don McGrath also had a contract. I also got BNP Paribas to sign three-year contracts that would make sure we would keep First Hawaiian's President Jack Tsui, CFO Howard Karr and Vice Chairman Don Horner.

Because we were being bought out, I didn't want to risk having Tsui, Karr and Horner lured away by our competitors in Hawaii. I wanted to offer them contracts because I thought it was in the buyer's best interest to have a stable management team. That created resentment because Bank of the West managers didn't have the same protection. My theory was that they didn't need it because they already had been BNP employees before these deals. But it did create awkward tension between senior executives of the two banks. BNP understood, but I wasn't popular in San Francisco for a while for doing that.

We took occasional grief locally after the deal was announced. Mike O'Neill, my counterpart at Bank of Hawaii, gave part of a Rotary Club speech in French and added, "Sorry, for a moment I was a little confused. I thought I was representing another bank in town." I've heard critics say, "Yeah, local management, but, at the end of the day, some guy in Paris pulls the trigger." Technically, that's true, but people don't understand that the shareholders—not local managers—own *any* company. Take Bank of Hawaii; more than 75 percent of its shares are owned by mutual funds and other institutional investors outside Hawaii. That's true of a lot of other publicly traded companies as well. Is there any difference to the social fabric of the institution if it is owned by shareholders in New York or a shareholder in Paris? I contend that there isn't a difference. Whether BNP Paribas ever takes a more active role in First Hawaiian is going to depend on performance, for sure. But have they pulled the trigger? In 17 years, they have not.

Of course, that's the benefit of hindsight. At the time we did the first deal with Bank of the West in 1998, we still had control of 55 percent of the stock. When we sold that 55 percent to BNP Paribas in 2001, we no longer had control. Despite that, I had no qualms about the deal offered to us. As a chief executive officer, your first obligation is to your shareholders. If you do that part of the job right as well as take care of your employees and your community, it will all work out. By the time we got to the second deal in 2001, I pretty much knew the character of BNP Paribas. I was comfortable that they were solid people whose word was good. Nobody can predict what's going to happen someday down the line. But, if it changes, it's not going to be because we at First Hawaiian didn't live up to our part of the bargain.

In the end, history has shown that we were very careful to protect the interests of everybody concerned—the customers, employees and the First Hawaiian shareholders who profited greatly from BNP's interest in our company. The change has been invisible to our customers. I wouldn't have wanted to do the deal if I wasn't sure that we'd continue to have the same "local" style that we had had since 1858.

People have asked me how I felt personally about the change. Certainly, on a personal level it was different. When you're CEO of a publicly held company that is doing OK, you're in charge. You don't have to report to anybody. Once that 2001 deal closed, I was working for BNP Paribas. But I didn't find it hard because, even though I had a boss, he left me alone. I never once had somebody from Paris tell me I should do X instead of Y.

Over the years, most bank mergers brought layoffs, branch closings and management changes. But our deal with BNP Paribas was totally different. First Hawaiian kept existing local management in place. Same name, same signs on the door, same employees at the same branches.

All these years later, that's still the way it is. Our senior managers average more than 25 years at First Hawaiian. We make our own banking decisions to help local consumers and businesses. On our board, 23 of 24 directors are Hawaii men and women. We're a 157-year-old Hawaii-chartered bank with a shareholder that is a very successful international banking company. BNP Paribas

> "BNP was very aware of the unique Hawaiian element. Jacques Wahl from BNP was on our board for a long time. I remember him telling us, 'You need to be careful of those guys in Hawaii. They are island people. Island people are different.' There's a sense of pride that 'we can do it as well as the guys on the Mainland can. We want to control things here.'"
>
> —Doug Grigsby, retired Bank of the West CFO

First Hawaiian's two deals with Bank of the West and BNP Paribas created a good partnership between myself and Don McGrath. Both of us are retired now, but our two banks and their BancWest holding company continue to thrive with the next generation of leaders.

is a wonderful shareholder to have. They are a long-term player, interested in growing our bank and having us succeed.

Doing these deals was a pretty exciting time for me. It was never easy, but I never had a lot of doubts. You try to use your best judgment, get professional advisers, but a deal doesn't always go well. Most of our earlier acquisitions were so much smaller than First Hawaiian that we never bet the bank. But when we did bet Bank of the West and First Hawaiian—that was a biggie. There was risk because we came together like a common-law marriage in which we exchanged stock. If Bank of the West had major problems, it would have affected us. We would inherit those problems.

To me the bigger risk, as I explained to our directors and shareholders, was not doing anything—remaining only in the small Hawaii market with a competitor across the street that was way larger than us.

Three years later, when we sold to BNP Paribas, we got all our money off the table, so there was no risk once we agreed on that. Even when I put that initial $2.5 billion price to them, I never had second thoughts about, "Gee, should I have said $2.7 billion?" I had done my share of transactions and had been ABA president, so I knew the range of prices; I was definitely at the upper end. Two or two-and-a-quarter times book value was the going rate; I was asking for three times book, as far on the upside as I could without creating warfare. In the end, BNP Paribas agreed, and all the analysts bought off on that number, so I felt comfortable.

I like doing deals, even to this day. Not just for ego, but I love to do a good deal and watch a company morph into a better company. I'm still doing them. I don't know where it came from. When I was a teenager, my deal was, "Could I become Aina Haina Service Station manager?" That was my life's goal. Even when I came to the bank, I was just a PR and ad guy, to start with. I don't know if it's instinctive or what.

I don't have a clue.

"In any acquisition you have to measure a whole bunch of variables. Is it the right thing for the community? Is it the right thing for employees? For the shareholders? Does our culture fit into their culture?

"I don't think anybody in the country could have pulled off the BNP deal except for Walter Dods. You were dealing with one of the largest corporations in the world. Michel Pebereau had to trust Walter, and so did Don McGrath. As much as the deal structure was important, it was a relationship deal, and Walter is a relationship guy. For them to agree to a standstill allowing no additional stock acquisition, they had to have a lot of confidence in Walter to put that kind of money in a company where he still had controlling interest. There was substantial trust on the part of the French investors, on the part of McGrath, and the part of Walter."

—*Don Horner, retired chairman & CEO, First Hawaiian Bank*

Over the years, First Hawaiian helped finance Aloha Airlines even though it struggled financially because Johnny Bellinger and I both felt that Hawaii was better served by having competing interisland airlines.

Honolulu Star-Advertiser photo, reprinted with permission.

CHAPTER 15

When Banking Could Extend a Hand

My years at First Hawaiian in many ways coincided with the heyday of community lending, the idea that there is more to a bank than a place to store and make money. Buried deep in most bankers' DNA is the idea that the bank is there to help the community grow and prosper. That may sound like a romantic idea out of the movie *It's a Wonderful Life,* but it's true.

Unfortunately, that era is coming to an end. Banking regulations, especially some of those that followed in the wake of the financial scandals of 2007–2008, have put the clamps on "handshake" loans in which the character of the borrower mattered as much as his or her bottom line. "Character loans" would be very difficult (if not impossible) to make today, which I think is too bad. Instead of deciding on the pros and cons of specific credits, banking regulators ought to look at the overall strength of an institution. I know I am going to get in trouble for saying this, but I believe that an institution with a strong balance sheet and a track record of generally good overall judgments should be allowed to make "character" loans from time to time for the benefit of the greater community. I have always felt that way, but it is really hard to do that in today's regulatory climate.

I probably got my thinking on this subject of character lending from Johnny Bellinger. A classic example of the breed is Aloha Airlines.

Aloha Airlines was a case to me of where sometimes the consensus of a community, the emotion of the community and our political leadership can be so far off. Both Johnny and I felt it was vital to the community to have two vibrant airlines flying between the islands. Some of the original financing Johnny extended to Aloha were pure character loans. Aloha Airlines had been in trouble many times over the years, and Hung Wo Ching, who was the main owner and who was running the airline, couldn't get a loan from Bank of Hawaii to save his soul. What was significant about that is Hung Wo Ching was on the board of Bank of Hawaii, yet still they turned him down, so he came across the street to see Johnny and told him the problem. Johnny said Aloha's finances couldn't stand up to scrutiny, but he was going to make the airline a loan anyway. He believed Ching would pay him back (which he did). In a broader sense, Johnny believed that it was important to the community to keep a second interisland airline going.

It was a running joke between Bellinger and Ching. They played golf together, and Johnny would tell Hung Wo, "Yeah, you may be a Bank of Hawaii director, but they won't loan you a dime." We had been helping Aloha Airlines off and on to keep them going, including helping them finance an unprecedented move to the Mainland with Boeing 737 aircraft. Flying that long over water with 737s had never been done.

What concerned me then and bothers me to this day is the impact of a third, upstart airline coming in and offering super-deep-discounted fares that by any stretch of the imagination you couldn't justify from a business standpoint. They were below cost; without a doubt, it was predatory pricing. That was one of the rare times when, I feel, government should have played a role.

Go! Airlines (yes, their name actually had an exclamation point in it!) entered the interisland air market with extremely low, unsustainable fares in 2006, during Gov. Linda Lingle's term in office. I fault her for not looking out for the community's long-term interest in this instance. The public was happy because they got cheap Neighbor Island fares, but people didn't realize Go! was driving out the competition. It broke my heart because I knew what the end was going to be. The proof is in the pudding. Aloha, the weaker of the other interisland carriers, folded in 2008. Go! stopped flying in 2014. Look at Neighbor Island fares today. Some days, you can go to Los Angeles or San Francisco for not much more than the price of flying to Hilo.

If state government had stepped in, I believe we might have a competitive interisland air market today. There are times when government should be involved and times when it shouldn't. This was a time when I felt the governor should have stepped in and said to Go!, "Cut this crap out. You can be competitive and challenge existing airlines, but you damn well better be charging fares that at least cover your cost. Otherwise, in the end you are going to hurt Hawaii far more than this joy of having $30 or $16 tickets for a temporary period." That's where you require strong leadership and are willing to put your cojones on the line.

The state could have jawboned Mesa Airlines, which owned Go!, by threatening to have the attorney general look into whether this was a predatory pricing scheme. Or she could have pointed out that, if you expect airline slots at the terminals, we

> "I doubt Aloha United Way would be around today if not for Walter Dods and Senator Inouye. When I was first named head of Aloha United Way, we were fading fast. Most people didn't expect us to last two years. One of the first things I did was call on Walter. He said he'd facilitate a meeting with Inouye and something like the top 30 CEOs in town, 'We'll be lucky if we get 12,' he said. All 30 showed up and Walter put each of them on the spot—'I knew your grandfather, you need to step up,' like that. In about a week we called the CEOs. Every single one agreed to come on the board because of Walter's help. Overnight, we had the most powerful board in town."
>
> —Kim Gennaula, former president of Aloha United Way

expect you to be a good corporate citizen. You may not win that case ultimately in court, but you put that flag out there, and people are going to have to look at it seriously.

By the way, Hawaiian Airlines is a good airline and they have done a great job. If I were sitting in their seat, I would fill that vacuum too. But it's not healthy, and a one-airline market could have been prevented with a little bit of gutsy governmental leadership. To me, this is a leadership lesson about the proper role of government. People get caught up in the moment and fail to look at the bigger ramifications.

I could say the same thing about the Thirty Meter Telescope controversy on the Big Island. The damage done to Hawaii's business reputation and its political reputation came at a very high cost. You have these very prominent universities on the West Coast and international astronomy researchers who came together and put up $1.4 billion for the project and then go through seven years of planning and hearings. All of a sudden, out of nowhere, you stop a project based on emotions. The long-term implication is that people who believe in science and believe in the community get turned off on Hawaii and they don't feel Hawaii's word is good.

I don't want to come across as a pro-development, "let's pave Hawaii and make it a parking lot" kind of person, because I am not. But when you start ignoring rule of law, the impact for your community and your state is big. I have heard it already in circles on the Mainland: "Hawaii can't be counted on to go by the rule of law."

One final thought on the place of government regulation. U.S. banks have been operating for nearly four decades under the Community Reinvestment Act (CRA), first

"I came to Hawaii in 1975 to be executive director of the HSTA, the teachers' union. A lot of people worked with me to turn the union around and improve its reputation and I left to do a variety of other work in labor and politics, including an unsuccessful run for Congress.

"By 1991 I was nearly broke, living in a rented house. Then my landlord, a Navy nuclear sub commander, told me he would need his home back. A friend told me about a new townhouse development by Queen Liliuokalani Park in Nuuanu, but my wife and I had no money for a down payment and no means of getting any. As I still inelegantly say, 'We did not have a pot to piss in, or a window to throw it out of.'

"So I screwed up my courage and made an appointment with Walter Dods, CEO of First Hawaiian Bank. Walt, like me, knew what not being born to money is all about.

"I told him my situation, and he said, 'John, you've paid your dues. You are a part of this community. Do you know the nicest thing about being CEO of this bank? I can loan money to whomever I want. I know you'll pay it back.'

"Walter Dods saved our family that day."

—*John Radcliffe, retired labor union leader and lobbyist*

> "When Walter commits to something, he might do more but he won't do less. When we were falling short on our capital campaign at Hawaii Public Television, I went to Walter. He was quite busy and suggested I find someone in the younger generation to help. I left feeling a bit glum. But then I ran into him and he said, 'You know what, I'll help you a little bit. We'll go in person.' He set up meetings with top people at places like Matson, A&B, Hawaiian Telcom and the bank. He went with me to help make our case. Within a short time, the money began rolling in and we made our goal."
>
> —Leslie Wilcox, president of PBS Hawaii

passed in 1977 and amended, changed and updated frequently over the years. CRA began primarily to stop redlining, the despicable practice in which banks would not make loans in poorer or minority neighborhoods.

As the CRA grew and changed over the years, however, the rules started to almost set quotas for community lending. That was offensive to me because I've always felt it's critical for a bank to serve all corners of your community. It was always in our bank's blood to be community-service oriented, but to pass legislation to say that you should make loans to your community, and do things for poor people, was kind of an insult to those of us who already were doing it.

Nationally, I understood why there was a need for CRA. There were banks across the U.S. that were redlining. I intellectually understood the need for the law. However, on a personal basis I was almost resentful of it. It was like telling you to brush your teeth, something you should be doing anyway. But I pledged that First Hawaiian would go all-out in that area because it would be easy; for us, that's what we do. I remember very early on telling CRA regulators, "I know you have to do your job and duty, but we pride ourselves on our diversity and our outreach. When you look at the ethnic extraction of our community and our employees, you'll find that they match. You'll find no redlining in this company." Pretty early on, First Hawaiian was rated "Outstanding"—the highest level for CRA performance, achieved by a small minority of banks.

I'm proud to say we've kept that rating for years and years.

Corky Trinidad cartoon, reprinted with permission of *Honolulu Star-Advertiser*.

CHAPTER 16

"If You Run, It's Gonna Kill You"

---

*"I think Walt would make an excellent governor;
he has probably the most spectacular business record in the state.
It would be a landslide."*

Honolulu Mayor Jeremy Harris, June 2002

As 2002 began, Democratic governors had been living in Washington Place for 39 years. Ben Cayetano's second term as governor was coming to an end, and he was barred by law from running again. Early on, the consensus was that the race for governor would be between Honolulu Mayor Jeremy Harris, a Democrat, and Republican Linda Lingle, the former Maui mayor who had barely lost to Ben four years earlier.

There was a longstanding tradition of incumbent lieutenant governors running for and winning the top job going back to 1974 when George Ariyoshi moved up. The pattern continued with John Waihee and Ben, but Harris looked like such a formidable candidate for 2002 that Lt. Gov. Mazie Hirono backed away from the race the year before. She announced she'd run for mayor instead, seeking the job Harris was expected to vacate to seek the governorship.

It didn't work out that way. In late May 2002, Harris stunned everybody by quitting his campaign for governor, saying new polls showed him too far behind Lingle to have any hope. He was also hampered by pending investigations into his campaign finances. (No charges ever resulted, but nobody knew that at the time.)

That left Democrats with two other candidates for governor—former Republican legislator D.G. (Andy) Anderson and state Rep. Ed Case. On the heels of the Harris announcement, Mazie Hirono switched gears and dropped back in to run for governor. Early in June, a week or so after Harris dropped out, I went to San Francisco to make a presentation to top executives of our parent company, BNP Paribas. As I flew home, I started thinking seriously about running for governor myself. I loved the bank, but I was 61 years old, getting near the end of my career at First Hawaiian. I thought it would be one more way to give back to the community. Hawaii had real economic challenges after 9/11 and needed strong leadership.

It was my own idea. Candidates like to talk about responding to the "call of the people," but nobody recruited me. Since I was a young man, I had thought of running for office someday. When the landscape seemed right in 2002, I considered it. It was fun to read news stories later about all these "invisible hands" manipulating me into the race.

> "The day Buster said he was not going to run for governor, if you looked at his face, I thought he was going to cry. He wanted to give back to the community and he was really torn. He had done everything he could do with the bank and he wanted to take the last step in his legacy."
>
> —brother Tommy Dods

In fact, I was the one who was soliciting support. I bounced the idea off people I knew and trusted. Most of them—starting with my old friends Dan Inouye and George Ariyoshi—encouraged me to run. I met with a half-dozen union leaders—Russell Okata from HGEA, Buzzy Hong from the construction unions, leaders at the ILWU, a few others. They all told me they would support me if I ran. For a business guy, that's pretty rare.

I felt that the support from the business and financial community and a lot of organized labor would have given me a unique base. I didn't have to go round up support; once word got out that I was thinking about it, people came out of the woodwork.

Not everybody thought it was a good idea, though. My old friend Wes Park told me I was crazy. He said, "People want you to run for their own selfish reasons." Gary Caulfield, the bank's top IT guy who had worked with me in several political campaigns over the years, also advised me not to run. Gerry Keir, my own PR guy at the bank, was against it, too.

Things were moving fast, but I really hadn't made up my mind. I asked Keir to draft different versions of a press release—one saying I was thinking about it, one that I wouldn't do it and a third announcing that I would be a candidate. If I announced, I had already decided I wanted to do it outside the Foodland in Aina Haina where I had started as a teenage bag boy. I needed to get away from the idea I was just some big-shot banker and talk about my roots.

As a courtesy, I called the other Democrats already in the race—Andy, Ed and Mazie—and told them I was thinking about it.

We had our annual bank retiree lunch about then. I was so close to running I toyed with the idea of saying something to them because I thought they'd be a great army of campaign workers. In the end I kept my mouth shut, which isn't easy for a Portagee.

Then the rumor finally hit the media. In a KHON lead story, Gregg Takayama said I was considering it—without any comment from me. The story had video of me standing behind Ben Cayetano at a news conference of the Economic Revitalization Task Force. And also, painfully, KHON showed film of me looking angry at a Thumbs Up Hawaii event from 1995, saying, "We're not idiots." (The Thumbs Up campaign was a poorly executed effort on my part to improve consumer confidence during a prolonged economic slump.) Gregg said I was a marketing genius, but my instincts failed me in Thumbs Up. He was right about the second part, and the news story gave me an idea of what the media spotlight is like in politics.

Once the story broke, it became a media feeding frenzy. My secretaries, Dorri Kuriki and Diane Yamashita, took 14 media calls in one day, and a KHON reporter and cameraman showed up unannounced to knock on the door of my 29th-floor office suite. Once the media aired the rumors, the flow of calls skyrocketed.

One reporter called to ask about a rumor that I had already resigned from the bank. Richard Borreca's front-page story in the *Star-Bulletin* quoted my old friend attorney Jeff Watanabe saying that I was "giving it very serious consideration."

The response was overwhelmingly positive. I bet I got 500 calls or emails saying I should enter the race from other business leaders, union leaders, legislators, old friends from school and a couple of well-known lobbyists. Johnny Bellinger's son, Neil, said, "Just tell me where to hold the sign." The most common message on my phone was "Go for it." Many of my fellow bank employees were encouraging, and I appreciated that.

Then others reacted. Andy Anderson said I would be a "formidable" candidate but didn't have "the basic fundamental understanding of government." Ed Case said he thought he could beat me. Jeremy Harris said I'd win easily. My old friend and business rival Larry Johnson across the street at Bank of Hawaii was kind enough to say I would be a strong candidate, but he also warned about the impact on my family.

Anyway, the story percolated in the media for a few days, and I was getting excited about the possibility, but I made one strategic error—not talking to my wife. I figured Diane would be against it, but I thought once I got enough support around town, I could convince her, so I left her to last. Big mistake. I talked her into having a family meeting because I was sure my kids would support me. We all got together, and she just sat there quietly. Finally, one of my sons looked me in the eye and said, "If you get elected, you're going to want to make big changes. When you tell people to do things at the bank, they listen. In government, they don't listen. Dad, you're stressed out, you're overweight. I don't want you to die." And the other kids chimed in "I agree. . . I agree." I ended up without *any* of the kids on my side. My wife didn't have to say a word.

One of them said, "You know, you're a great dad, but you've never spent the kind of time with us we'd really like." That's pretty tough to take. In the end, I think I have given a lot to the community, but there is no doubt I haven't given the time I should have given to my own family. Diane bore the burden of that.

"Most of Walt's friends supported him running for governor, but I told him I thought he was out of his mind. I thought he could win and would be a good governor. I just thought he would be miserable in the job.

"At the bank, when he has a good idea, he can get it done without going through 76 legislators. With the exception of the Thumbs Up debacle, he had a lifetime of positive, supportive media coverage. All that would change if he moved into the Capitol. He would have found it immensely frustrating. I'm glad he didn't run."

—*Gerry Keir,*
former Advertiser *editor, retired head of Corporate Communications at First Hawaiian Bank*

> "Dods (is)... too rich for the blood of some Democrats. It's an ugly reverse snobbery that mistrusts some of our best as 'too' successful—the old *alamihi* crab syndrome of trying to climb out of the bucket—that holds Hawaii back from realizing its potential.
>
> "Dods takes the responsibilities of his wealth seriously. He and his wife, Diane, funded a $1 million scholarship fund at UH to benefit graduates of Hawaii public schools. He's given his time as well as his money to efforts to reinforce the social safety net so dear to Democrats. Dods always answered honorably when called. It's the kind of local success story that should be celebrated, not viewed with suspicion.
>
> "It's impossible to say whether Dods would have made a good governor—or even a good candidate. Dods doesn't like to be criticized. We saw his thin skin when he bristled at the heat he took for the infamous 'Thumbs Up Hawaii' campaign he helped launch.
>
> "Still, it would have been much to our benefit to hear what he had to say. After all, it's been more than 40 years since Hawaii elected a governor who came to the job with a record of real accomplishment in another life, who saw politics as a calling rather than a career opportunity."
>
> —David Shapiro, Honolulu Advertiser *columnist*, June 2002

Absolutely, I think I could have won, but family comes first. My wife and children have been in the public view for years because of my position in the community. They would have lost even more of their privacy, and I'd have even less time to spend with them if I were in political office.

I look back on it now, and my kids were right—the decision not to run probably did save my life. I would have taken things too personally. I have no regrets about not running.

It turned out the Democrats were in trouble that year. Mazie Hirono won the primary but lost to Linda Lingle by almost 20,000 votes, and the Republicans were in Washington Place for the first time since 1962.

But I learned a few things from my brief career as a candidate:

1. Apparently, you can be too rich. One thing that bothered me was the suggestion from some people (including a newspaper columnist or two) that I shouldn't run because I'm too well off to be a credible candidate for the Democratic Party. That is a very bad message to Hawaii's young people: "If you've made it, you shouldn't run for public office because it runs counter to the values of a democratic society." That's wrong. We should be trying to convince our kids that a local boy or girl can work hard, make it financially, and still give back to the community in public service. I know what it is to be poor. I think it's a tragedy that if you start out as a mail boy, with a dad who was raised in an orphanage and a mother who never finished high school, and you work really hard, that you should not be eligible for public service because now you're a millionaire. It's almost like, "Let's keep people down on the plantation," and as a local boy I resent that. That's wrong.

2. Campaign finances needs cleaning up. The flaws of our campaign finance system stared me straight in the face as I thought about having to raise big bucks to run for governor. The flood of money from architects, engineers or consultants who do business with government has bred contempt for the political system and politicians. If I had run, I would have accepted no money from those doing government business. That would have been an easy stand to take because I could have used my own money to finance my campaign. But that's not fair, either. Most candidates are not wealthy; they must rely on contributions. I don't think being rich should bar you from politics, but it's terrible if not being rich makes it impossible to run a credible campaign without built-in conflicts of interest from donors.

No thinking person can possibly be in favor of the way things are now. Obscene amounts of money are raised and spent by candidates for major office—even worse now, thanks to the Supreme Court's Citizens United decision, than it was in 2002. The public assumes the worst, that elected officials are in the pocket of special interests and that contributors get preferential treatment.

Despite my many misgivings about the world of politics, I continued to stay involved, primarily through helping my good friend Sen. Dan Inouye, right up until the day he died.

> "I'm surprised Dods would even think of running. He's got it all: money, influence, a big heart, respect in his community. Dods has never forgotten his roots in Hawaii. ... Why bring an otherwise magnificently successful career to a close with a highly problematic foray into politics? It doesn't compute."
>
> —Dan Boylan,
> Midweek *columnist*

Flying back from the Democratic Party Primary Eve rally in Hilo, with Sen. Inouye, Maggie and in the back, Inouye aides Jennifer Sabas and Henry Giugni.

Celebrating another win to add to Dan's undefeated political career.

CHAPTER 17

Our Man in Washington

> "(Dods) is one of those guys who fit the bill as the political insider whom you would always go to. People used Walter as a surrogate for Dan Inouye."
>
> *Former U.S. Rep. Colleen Hanabusa*

One of the saddest days of my life was December 17, 2012. Diane and I were in a car headed to the airport for a flight to the Mainland when I got a call from Inouye aide Jennifer Sabas in Washington telling me that Sen. Dan Inouye had just passed away.

We were devastated. I don't mind admitting that we both had tears in our eyes as we tried to digest the news. Inouye was a personal friend as well as an icon, both in Hawaii and in Washington. We knew that Inouye was ill—probably in worse shape than most people realized, but no one expected the news this soon. His staff kept saying that, while he was in the hospital under close care, he was still writing notes (he couldn't speak because of a breathing apparatus) and issuing instructions.

Several months before Dan died of respiratory complications, I happened to be one of the first to know that his deteriorating health was more serious than most people suspected. He was in town and called to ask me to have lunch with him at the Bankers Club upstairs from my office. He said, "I have an appointment with the doctors at Tripler and may be a little late, but I'll come right afterwards."

When he arrived, he said, "We'll talk about a bunch of things, but I need to tell you I just came from Tripler and I now realize that these doctors at Walter Reed pretty much have been blowing smoke up my ass." (Walter Reed is the national military hospital in Bethesda, Md., not far from where Dan lived.) "They tell me, 'You're great, you're feeling good, your heartbeat is so great and all the rest of it.' This is the first time I ran across a doctor at Tripler, and he told me that I have serious problems with my breathing."

He said he was going to have to start going around with oxygen more. Then he told me: "It's clear now that I'm not going to be around forever and I want to do everything I can to position Colleen (Hanabusa) because . . ." (This is the part people don't understand, people are going to say it's the old guys trying to keep in power, but what Dan said to me was: "I've had the chance to look at all the people involved, and Colleen clearly is the one that should be there." Meaning there in the Senate to succeed him.)

He said, "Please let me know anything that I can do, anything that would be helpful to Colleen."

He was almost 88 years old and until that day had *always* talked about the next election. The last time he ran, in 2010, after it was over we were all tired, but the next day at breakfast, it was, "I'm going to run again in six years." That day at lunch was the first time I knew he wasn't thinking that way. This was the first time he indicated, "I'm not going to be there, and we need to make sure Colleen is ready."

After that, I was told by the staff and his second wife, Irene Hirano Inouye, that he was starting to get on oxygen pretty heavily. He wouldn't use it when he walked out to the Senate floor or at public hearings. Even in Honolulu the Secret Service bodyguards who were always with him (as Senate president pro tem, he was third in line to the presidency) found ways to drive him almost to the door of wherever he had to be. For instance, at the Hilton Hawaiian Village, you can take that ramp all the way up, almost to the entrance of the Coral Ballroom. Then he would be without oxygen for a short period of time in public, but he was on it much more than people thought. In the car, at home, even in the office, quietly.

When he went into Walter Reed nine days before he died, it became more widely known that he was using oxygen and, sometimes, a wheelchair. His staff attributed the need for oxygen to being misdiagnosed with lung cancer in the late 1960s and having part of a lung removed.

Just hours before hearing of his death, my friend Jeff Watanabe and I had delivered a letter to Gov. Neil Abercrombie on the senator's behalf. It contained, to no one's surprise, Inouye's wish that Abercrombie appoint then-U.S. Rep. Colleen Hanabusa as his replacement. There have been stories that the letter was fabricated by Inouye's staff after he was no longer able to function, but I don't buy that. After all, it was already well known that Inouye wanted Hanabusa to succeed him.

I remember that meeting vividly. Jeff and I were kept waiting in the governor's outer office for quite some time; we were told that the governor was stuck in traffic coming back from an outside appointment. Ironically, given the way things turned out, while we were waiting there, Lt. Gov. Brian Schatz came rushing in. He said, "Oh, what are you guys doing here?" Surprise!

When we were finally called into Abercrombie's office, he was not alone. Attorney General David Louie, his top political adviser, Marvin Wong, and his chief of staff, Bruce Coppa, were there with him.

There's no question the governor knew what we were there for and what the letter would say. Abercrombie's hands were trembling as he took and read it. The letter put him in a terrible box: If he followed Inouye's wish, he would be seen as not his own man and would have little by way of gratitude from the new senator. If he disregarded the letter, he would be seen as ignoring the last wish of Hawaii's most popular and revered political figure.

Abercrombie said he intended to keep the letter confidential and asked if we would do the same. We immediately agreed, but it didn't matter: the contents quickly became public through channels in Washington. Jeff and I had nothing to do with its release. This was not the way I anticipated my long friendship with the senator would end.

Once word of the letter got out, there were whispers that Inouye was already dead by the time the letter was produced. That's not so. In the end, I believe the community turned against Abercrombie over the whole sequence of events. I think that's why Abercrombie got killed by David Ige in the Democratic primary. The entire Japanese community turned on Neil, it's very clear. If you watched the last part of the campaign, Japanese faces started to appear in all of his ads. Then the haole community deserted him. The environmentalists deserted him. The teachers, too. In the end, there was no hope for Neil.

Diane and I went back to D.C. for the senator's funeral, an experience I'll never forget. They had him lying in state in the Capitol Rotunda. We got off the plane late at night and went directly from the airport to the Capitol. One of Dan Inouye's aides escorted us down to the Rotunda to pay our respects. To see him there, in the dark, was just overwhelming.

One story about that ceremony sticks with me. I didn't see it, but I wish I had because everybody was talking about it. Former Sen. Bob Dole, who is a Republican but also a close friend of Dan's dating to when they were hospitalized together after World War II, arrived at the Rotunda in a wheelchair. He didn't want Dan to see him in a wheelchair, he said, so he got up and went inside the ropes, up to the 200-year-old catafalque. And he quietly put his hand on Dan's casket.

I had known Inouye generally for years. We used to eat together with a bunch of other people

"Soon after Walt and I delivered the senator's letter to Governor Abercrombie, the word on the street, which Neil's people put out, was that it really wasn't the senator who wrote it, that Walt and I wrote it. Stupid. We weren't even told what the letter was going to say until we agreed to take it; we were just messengers.

"The governor didn't say anything to us about whether he would respect the senator's wishes to appoint Colleen. When he saw the senator's widow before the services, he went up to her and said, 'Irene, I got the senator's letter, and we are going to do the right thing.' Stupid. Later, he talked to an *L.A. Times* reporter, and that bounced back to Irene, and she said, 'Well, we are really hurt, and in fact, the governor told me he would do the right thing.' It was badly handled.

"Neil and the senator never got along. Even when they were part of the congressional team, they weren't buddies. The senator was always banging him on the head for one reason or another. I think he knew he was going to be put in a no-win position."

—*Jeff Watanabe, attorney and longtime friend of Inouye and Dods*

after political rallies like the traditional campaign closer at the Mooheau Bandstand in Hilo. I became much closer after he asked me to be an honorary chairman of his reelection campaign in 1986, although I had little to do with the actual campaign that time around. I was a political junkie and remember admiring Stuart Ho and Fred Trotter for each having run one of Inouye's prior campaigns. Accepting the chairmanship of a campaign was supposed to be a community honor; there wasn't supposed to be any work involved. If anything, I was able to give some media advertising advice.

People might say Inouye was the last candidate in the world to need advertising or advice. But Dan was a smart guy. He said to me many times, "You know, when you run only once every six years, there is a new generation after a while that doesn't know all of these things." He never took for granted any election and he knew you had to get out there. He really worked at it. The one thing he really worked his butt off at was high school graduation speeches. He felt he had to reintroduce himself every year to a new set of people and, over two campaigns, that's almost a generation.

If you start early and strong, you discourage people from even thinking about running against you. He always felt you had to run a hard campaign, raise money, get out there, get to the Neighbor Islands, get to the younger people.

The 1986 campaign went fairly smoothly, not at all like the next one, in 1992, which I will discuss a little later.

Inouye was always—I don't want to say cocky—but full of confidence. That was his public persona, but there was a deeper, more somber side to him that you didn't often see. When there were just a few of us at dinner, he would have a couple of drinks and tell war stories about how he killed people in Europe in World War II. He would go into intricate details that I had never heard mentioned before, and every once in a while he would go off on a tangent and really get into some bloody stuff. It was a revelation to me, but you could see it was deep-seated. He could only let it out once in a while.

He described one time a young German guy on the other side who was peeing. He shot him. He never talked about charging the hill in Italy, the battle that won him the Medal of Honor. He was talking about one-on-one killings. It was obvious this was always somewhere in his mind. He had—for want of a better word—a fatalistic worldview.

Another thing he would talk about was his admiration for Israel and many of its leaders. When we went out to eat—either at Zippy's or Chinese food—he would talk about Israel and his defense relationships with them. This is no secret, but for a while he seriously considered converting to Judaism. In the end, he told me that his mother was so strong a Methodist that he couldn't do that in honor of her, but he had come very close to converting.

When you talk about Inouye, you have to talk about his best friend and closest confidante, Henry Giugni. If Inouye was somber and proper—at least in public—Henry

I didn't meet with Inouye that often, but when he was in town we would get together for breakfast or lunch, often at Zippy's, his favorite local hangout.

was the opposite. He was brash, boisterous, with a rascal look that suggested he knew a great secret he couldn't quite tell you.

I felt I came to know Inouye fairly well, but that was nothing compared to the bond between Dan and Henry. It was an incredible relationship, much deeper or fuller than people realized. At one level, Henry was his punching bag; at another level, Henry did all of his dirty work, including being willing to take a fall for the senator.

That's exactly what he did when Inouye—then chairman of the Senatorial Campaign Committee—got caught up in two relatively minor campaign fundraising violations. In 1974, the senator's campaign was charged with violating a federal campaign spending law by not reporting a $5,650 contribution that Giugni accepted from shipbuilding magnate and New York Yankees owner George Steinbrenner. In 1976, Giugni, in exchange for immunity, admitted taking an illegal $5,000 contribution from an oil company lobbyist and lying to a federal grand jury. The lobbyist was acquitted.

In both cases, Giugni "took the bullet" to insulate his boss from legal troubles. He could have gone to jail. If he had to go to jail, he would have. Henry was like that. He was a tough guy, and he would have gone. He also had a big bark, but he was a softie underneath.

Even that hardly captures the depth of their relationship. Inouye used to joke that Giugni was literally his "right-hand man" who would hold his briefcase when Inouye had to use the men's room when they were traveling together. They were like frat buddies who immensely enjoyed each other's company. They used to play off each other and loved gossiping. You know, talk about who is up and who is down in Washington's power games.

Henry was with Inouye from his early days in the Territorial Legislature, when, as a cop, he was assigned to drive for Inouye because of his losing his arm during World War II. He went with Dan to Washington and stayed close through many a political battle until 1987, when he was appointed—thanks to Inouye—as Senate sergeant-at-arms. That made Henry responsible for Capitol security, for diplomatic duties such as ushering VIP visitors around and, of course, leading the president into the House Chamber for his annual State of the Union address.

In some ways, I think I was closer to Henry than I was to the senator. Henry had a way of drawing you into his confidence. I remember Dan was upset with me once

Henry Giugni, the consummate Washington insider, still enjoyed his trips home. He's shown here greeting me at a Boy Scouts fundraising dinner in Waikiki.

because Henry became sergeant-at-arms on the same day the U.S. senators got sworn in. I went to Henry's swearing-in instead of the Senate ceremony. For years Dan ribbed me about that. He said, "You can come up here for Henry Giugni's thing, but you can't come up for my swearing-in." He used to give me all kinds of grief over that.

It was obvious to anyone that the sergeant-at-arms job was the high point of Henry's life. He loved the authority, the prestige, perks like a private car and driver and an office with a view down the Capitol Mall. He loved to show me his office and the gun he was authorized to carry. His office had one of the very few fireplaces in the Capitol. He was proud of that and loved to show me it whenever I visited.

Inouye was also proud of Henry's role as sergeant-at-arms. However, when Henry left Inouye's office to become sergeant-at-arms and then left that to go with a Washington lobbying firm, Dan took it pretty hard. He no longer had his alter ego. Henry would visit Inouye on occasions, but it was totally different, and that was a hard period for Inouye. Among other things, Henry was the one in the Senate office who was there to kind of whip people into shape and cover up what needed to be covered up in the sense of keeping things going in the right direction. That was a lonely period for Dan. When Henry passed away, that was hard on him. He really cared for Henry.

As I became involved in Inouye's campaigns, I had to deal with Henry and, while I thought he was a great guy, it wasn't always easy. Essentially, Henry and some others took care of the grassroots and organizing. I was in charge of media and "message."

It's been said that Inouye didn't have much of a grassroots organization, but that wasn't entirely true. A core group—some going back to his McKinley High School days—were always with him. One of the few things Inouye insisted on was that his campaign colors, things like bumper stickers and T-shirts, had to be black and yellow, his McKinley colors, which is not a great advertising color scheme! His grassroots guys became known as the "black shirt gang," and to this day they stick together and work on various campaigns. They were Dan's "sparrows."

At one point I wanted to do a film, but Henry didn't want a "Dan Inouye film." Eventually I got my way because Dan trusted me on the media side of the campaign. Henry backed down eventually but grumbled the whole time and then, when it turned out well, he would come around and say, "OK, I was wrong." But it didn't stop him from trying to poke holes in every ad I ever did. However, he did support me in

> "When the issue about the barber first came out, our advice to the senator was: 'Look, whatever you do, don't attack her. You can say it didn't happen and leave it at that.' Of course, some reporter stuck a microphone in his face one day and asked, 'Why do you think she is doing this, Senator?' And he said something like, 'I don't know; maybe she is making it up.' And then the shit hit the fan. Every women's group around surfaced."
>
> —Jeff Watanabe

> "We were very D.C.-centric in the 1992 campaign. There was not much political capacity in Hawaii, so we called Jeff Watanabe and Walter to get eyes and ears on the ground. We didn't have a ground game and ground troops and needed them to kind of restart things. Walt could smell something was up. He knew we needed help."

> "The senator was kind of in denial. Walter had the presence of mind to say we needed to use Maggie. Walter pressed him because the issue was heating up. 'We have to get Maggie home, and she's got to be standing with him, publicly,' he said. 'We can't do it if she's not home.' Walter could deliver the tough news and what had to be done. There was no one else. He was willing to do it.

> "Walter has this sense, a local sense. You can have talented Mainland PR firms, but unless you have the intuitive gut sense of what's going to play for local people, you can't move. He has this amazing sense of what would play depending on the candidate. Plus he had so much credibility and heart."
>
> —Jennifer Sabas, former Inouye chief of staff

what was surely the toughest political issue I ever had to deal with concerning Inouye.

It was 1992 and Inouye seemed to be coasting to yet another easy victory. Then his opponent, Republican state Sen. Rick Reed, launched a series of television ads alleging that Inouye had molested his Honolulu barber and had forced her to have sex with him 17 years before and molested her over the years as she continued to work as his barber. The ads were based on clandestine recordings of the barber, Lenore Kwock, made by a young woman who had been associated with the Reed campaign.

That year, I took a much more active role in the campaign. With Inouye's rising national status, they had shifted most of his staff resources to Washington and didn't have many people with political eyes and ears on the ground in Hawaii. They had asked Jeff Watanabe and me to get involved, but none of us expected something like this!

I was on a plane sitting on the tarmac when Donna Tanoue, the former Hawaii banking commissioner who was running day-to-day operations for the Inouye campaign, called me to say that the barber's allegations had gone public. My initial reaction was to say, "Don't worry, this will blow over in a day or two." Boy, was I wrong.

Kwock, who initially denied the story, held a news conference to say it was true. The senator denied it, but I knew we had to do something more. I wanted to make a television ad featuring Inouye's first wife, Maggie, declaring her belief in and support for her husband. Inouye would have none of it, saying he was not the kind of man who would "hide behind a woman's skirts. My wife has nothing to do with this."

There was quite a battle, but eventually he agreed. Our campaign offices were in the old First Hawaiian building, which was being vacated in preparation for the move to our new building. We had lots of space, and Inouye had his own private office. He and I had a fairly tense meeting; afterward, he came out said:

"When this issue came up about Maggie, I was against it. And you know, frankly, I'm still against it. But, goddamn it, Walter's the chairman of my campaign and he wants to do it. I'm not going to stand in his way." Henry supported me on that. He knew it had to be done.

Maggie agreed to do the ad, but she said she would only do it if I was the only person in the room besides the cameraman. I never talked to her in detail about the barber and the ugliness of the rumors. I just said this was disruptive to the campaign, the cheap shots were unfair, and she could help us get on top of it. I wrote, produced and directed the spot, which we filmed in Makiki, at my neighbor Dr. Steve Berman's house. It was very effective. Maggie wore white and spoke directly to the camera. The ad was produced and shown, the controversy faded within a few days of the ad, and we were back on track. We had been doing polls, and while we were still way up there, we were slipping and down to 55 percent or so. Immediately, the polls flattened out and started going back up. There was a definite cause-and-effect relationship.

(Dan Inouye proposed to Maggie on their second date and they had been married for 57 years at the time of her death in 2006. The senator married Irene Hirano, then CEO of the Japanese American National Museum in Los Angeles, in 2008.)

Nonetheless, we were ready for more attacks. We put together another ad—which we never used—that showed a dirty alley in Chinatown somewhere with rats running around. Then someone slammed a lid on a garbage can and a voice said, "Let's stop all this dirty stuff." In our campaigns, we almost always had something like this on standby if things got really negative, but we didn't have to use it. Still, the accusations must have had some impact because while Inouye won handily, his vote was only 57 percent, the lowest of his career. It was the only time his vote share was less than 69 percent.

Inouye's years of service in the Senate and the friendships he developed gave him a unique kind of clout. By chance, I was able to see how this worked on two different occasions.

At one point during the administration of George W. Bush, I was sitting in Inouye's Washington office, and his secretary comes running in: "Vice President Cheney is on the line!" I asked Dan if he wanted me to leave the room, and he said, "Of course not, stay right there."

It wasn't on the speaker phone, but I could still hear it clearly:

"Danny, I need your help."

"Yes, Mr. Vice President, what can I do for you?"

"I can't get my vice president budget approved. The senators have locked it up, and I'm desperate; I have to operate this office. I can't get it approved, Danny, and I know we are on opposite sides, but you have always been a good man, and I really need your help."

"OK, Dick, I will find a way to make it happen."

"I'm forever grateful to you, Danny."

I'm sitting there, this kid from Hawaii, and the vice president is basically on his hands and knees asking Dan Inouye to get his budget approved. That stuck in my mind, big time.

Oddly enough, a similar thing happened earlier, in 1995. I was also in Dan's office when the secretary came rushing in and said, "Senator D'Amato, urgent call." The senator asked me to stay and put D'Amato, a Republican from New York, on the speaker phone.

D'Amato said, "Danny, I need you to save me. This is urgent." He had been under fire for a radio interview where he used a fake Asian accent to criticize Judge Lance Ito, who was presiding over the O.J. Simpson murder trial. The Japanese-American Anti-Defamation League and other civil rights groups were calling D'Amato a racist, and he said, "Danny, you are the only guy that can save my ass."

Dan loved the Senate as an institution and said, "Alfonse, I'll take care of it." He made a statement that D'Amato was a strong supporter of Asian Americans and Japanese in particular. D'Amato was pretty grateful.

Fast forward to 1997 when Clinton administration people were looking to diversify their appointments and wanted to find a regulator who was a minority. Senator Dan recommended Donna Tanoue, who had been the banking commissioner in Hawaii, to chair the FDIC, a very big job. President Clinton nominated her.

My daughter Lauren with the senator and me.

At the time, D'Amato was chairing the Banking Committee and was mad at Clinton. D'Amato had said, "No appointment for the Clinton administration is going to get a hearing in my committee." Just by coincidence, I was in D.C. having lunch with Dan Inouye in the Senate dining room, and D'Amato came over to the table and said, "Dan, I will never, ever forget what you did for me. If there is anything I could ever do for you, please let me know."

"Well, there's this one little thing . . ." Pretty quickly, there was a hearing, Inouye and Sen. Dan Akaka testified, and Donna was confirmed. I just happened to see that fascinating slice of history. Whether the Judge Ito episode played any role, I don't know, but that same year D'Amato lost to Chuck Schumer in New York.

You know, the Senate has rules, but just as important—maybe more—are the relationships senators develop with one another. Inouye was a master of this. Of course, his most famous relationship was with Ted Stevens, the Republican from Alaska.

They were both on the Appropriations Committee and shared power equally, no matter which party was in the majority in the Senate.

When Stevens was in charge, and I can't remember who went first, he said to Inouye, "We have an equal voice," and when the Senate switched over to a Democratic majority, Dan called Stevens and said, "Same deal." They considered that they were equals no matter who was in charge. They had the most unbelievable relationship. They were a rare combination, and they took care of two small-population states, both of which benefited greatly.

I don't think people will ever see that again.

People think of me as a serious banker, but I'm always good for a yak. This photo was taken during a trip to China after my retirement from the bank.

CHAPTER 18

From the Banking Frying Pan into a Telecom Fire

There I was, at an early board meeting for the proposed Daniel K. Inouye Center at the University of Hawaii. We were to introduce our occupation and ourselves, and when my turn came, I said, "Walter Dods. Retired." There was a roar of laughter, and I began to realize that people see me differently than I see myself.

One of the questions I get asked most often is, "Why did you retire?" There are two answers. The first is that, at the age of 63, I felt I had accomplished almost everything I could at the bank and was ready to move on to other things. The second was that I saw business opportunities that might benefit me and my family, and benefit the community at the same time. I wanted to try that out. So I left as CEO of the bank at the end of 2004.

I announced my plans early that year, along with Don Horner's selection as my successor. I wanted our employees to know that the local leadership team was still in place, despite our foreign ownership, and that First Hawaiian Bank is still just that—Hawaiian *first*!

While that shift into retirement led to a lot of success and achievement, it also led to what has to be my biggest business failure. And there's a lesson in that. I will discuss that "failure" and the lesson it taught me later, but first: Why did I leave the bank at the pinnacle of my unlikely success? I didn't want to die in the saddle the way my predecessor had. I had put together a solid succession plan, and it was time to move on. As a side issue, I didn't want to continue traveling to Europe for business, but that wasn't a primary motivation. I had already been at the bank a long time. The average CEO nationally serves about four and a half years; in Hawaii, it's maybe a bit longer. I had been CEO for 15 years.

When the cycle started coming around again—the annual budget, setting goals—and I started to dread another battle with departments over the budget, I felt internally it was time. I didn't consult anybody; one day I just said to myself, "I'm going to retire." There was no pressure from anybody. I think Don McGrath, my counterpart in California, wanted at some point to take over the BancWest holding company, but he wasn't pushing me.

Our French owners at BNP Paribas were not eager to get me out either. The proof is in the pudding. When I first did the transaction with them in 1998 and then the final transaction three years later, they asked me to stay as CEO. When I announced my retirement in 2004, they asked me to continue as chairman of First Hawaiian and

> "Though he retired from the bank, I still call Walt and ask for advice on politics, personalities, just about anything. People trust him. They know he'll give you honest advice. If he has a bias, he will tell you about it up front. That kind of input is hard to come by."
>
> —*Bob Harrison, chairman & CEO, First Hawaiian Bank*

BancWest for an additional three years, which you don't do if you are pissed.

I knew I would probably stay on a couple of public service boards and a couple of corporate boards. However, I never dreamed that I would have such an active and financially rewarding post-bank career. It's a second career that has had substantial risks, as I will explain below, but also substantial opportunities to make money and help the community.

In many ways, the most dramatic—some might say, traumatic—experience of my post-retirement years involved the telephone company. The history of Hawaii's phone company dates back to its founding in the Kingdom of Hawaii in the 19th century. It was originally Mutual Telephone Co. but had been called Hawaiian Telephone in modern times until 1967 when it was bought by GTE Corp. and renamed GTE Hawaiian Tel. My own ties to the company began when I was on its board under GTE and also went onto the boards of GTE California and GTE Pacific Northwest. That was a wonderful learning experience for me. After a Mainland merger involving GTE, the local company was renamed Verizon Hawaii in 2000, and I ended up being on an advisory board in Hawaii for Verizon.

Around the time of my bank retirement in 2004, people from The Carlyle Group, a huge private equity manager based in Washington that does leveraged buyouts all over the world, approached me and said they were interested in buying Verizon Hawaii. They asked me if I would advise them, and I said, "I'm happy to give you advice, but if it's going to be sold, I would like it to go to responsible people." I must admit I took a liking to the team they put in place here. One was Jim Attwood, who had been a former president of GTE, and the other was Bill Kennard, a former chairman of the Federal Communications Commission under Bill Clinton.

After Carlyle became the winning bidder for Verizon Hawaii, they asked me if I would be interested in investing in the deal. Carlyle renamed the company Hawaiian Telcom, and I agreed to go on its board in 2005. The whole deal was for $1.6 billion, and the cash portion was $300 million. I invested myself and agreed to find other local investors to put up 10 percent of that total, $30 million. The idea of having at least some local ownership of this venerable Hawaii company appealed to me. My investment was $2 million, and a lot of my friends also put in significant money. It was the one time in my business career that I did not do my own due diligence. Why not? Simply because Carlyle had the smartest, fastest, best guys in the United States. The biggest brains. I felt, "Why should I do my own due diligence?"

Many will remember the story. The conversion of management went poorly. With Verizon out of the picture, the newly renamed Hawaiian Telcom had to create its own back-office operations to handle administrative tasks such as accounting, billing, public relations and human resources. The company went through a terrible period of bad publicity, with headlines about overbilling, long wait times for customer service and other problems.

The picture wasn't pretty. By 2008, I knew the company was heading toward bankruptcy. The problem was Carlyle had over-leveraged. They had paid too much and borrowed way too much. The basic company was a fine company, but they loaded it up with too much debt. It could have handled maybe $300 million of debt, but they borrowed over a billion dollars and couldn't make the payments. It was that simple.

Their projections said they were going to increase their revenues while at the same time the world was eliminating telephone landlines. It was a perfect storm of bad conditions. Nobody knew landlines were going to disappear as fast as they did. Their debt was humongous, they were expecting revenues to go up to pay the debt, but instead their revenues were going down. It didn't work. They had very smart guys with rosy projections, but it just didn't turn out.

Carlyle had appointed Dan Ackerson as chairman of the Hawaiian Telcom board. He was the chairman of Carlyle's U.S. Equity Fund, which meant he had the final say on every major deal they made in the United States. Their top guy! Plus, he was a former telecommunications executive with MCI and Nextel. However, when things got a little rocky and he had a lot of other things on his plate, he asked me to replace him as chairman of Hawaiian Telcom in 2008.

I told Ackerson I didn't want to become chairman, but eventually I said I would do it if I got to select the new CEO. I said, "We have to bring in a

> "I was surprised that Walt wanted to retire so young, but I think maybe he thought of what had happened to Bellinger. He felt good about leaving the bank in good shape. When he retired as CEO, he continued as board chairman and asked me to stay with him. I didn't know if I could do it myself because there had been two of us working for him as CEO, but he said, 'Don't worry, you're going to be reading newspapers.'
>
> "I was right to worry because after he retired, from Day One he went on to do all those big deals, several projects at the same time. The phone would constantly ring, emails, people wanting to meet with him because they thought he was no longer busy. 'Walt, can you join our board, can you chair this fundraising dinner?'
>
> "It was so hectic that twice I told him I wanted to quit. He didn't want me to and said, 'What can I do to help?' I said, 'Start declining some things instead of saying OK to everything.' After that, he was very selective. He started answering his own phone and trying to lighten my workload."
>
> —*Dorri Kuriki, Walt's administrative assistant, 1999-2009*

> "I had just become chief operating officer of Hawaiian Electric when Walter called in April 2008. He and I had only met on two brief occasions, but he asked me to come to his office. He said, 'Hawaiian Telcom is going through a challenging time. They've asked me, the only local director, to chair the board. I told them I would do it if they let me pick the CEO. Would you be interested in being CEO of Hawaiian Telcom?'
>
> "I said, 'Walter, I'm flattered, but why would I do this?' He said, 'Just hear us out.' I thought I would meet with the Carlyle guys who own the company, then tell Walter I'm not going to do it. They made a compelling case and put an offer on the table. I told Walter I would sign up to be president and CEO of Hawaiian Telcom at a time that it was bankrupt but not yet in bankruptcy.
>
> "Walter said, 'Eric, although I'm board chairman, you're the boss. If you ask, I'll give you my honest opinion. If you follow my advice, I'll support you 100 percent. If you do something different, I'll support you 100 percent.' He lived up to it."
>
> —*Eric Yeaman, former Hawaiian Telcom CEO, now president of First Hawaiian Bank*

better person to run it." (A bit of trivia about Dan Ackerson. He left a struggling telephone company out in Hawaii and became chairman of General Motors. He is the guy that turned around GM, which was in terrible trouble at the time. So I tell everybody that I replaced the guy who became chairman of General Motors.)

I decided to approach Eric Yeaman, the chief operating officer at Hawaiian Electric Co., whom I really didn't know well, for the Hawaiian Telcom job. I called him on April 1, 2008, the day after Aloha Airlines filed for Chapter 7 liquidation. That was a catalyst. I said, "I'm not going to let this happen to another long-term Hawaii company."

I had met Eric only briefly, but I followed his career from afar and was impressed. He had helped restructure Kamehameha Schools and had moved up fast to COO at Hawaiian Electric, a major institution. I knew people who had him on their radar screens as a comer. I knew he had all the qualities—leadership, compassion, accounting background and financial skills—that would help Telcom, where employee morale was pretty bad because of all its problems.

As it turned out, Hawaiian Telcom did declare bankruptcy in late 2008. It was the only time in my career that I lost any real money. All of it! Between my friends and me, we lost the whole $30 million. There were a few investors in the couple-million-dollar category, but most were less than that. They were all what we call sophisticated investors. To do this kind of deal, it can't be your life's savings. Most of them write it off for taxes, so they lost about half of what they put in. Most of them were doing pretty well in other investments as well, and the market was pretty good at the time.

I have not had one of them tell me to my face, "I will never forgive you." I'm sometimes amazed that they remained my friends, but they did. Two of them still do deals with me, in a rather unusual business partnership that I will get into in the next chapter.

Nobody likes to lose money, including myself. It was a tough experience and it taught me a great lesson that, even in the best of deals, you should try to do your own diligence. People lost their money, but they were big about it, they are sophisticated investors, and they had access to the same information and went to the same presentations as I did. I didn't force anyone to go into it.

Even at that, we could have done all right, but we made a decision to keep our investment 100 percent local. The way we got hurt is they had a fund called Carlyle Four, which would buy 40 different companies; some make it and some don't, but overall you are making money. We bought just the Hawaiian Telcom portion of that overall fund. If we had gone into the overall fund, we all would have made money. However, we said, "We know Hawaii; we don't know all these other chemical companies you are buying in Ethiopia; we just want to be a part of this one."

It turned out to have been a bad bet.

After the Chapter 11 bankruptcy and reorganization, the banks became Hawaiian Telcom's owners, and they got rid of the board in 2010 to make a fresh start. Then, within a couple of months, they realized they didn't have the Hawaii connection and asked me to go back onto the board. I told them, "Not in a million years." It was a very tough year and a half fighting with the labor unions and the bankruptcy, the hearings, the critical newspaper stories. It was a brutal period, and at that point I hated it. I retired for this? I did it to help out the community and bring the phone company back home. Of course, I was hoping to make a dollar or two as well. It was a pretty tough experience. So I had zero interest in going back.

Then Eric Yeaman called me up and said, "Hey Walt, you recruited me for this job. I'm in here and I need you back." I couldn't turn that down, so I did go back on and have served on the board ever since.

Eric did a wonderful job; he turned the company around dramatically. The company is doing very well and now has a good balance sheet. In mid-2015, when Eric left to become president of First Hawaiian Bank, its market capitalization was over $260 million, up from zero when he took it through bankruptcy. It has become more of a telecommunications company than a telephone company.

As for me, while I lost some money, I learned an important lesson about trusting your own instincts. However, not all my investments have played out so publicly, or badly. More on that in the next chapter about a little-known three-member *hui* of dealmakers.

> "He trusted his instincts on his investment in Verizon Hawaii, and maybe one out of a thousand, I guess it didn't work. I know he didn't feel good about it, not because of the money he lost but because of the friends that he got involved. Probably one of the hardest things for him was the fact that his friends lost money."
>
> —Eric Yeaman

Since retiring as CEO of First Hawaiian, I've been involved in several business deals in an under-the-radar, informal hui that includes David Hulihee (left) and Bill Mills.

CHAPTER 19

Trust, Friendship and the Art of the Deal

> "The combination of David Hulihee, Bill Mills and I somehow works magic."
>
> Walter Dods Jr.

I don't play much golf any more. I have limited patience with lying around in a hammock or taking fancy cruises. So what do I do with myself after my retirement from the bank?

The short answer: I make deals.

Sometimes the deals involve my work on corporate boards, such as the separation of Matson Navigation Co. from its parent, Alexander & Baldwin Inc., in 2012. I served as chair of A&B and, after the separation, I still chair the board of Matson.

When I was chairing the A&B board, CEO Stan Kuriyama would tell me about his meetings with shareholders, stock analysts and prospective shareholders. More and more they would tell him, "OK, we get historically why a shipping company (Matson) and real estate company (A&B) are together because of the need to ship sugar. But why does it make sense to keep them together today?" After a while, Stan realized there was no logical business reason.

In 2011 Stan told the board, "The time has come. I can't justify keeping these two companies together." I agreed. Initially there were others on the board who weren't as supportive, though in the end they all came around. Splitting up allowed each company to focus on its area of expertise (Matson on shipping, A&B on land development and agriculture) and eliminated internal competition for corporate resources between them.

> "When A&B was preparing to separate from Matson, Walt said, 'One person you have to tell in advance is Dan Inouye. I'll go with you, Stan. I want to be there, and let's ask Jeff Watanabe to join us.' We went two days before we announced because Walt said, 'In case Dan for some reason doesn't like it, we'll have a couple of days to regroup.' The three of us flew to D.C., had a 40-minute meeting with the senator, then flew right back. We spent three days for a 40-minute meeting. Anyone else would have said, 'Oh, just give him a call.' For Walt, being there in person was critical."
>
> —Stan Kuriyama, chairman & CEO of Alexander & Baldwin, Inc.

That was a highly public and successful deal that turned out very well for both companies and their stockholders. A&B's market capitalization was $1.6 billion on the day we announced the split of the two companies; three years after the split, in which the owner of every share of A&B stock also received a share of the independent Matson, the combined market value of the two companies totaled nearly $4 billion. Clearly, the spinoff of Matson was very effective in building value for holders of A&B stock.

A&B is the last remaining active member of the Big Five still operating in Honolulu. (The other four were Castle & Cooke, C. Brewer Co., American Factors, now known as Amfac, and Theo H. Davies & Co.) Alexander & Baldwin is a kamaaina company that had interests in agriculture, real estate development and shipping, among others. First Hawaiian had long held a seat on the A&B board and, when Johnny Bellinger died and I took over at the bank, I was asked to take his seat on that board. One thing that appealed to me about the company is that it had (and still has) a local heart; it respected and honored its 145-year-old roots in the Islands.

> "It was obvious to everyone at Matson that Walter was the most important member (of the board). People held him in awe. Everyone was on their toes when they presented to Walter. He's never rude but always on his toes, a force and candid."
>
> —Matt Cox, Matson CEO

That heritage came through clearly in A&B's attitude toward sugar, which along with pineapple had always been an economic backbone of the Big Five. Beginning in the 1980s and '90s, plantations began closing down due to rising costs and cheaper overseas competition. When Kauai's Gay & Robinson closed in 2009, Hawaiian Commercial and Sugar on Maui (owned by A&B) became the last surviving plantation in Hawaii. Despite some advantages in water availability and quality of land, it hasn't been an easy proposition keeping those 36,000 acres of sugar and other crops in production.

Being the last survivor in the industry, A&B no longer has the synergies available when it worked with the other four of the Big Five as it did in the old days when all five used to cooperate in shipping and in supporting research at the Hawaiian Sugar Planters Association (HSPA). When there is only one remaining sugar producer, as there is today, there can be no sharing of industry costs among all of the companies. With declining world prices for sugar, it just gets more difficult. Still, those of us who've been around for a while feel that it has a place as long as we can sustain it and survive.

Philosophically, we felt that, as long as HC&S could break even or be limited to modest losses, it was helpful to the community. It supported A&B's overall projects in the community and created goodwill by maintaining green open space. However, even that goodwill is getting challenged today. For example, people who were attacking the smoke from burning cane have gone to court trying to put an end to the practice. The fact of the matter is HC&S works very hard to control those burns. We have

200 of these controlled fires a year and, every once in a while, the wind will change after the burn starts. That's not going to change.

Nonetheless, it gets harder and harder to sustain sugar even with the best of intentions.

From my perspective, sugar is a nice balance and complement to A&B's other operations, such as housing and resort development, but not everyone thinks that way. A&B's institutional shareholders say, "Hey, you're not utilizing the stockholders' money the best way." There is a challenge of leadership in balancing community interest and shareholder interest. Management works for the shareholder, but the company doesn't exist in a vacuum. It must rely on the goodwill of the community. There are trade-offs. A lot of times, a stock analyst in New York doesn't have a clue about that balance.

In Hawaii—and probably elsewhere—a big company can have too much expected of it. That's what the investor in New York doesn't understand. They look at the land A&B owns, take a value per acre and multiply by A&B's 80,000 acres on Maui and say, "Wow, the company should be worth *this* and not *this*," not understanding what A&B would have to do to make this land worth more. It could take the company 20 years to get rezoning and rights to develop the land into, say, housing. It's a pretty tough deal. A&B has done a good job. We're lucky that Hawaii has a few civic-minded, responsible corporate citizens like that around.

Still, when the losses become substantial, management has a real challenge. That has happened cyclically over the years; each time, A&B came very close to having to take more severe actions. Obviously, that sugar land could go into development someday, but, right now, the community of Maui loves the open space sugar provides. The company must develop in a measured, carefully planned way. There's a tremendous economic handicap that comes with having bad will in the community. Obviously, that land needs to be developed to get its best and highest use. However, I can make a case that if A&B doesn't approach it the right way, loses the community goodwill and is turned down for development, all that land becomes a barren wasteland, a dust bowl. Is that what Maui wants?

However, not all my deals are so huge or so public as A&B/Matson. I also have a quiet relationship with two other business leaders that has led to a great deal of personal satisfaction as well as nice profits and long-lasting community benefits. The common thread among the three members of our hui is looking for deals that are good for us, obviously, as well as good for Hawaii. These deals have taken me out of my comfort zone as a banker and marketer, while deepening my friendships with

> "Even after retirement, whatever he did, he did passionately—200 percent. So he would get a lot of stress and his blood pressure would go up. But he always had a handle on things, never out of control. I hardly ever saw him lose his temper in 10 years. On very rare occasions, he might blow his stack over somebody he had respected showing a lack of character. Character and trust are important to him."
>
> —*Dorri Kuriki, Walt's administrative assistant, 1998–2009*

> "We were in Shanghai together and wanted to pay a visit to one of our ships that was in dry dock at the COSCO facility in Nantong. The ship was out of the water, and it was a super-warm, humid day. There was no air-conditioning, but I could not get Walter off that ship. He was into every compartment—'Let's go up these stairs, down there!' We were dripping with sweat, but he had to look in every nook and cranny. That was fun."
>
> —Matt Cox

the other two members of our under-the-radar hui—Bill Mills (a business executive who first came to Hawaii with Castle & Cooke) and David Hulihee (who runs his family company, Royal Contracting). Here's how our relationship evolved:

Years ago, First Hawaiian had a client named Pacific Concrete and Rock, a good company. It was like the Ameron of today. It had a quarry up at Makakilo and delivered concrete to construction sites. I was a young guy at the bank and was asked to go on their board.

Later, it was sold to Grace Brothers, which was run by Dwayne Steele. I didn't know him then, but he became a close friend. Dwayne kept only two of Pacific Concrete's directors, myself and Jeff Watanabe. It's rare to find people like Dwayne in life. He came here in the 1950s, kind of a bumpkin from Kansas, and worked as a steamroller operator. He moved up the ranks to become president of Grace Brothers. When they bought Pacific Concrete, they renamed it Grace Pacific. Now he owned a successful paving company and also one of the biggest quarries on the island—a powerhouse. Under Dwayne's leadership, Grace Pacific grew and grew. Its annual sales soared from $8 million to $135 million, and the payroll went from 50 employees to 500.

What really made Dwayne interesting, besides his generosity to his employees and to local charities, was his intense interest in all things Hawaiian. He learned to play the guitar and slack key from the late Johnny Almeida, the blind musician. He learned Hawaiian music, then studied intently to learn the Hawaiian language.

As he became more and more successful, he became an investor in the Hawaiian community. For example, he paid to translate all the old Hawaiian newspapers into English for research and community use. He traveled to libraries around the world to look at Hawaiian periodicals and get them translated. He went to the University of Hawaii, studied advanced Hawaiian, and became an expert in understanding Hawaii title law and properties. He would debate professors in the Hawaiian studies program and eat their lunch when it came to the kingdom and who really owned the crown lands. Even they came to respect Dwayne. He read, wrote and spoke Hawaiian like hardly any Hawaiian.

He was also a solid businessman. I named him to the First Hawaiian Bank board along with another construction guy, David Hulihee, head of his family's contracting business. Both Dwayne and David had bought a lot of First Hawaiian stock over the years, so when the sale to the French went through in 2001, they both did very well. At the board meeting where the sale was being discussed, Dwayne leaned over to David before the meeting started and said, "You're like me. You have a Hawaiian heart and you understand the community. I want you to take over my company." Without blinking an eye—this is big money, remember—David said, "OK, if you want me to, Dwayne, I'll do it." David bought more and more of Grace Pacific. When Dwayne passed away in 2006, we asked David to become CEO of Grace Pacific. He did and took it to the next level. I stayed on their board after retiring from the bank.

Among the three of us, David, Bill Mills and I owned 70 percent of Grace Pacific. The company wasn't for sale, but one day David and I were talking to A&B's Stan Kuriyama. We mentioned that we were buying out a fairly large bloc of Grace Pacific stock held by a Japanese company. A&B had just separated from Matson, and Stan was actively looking for growth investment opportunities in the state. He said, "How about selling us an interest in Grace Pacific?" We thought about it for a few days and then I said to Stan, "If you have an interest in buying *all* of Grace Pacific, let's talk."

David, Bill and I are in our 60s or 70s. Exiting from ownership of Grace wasn't a bad idea for us, but the issue was more than just being able to sell at the right price. Grace is a longtime local company with 500 employees, and we wanted to make sure it ended up in the right hands. Also, we had a very low tax basis in Grace Pacific stock. What worked best for us to lower our tax bite was to trade the Grace stock for another company's stock, rather than selling for cash. A&B had its own stock, so we liked that.

We also knew that Grace would be in good hands. We probably would not have sold to any company other than A&B because we wanted to honor Dwayne's tradition of community service and corporate involvement. Grace Pacific wasn't a commodity we could just sell to anybody, but A&B had the same community spirit and commitment.

Hawaii is a small place, and if you are involved in big business, you're always going to run into conflicts of interest. It's how you deal with them that matters. Both Jeff Watanabe and I were on both the A&B and Grace boards and had to step aside and let the non-interested directors work out the sale. The deal was approved in 2013. We had taken a

> "When A&B was deciding whether to buy Grace Pacific, we had several conflicting interests among our directors. Walter and Jeff Watanabe were on the boards of both companies, so they couldn't participate in the decision. Neither could Bob Harrison, CEO of First Hawaiian Bank, because the bank was the largest lender to both Grace and A&B, so he had a conflict. A fourth A&B director with a conflict was Eric Yeaman, who was running Hawaiian Telcom at the time. Walter was chairman of Telcom's compensation committee, so because he controlled Eric's purse strings, Eric couldn't participate on the Grace matter, either.
>
> "Suddenly, four of the nine A&B directors couldn't participate in this $300 million-plus deal. The remaining five had to pretty much unanimously agree. It was not a slam dunk, for sure."
>
> —Stan Kuriyama

company that, when Dwayne first had it, was worth maybe $10 or $20 million and sold it for $277 million.

As a result, David Hulihee, who is not very widely known in the media, became the largest individual shareholder in A&B. He's one of those guys who operates under the radar. He looks like a tough Hawaiian construction guy, but after Iolani, where he played basketball, he went on to Syracuse University, where he earned a degree in accounting. Most of the time he's the most quiet, humble guy in the room. He'll rarely say anything, but when he speaks, listen carefully. He knows what he's talking about.

When Grace Pacific was sold to A&B, the people who controlled the company were David Hulihee, Bill Mills and myself. We've since gone on to be partners in a lot of other deals, too, always on a handshake basis. Over the years of investing together, we've never had a single disagreement. Our only real loss was that Hawaiian Telcom deal that I discussed in the previous chapter. The way we'd work is that any one of the three of us could speak for the rest and make commitments for the others.

Bill Mills is one of the most brilliant guys I have ever met. He has a near-photographic memory; he still remembers his high school locker combination. That one always baffles me. He's a self-made guy who had a tough childhood and started out as a carpenter but went on to a successful construction and real estate career on the Mainland. He came to Hawaii in 1985 to become chairman of Oceanic Properties/Castle & Cooke Land. I had known Bill for a long time through banking, but it was during board meetings at Grace Pacific where we really bonded.

We each have our own individual investments, but also do deals together, sometimes two of us and sometimes all three. We have our own little hui where we invest individually but think collectively. We do it all on an informal basis. One of us will call the others and say, "I heard about a good deal, do you want in?" We check it out and, if it looks good, we're in. No lawyers or lengthy meetings. We don't get experts involved. We analyze it ourselves and, if we like it, we do it. Then we bring the experts in to legally put it together—but *not* to give us business advice.

Here's a suggestion I give my friends: Understand specialists and their purposes, but don't look to outside people to make your business decisions. Make your own decisions. Believe in what you're doing or you shouldn't be involved in it. If you start going to outside people who don't have skin in the game, except for their fees, and ask them to make business decisions, it's a very bad thing. Yes, ask them how to financially structure it from a tax

> "It's unbelievably refreshing to deal with Walter and David. It's the old way of doing business. Their word is their bond. Also, it's done in a non-adversarial, non-contentious way. We want to do deals that are based in Hawaii. We want to keep certain values, so we hire local guys to run the companies we invest in. We're not bringing people in from the Mainland. We do things that will create jobs."
>
> —*Bill Mills, investment partner with Walter and David Hulihee*

and accounting standpoint, but never go to them and ask them whether to do a deal or not. That's one reason I don't think we've ever had a business meeting that lasted more than an hour.

David, Bill and I are different in our personalities, how we approach things, just about everything. But the combination of the three of us somehow works magic. We don't have a name like the Three Musketeers or anything like that, but we're a tight-knit group. While we do business together, it's also a social thing. Our families are close. We get together, have a few drinks, watch the Super Bowl. Everyone is always invited.

A classic example of our relationship is the story of Mid Pac Petroleum, which used to be part of the Gas Company. They're the ones with the Union 76 stations. One day, I got a call from Jim Yates, who was Mid Pac CEO. He said, "You know, the owners (headed by former U.S. Ambassador to Singapore Steven Green) are selling the Gas Company, but they want to sell Mid Pac Petroleum separately. I think it's a little gem and I'd love to do it, but I can't afford it. Would you be interested?"

> "We don't get too big and we're not out there trying to get attention. Very low key about everything we do. We don't care if nobody knows who we are.
>
> "Walt, Bill and I get together at least once a week, just to talk. We're good friends on the side, not just business partners. We talk about our problems, how our families are doing. Everything's open with us. We have trust in each other, ask for advice. It's not just business, it's all-encompassing."
>
> —David Hulihee, investment partner with Dods and Mills

I told him to bring the numbers over and we would talk. I looked at the numbers and thought, *Wow, that's interesting*. I called up Bill and David and said, "Hey, here's a transaction that makes a lot of sense. It would require each of us to put up close to $5 million to contribute $14 million in cash toward the deal. Jim Yates will come in as an equal partner, and his equity will be sweat, running the company. The total bid would be $44 million—our $14 million in cash and the rest borrowed against Mid Pac assets, largely the land under the 76 stations."

Bill and David asked, "Do you like the numbers?" I said, "Yeah," so they said, "Go!" That was it, just the trust the three of us had with each other. I called Jim Yates back in about an hour and said, "We got the money." He said, "What the hell are you talking about? This will take months!" "No," I said. "I talked to two guys and we have the money." He was shocked. We had a package, but I knew we would have to bid against other buyers. And here's where the story gets funny. . . talk about living under a lucky star.

I never let my house be used for political functions. Well, almost never. This one time, I was chairing an Inouye campaign and I let my house be used for one of those $2,000-a-ticket fundraisers. By pure coincidence, Ambassador Green—head of the Gas Company ownership group—happened to be in town. Green is a smart guy, a philanthropist and canny investor. He had money and wanted to become an

> "He'll never ask somebody to do something that he wouldn't do himself. He has a tremendous sense of integrity, and so people trust him. He works unbelievably hard, so when you see somebody that's into the office first and out last, people respond to that."
>
> —Bill Mills

ambassador, so, as we do in America, he donated a lot to a presidential candidate and he was in. Their company bought some tickets to the Inouye function, and he came to my home. It was twilight, and I remember standing in the cool breeze by the ocean and talking with him. He and I hit it off.

Green was a great admirer of Inouye. He was Jewish and had a fine appreciation for the work Inouye had done for Israel and the Jewish people. He was amazed to see Dan sitting in my backyard in an aloha shirt and slacks. Then I gave the speech for Inouye and introduced him to the ambassador. They hit it off really well, too.

When the old owners put Mid Pac Petroleum out to bid, we were one of many bidders. But that night at the Inouye fundraiser, I had seen that sparkle in Green's eye and thought, *If we have a chance, he'd give it to us*. No one else thought we had a chance to win it.

Some time passed, and then I was in Washington. As luck would have it, I was sitting in Inouye's office. I didn't go there very often. All the time I worked for him, I probably went there 10 times. The secretary comes in and says I have a call. It's Green. He says to me, "You guys came in third in the bidding, but the other two are fierce competitors that we've had problems with over the years. If you will guarantee me, right now over the phone, that if I give you this deal you'll close come hell or high water, I will tell them to give you guys this transaction because I don't want to sell to my competitors." I said, "Ambassador, you have my word. I'll close."

I hadn't talked to Hulihee or Mills yet, so I answered unilaterally for the three of us. That's how we worked.

We closed, and Jim Yates did a great job with the company. Ultimately, we rolled it into Grace Pacific on the theory that we would put two natural resource companies together, making it stronger, and more marketable, than either company alone. However, when A&B bought Grace, Mid Pac didn't fit their model, so they offered to sell it back to us, at book. We took it back at about $44 million because we had great faith in the company. Then, we sold it a year later for $107 million to Par Petroleum, which already owned Hawaii's biggest refinery.

Which leads to another funny story. One of the owners of Par Petroleum, based in Houston, is the billionaire Sam Zell. Shortly after we closed the deal, the Par people came and said, "We don't have a really good feel for Hawaii. We understand the oil business, but we need a Hawaii director. Would you serve?" I said, "Hey, I'm turning 74. I'm way too old to be director of another company." They insisted, and Jim Yates pushed for it too, saying it would help him to have somebody they would listen to from Hawaii. I agreed, but I said, "Make sure Mr. Zell knows how old I am." Next day, I get the word back that Mr. Zell said, "As far as I'm concerned, wisdom doesn't start 'til you're 70." (Zell was 74, too.)

The Mid Pac saga is a good example of how we work. And most of the time, it pans out. Of course, the Hawaiian Telcom deal didn't go so well, and there have been a few other instances. One involved a deal David Hulihee proposed in California.

David had a close college friend in Los Angeles who had found a real estate deal. David was asked to put up $1.5 million. The guy, an accountant, came in from the Mainland and made his presentation to the three of us. Bill and I started peppering him with questions that he couldn't answer. The pricing wasn't right, so we told David afterward, "Don't do the deal. It's not a good deal." We walked away. About a week later, we found out David put the whole amount up out of obligation to his friend. He said, "Don't worry. I made the deal." Bill and I got together and said, "Hey, brother's out there, and it's not a good deal. We can't let him do that."

We called up David and said, "No, that's not right. I'll put up $500,000, Bill will put up $500,000, and you put up $500,000." He had made the commitment to put it all up himself. We made the loan together and we lost it all. That was the way our partnership works. We weren't going to let him take the hit. He even tried to pay us back, but we refused. It really was Three Musketeers. We stood up for him because that's the way we operate. It's really been a remarkable friendship. We share in all the good deals, so we share when there is a misfire.

What we did on the others was so good that it made that one look almost like coffee money.

"One of my small investments during retirement got me into an embarrassing fix.

"I built a cute little two-story building next to the old First Interstate Building on South King Street. We had just finished construction but didn't have tenants. I went in on a Saturday morning to inspect the building, and nobody was there. I had to pee so I went into one of the bathrooms and shut the door. I finished peeing, washed my hands and hit the door handle to go out. The handle spun 360 degrees. It was busted! No way to get out, and nobody in the world knows I'm in the building.

"I called the First Interstate Building next door, tracked down a maintenance man and told him what happened. Fortunately, I had left my building's main door unlocked, so the guy was able to come up to the bathroom. I slid the key through the crack under the door, he opened it and came in.

"I'm thanking him so much and said, 'Let me show you what happened.' Like an idiot, I shut the door and this guy looked at me funny. Now the two of us are trapped in the bathroom! I felt like an ass. Then I remembered my son Peter's business, Easy Music, was next door. I called, and fortunately there was one kid there before they opened. He came up, and I slid the key under again. He opened it up and saw me with this janitor in the bathroom. He must have been thinking, 'Peter Dods' dad is the weirdest guy I've ever seen.'"

—*Walter Dods Jr.*

Jimmy Carter, shown meeting my wife Diane and me on an island stopover, was one of eight U.S. presidents I have met.

CHAPTER 20

Some People I've Known

"Walt knows everybody. He has the best Rolodex in town."
Jack Tsui, retired president of First Hawaiian Bank

I've been blessed to meet many leaders whose names you would recognize from the headlines and history books. I met Jordan's King Hussein, German Chancellor Helmut Kohl and Chinese leaders Deng Xiaoping and Zhang Zemin. As president of the American Bankers Association, I attended the World Economic Forum in Davos, Switzerland.

Thanks to my work in my own industry and in politics, I have met every U.S. president since Nixon, several vice presidents and quite a few treasury secretaries. I spent three years on an advisory council that met regularly with Federal Reserve Chairman Alan Greenspan and his board. I've known every Hawaii governor since Statehood; some of them are close friends.

Here are a few of the memorable characters I've known and worked with here in the Islands:

Robert (Bobby) Pfeiffer, longtime CEO of Alexander & Baldwin

Bobby Pfeiffer was a good friend. I served on his A&B board of directors, and he was on the First Hawaiian board. Bobby came from a long line of sailors. His grandfather shipped out of Hamburg in his own schooner to trade in the South Pacific. His father became a plantation manager in Fiji and captain of a Fijian interisland schooner. Bobby was born in Fiji, but the family moved to Hawaii when he was an infant. By age 12 he was working summers as a deckhand on a Honolulu harbor tug.

After World War II service in the Navy, Bobby came home and worked up through the ranks at Matson Navigation Co., eventually running both Matson and its parent, A&B. He helped negotiate the historic labor agreement that made containerized cargo possible and made Matson one of the world's most efficient shipping companies. He recognized that A&B's landholdings could be a "third leg" for the company, alongside Matson and sugar. There was more to the man than Bobby the sailor or Bobby the successful CEO. There was also Bobby the philanthropist. Under his leadership, A&B adopted a policy of making charitable contributions equal to 2 percent of pre-tax income.

He had a flair for music. He loved to dance the hula and sang and played the *ukulele*. After getting a pilot's license at age 45, he used to pilot A&B's own corporate jet on business trips.

Because I liked and admired him so much, one of the toughest business decisions I ever made was going against Bobby's wishes in 1998 when A&B was picking its next CEO. Three finalists made presentations to the board in a meeting in San Francisco —Brad Mulholland, CEO of Matson; Glenn Rogers, chief financial officer of A&B, and A&B's head of real estate, Allen Doane.

Bobby—a shipping guy himself—recommended Mulholland, the Matson CEO, to succeed him. We were going to vote the next day. However, several of us directors thought Doane was the strongest candidate. Remember, Bobby was one of those who stood up for me when I became CEO of First Hawaiian after a bit of a board struggle. He was a special human being, but when you are a director of a public company, your responsibility is to the shareholders, employees and community.

A few of us directors who were uneasy about Bobby's choice had drinks at the Big 4 Restaurant on Nob Hill. We all agreed that Allen was the better man. He had a vision, he was smart, he knew his stuff. The next day we went in to tell Bobby, who took it quite hard. We laid out our case and, to his credit, when he realized that we all felt the same way, he accepted it. That's how Allen Doane became CEO of A&B.

Everybody knew Bobby's motto was the Hawaiian expression, *i mua!*—"forward." And he was *always* moving forward. Years later, Bobby came to tell me that he took it hard at the time, but on reflection Allen was the right choice. That helped me a lot because I had been feeling badly about it ever since.

Chris Hemmeter, developer of Island megaresorts
The early 1980s was the heyday of Chris Hemmeter, developer of the Hyatt Regency in Waikiki, the Hyatt in Waikoloa on the Big Island and other megaresorts on Maui and Kauai. Chris was one of the world's great optimists. He was a dreamer, very handsome, charming and personable. He made the *Forbes* list of the 400 richest Americans in 1988. He did have many problems later in his career, but the hotels he built in Hawaii remain key tourism facilities in the Islands today. They never would have been built without a guy, like Chris Hemmeter, who took that level of entrepreneurial risk.

You could not build those hotels today—the numbers just don't come out. As a matter of fact, even in that period they didn't come out. Chris was fortunate to sell off most of his properties in the late 1980s at the height of the Japanese investment bubble. The Japanese put up most of the money for financing, and then many of them either went bankrupt, foreclosed or were resold. The second or third owner, by acquiring them at a much lower price than the original development cost, made out OK financially. Although many people took financial hits along the way, those projects stayed, and the Hawaii tourism industry was the beneficiary of Hemmeter's *chutzpah*.

Diane and I meeting with Jordan King Hussein and Governor Ariyoshi at Washington Place. At far right is Maurice (Sully) Sullivan, founder of Foodland.

First Hawaiian, fortunately, was not one of the banks that took hits from those projects by Hemmeter. Johnny Bellinger and I recognized that they may have been creative and exciting, but we couldn't see how the numbers could work out. We agreed to be the lead bank in coordinating the loans and agreed to accept the deposits, but we kept our loan amounts to a minimum. We never lost money, though a lot of other banks did.

Hemmeter left Hawaii after he lost out on the state contract for the Aloha Tower redevelopment. Chris had a typical, grandiose billion-dollar plan with a Venetian canal and gondolas going up River Street and through Chinatown. But having built our own building downtown, I learned a little bit about underground water in Honolulu. His idea probably would have been a disaster. Of course, the development the state chose over the Hemmeter plan—and over a competing plan by Jack Myers, who was also bitter about losing—turned into a financial disaster itself.

After Hemmeter left Hawaii, he got into financial trouble trying to build a casino in New Orleans. Unfortunately, he died too young, at 64.

Dr. Fujio Matsuda, former UH president and longtime First Hawaiian Bank director

Fuj and I are close. I've always admired him. He ran the state Department of Transportation (DOT) for Governor Burns and then was University of Hawaii president for years. After retiring from UH, he ran PICHTR (Pacific International Center for High Technology Research), then JAIMS (Japan-America Institute of Management Science) in Hawaii Kai. I tease him that he's even worse at retiring than I am.

When he was UH president, I used to help him out with PR crises. He'd call me at 3 a.m. when there was an NCAA investigation into UH sports or some other major crisis. I'd go and give him my best advice. We also worked together publicly in 1974 when Ariyoshi was acting governor, Fuj was running DOT and there was a gas crisis in Hawaii and nationwide due to the Arab oil embargo. Hawaii service stations had long, long lines of people wanting to top off their tanks because they were afraid supplies would run out.

I came up with a campaign called Gas Plan and worked with Fuj on a task force to implement it. The rule was, if your license plate ended in an odd number, you could only fill up on odd-numbered days. Even-numbered plate, same rule. Almost overnight, the gas lines disappeared.

Maybe the most memorable time I met with Fuj was when he was coping with a football coach issue. Larry Price, then UH coach and now a radio personality, was being replaced after a losing season. (He wasn't given as much leeway as Norm Chow.) Fuj wasn't prepared to handle the PR fallout as UH was trying to find a replacement and also find Larry something else to do. It was a delicate situation.

I was called to Washington Place one rainy night to meet with Fuj along with George Ariyoshi, who was acting governor, and Wally Fujiyama, chair of the UH Board of Regents. They didn't ask me to tell them what decision to make, but how to present it to the public. My advice was, as it always is when problems arise: "Make a decision and put it out there. Take the hit; don't dribble it out."

After the meeting, we all went out in the rain to go home. Fuj's car wouldn't start and the governor, the chair of the Regents and I helped push the car to get it started. That would have been a picture!

Evan Dobelle, former UH president

I was on the search committee that selected Evan Dobelle to become UH president in 2001. He had excellent credentials. Given all the trouble he got in later here and in Massachusetts, some members of the committee wanted to disown him later, but the fact is that after reviewing all the candidates, our choice was unanimous. He was bright, eloquent, smooth-talking, political, a breath of fresh air. And then his ego caught up with him.

My first warning sign was when he had one of his political friends from his days as a White House aide come here and do a poll to test his popularity in Hawaii. The poll actually had one question asking how Evan would do if he ran for governor. This was early on in his tenure when he was getting all positive publicity in the papers. That was an early warning sign to me that he was getting out of hand.

I had a serious confrontation with him when he endorsed Democrat Mazie Hirono for governor in 2002. I told him, "Dobelle, Mazie is a friend of mine, and I'm a Democrat, but you are the president of the University of Hawaii. You can't be endorsing anybody because you're *everybody's* president." But he ignored me because he was so sure Mazie was going to win (she lost to Linda Lingle) and he would become more powerful. That was the beginning of his downfall. The Lingle people were determined to get him, but he didn't need anybody else to get him. He was doing it all on his own. It's really sad.

The way the Board of Regents mishandled his firing in 2004 was also sad. The mess cost UH a $1.6 million cash settlement and other side benefits for Dobelle.

Frank Fasi, six-term mayor of Honolulu

Frank and I got to know each other quite well, although we were always on opposite sides of political campaigns. I worked for Neal Blaisdell, his predecessor as mayor of Honolulu; I worked for George Ariyoshi in three campaigns for governor against Fasi (which George won); I worked for Eileen Anderson in 1980 when she surprisingly ousted Fasi from the mayor's office for a term. So, in election years, we were always enemies.

But you have to give credit where credit is due. He was Honolulu's longest-serving mayor, serving six terms between 1968 and 1996.

Toward the end, I came to grudgingly admire him for having the guts to stand up for what he

Fasi makes a surprise appearance at my Salesman of the Year lunch. I battled Frank Fasi throughout his political career but I developed a grudging respect for him.

believed in and for actually getting things done. Two episodes turned my grudging respect into a warmer feeling. One, he showed up at my father's funeral and stayed for the entire service. The typical politician comes in, works the crowd and leaves, but his staying left a warm spot in my heart. Second, when I was given the Salesman of the Year award in 1992 by the Sales and Marketing Executives of Honolulu, he showed up, uninvited, and asked to get onto the podium to present me a plaque. He read through a long citation and finished up by saying, "Walt has beat me more times than I can remember, so that alone should make him Salesman of the Year."

> "The first time I got involved with Walter was 1974, when George Ariyoshi encouraged me to run for lieutenant governor. Walter was with Ariyoshi, and I first met him because he came out to help me. It was a blessing that I didn't win, but from then on Walter was always a big help.
>
> "Later, when I ran for the Senate, he helped me in so many ways, so generous with his money and his time. And he knew so many people. Whenever he wants to do something, he really puts his heart and soul in it. That's what he did in my campaign.
>
> "In politics, people normally help you because they want something in return. Walter was not that kind of guy. He never came to ask me for things. But he always made time for me. If I ever wanted to talk, he was available."
>
> —Retired U.S. Senator Dan Akaka

Dan Akaka, retired U.S. senator

I had known Dan for years and worked in his campaigns for the U.S. House and then the Senate. We became very close when he was challenged by U.S. Rep. Ed Case in the 2006 Democratic primary for the Senate, and Dan's chances were looking slim.

Dan Inouye seconded me over to Akaka's campaign to unofficially reorganize it. A big issue was whether Akaka would agree to a televised debate. Case was insisting on it; Akaka was ducking it. I said to Akaka's campaign committee, "The senator has to debate Case because our polls are showing him getting killed on the subject." Most of Dan's brain trust didn't want to do that. I said to them, "We have to pay a debate tax." We tried to design the debate to occur early in the campaign and to be on public television so it couldn't be rebroadcast, but we had to do it.

The committee finally agreed, but they said I'd have to persuade the senator and his wife. I met for breakfast with Dan and Millie at Waialae Country Club. I laid out my case for them, and in the end he said, "If you feel I have to do it and you will work with me on it, I'll do it." It was a hard decision for him because debating wasn't his strength. He was better one-on-one.

One of the people in Akaka's campaign was George Ariyoshi's son. He was vehemently against debating and talked to his father. George called me and said, "Why are you doing this?" I explained my reasons, and George ended up siding with me, but that was a heavy political decision. If the debate had been a flop, that could've cost Dan the election. It didn't, fortunately.

We became very close. He made his own decision not to run in 2012, but he did come to talk to me about that as well. I agreed with him that it was the right decision. He's a special human being. People say he's not much of a public speaker, but in Congress he did have a following of people who respected and liked him. In his own way, he helped Hawaii a lot. He could never get the Akaka Bill on Hawaiian sovereignty through, but, in fairness, neither could Dan Inouye.

Larry Johnson, retired Bank of Hawaii CEO

Larry Johnson and I grew up in banking together. I was interviewed for a story in 1971 in *Honolulu Magazine*, and the writer asked me who I thought were Hawaii's future leaders. I threw out a half-dozen names, and one of them was Larry, who was Bankoh's Waikiki branch manager at the time.

He and I were fierce competitors. We'd beat each other's brains out over customers, but after hours, we'd work well together in community affairs. We always kept an open line of communications. He was one of those who had my back and stood up for me when the Thumbs Up campaign went into the tank. We had a great respect for each other.

He went through some hard times at Bank of Hawaii when they were struggling in the Asia and Pacific markets. I never gloated about that. I felt sorry for him because I felt some of that was thrust on him by others. In the end he took the hit for it.

To this day we're good friends. We've been in the same Saturday morning golf group at Waialae for 30 years. We have several foursomes, but we hardly ever play in the same group because we go by skill levels, so he was in the A group with the other really good golfers. I was in either the C or D group.

Walter Kupau, longtime Carpenters' Union leader

Walter and I went head-to-head in 1996 when he very publicly pulled all of the Carpenters Union pension fund money out of First Hawaiian.

I always took the position that we should encourage bank employees to get involved in public service and, if they do, we shouldn't dictate how they make their decisions about elected office. Sometimes it comes back to bite a company in the ass, as it did in this incident with Kupau, but we stuck with that position.

The flap involved a bank officer named Arnold Morgado, who was on the City Council. Arnold was against the proposed rail transit project, which caused a lot of heartburn for the bank because a lot of our customers such as construction labor unions and big contractors were eager for rail to move ahead. Also, the bank supported rail, and I personally supported it.

Walter Kupau's union had millions of dollars in pension funds with First Hawaiian. He called me and said, "Either you get Arnold to change his Council vote or we'll pull all our funds out of the bank." I said, "No, we won't do that. Arnold doesn't tell us how to run the bank, and I don't tell him how to run the City Council. I can't have you telling me how to run my bank and have people around town think they can do the same thing over some other issue."

He had the union picket First Hawaiian Bank with big hats on that said "ABA, Anybody but Arnold." He took all the business out to Central Pacific Bank. Years later, after Walter left the union, a lot of that business came back, but in between it was a very painful time.

Harry Weinberg, local investor, posthumous philanthropist

Harry Weinberg, a billionaire investor who lived the last two decades of his life in Honolulu, was a tough guy with a gravelly voice who could be a son of a bitch to deal with. Since his death in 1990, he has become one of the greatest philanthropists in the history of Hawaii through his Harry and Jeanette Weinberg Foundation. Ironically, "generous" was not what you would call him in life. When I first met him in about 1980, it was hard to get him to give money to charity.

I was working with Johnny Bellinger and Bobby Pfeiffer, co-chairs of a campaign to raise money for a Palama Settlement building. I went with Bellinger to ask Weinberg for money. Harry's office was a hovel down on Nimitz Highway. The Palama project touched him because it was to help poor kids, so he said to Johnny, "I'll give $100,000, but I expect A&B and First Hawaiian to give $100,000 each, too. And you tell the other guys in town, 'If a Jew can give $100,000, they can do better than that.'"

His was a classic Horatio Alger story—a poor European immigrant who left school at age 12, worked in his father's auto repair shop and built enormous wealth with an aggressive investment style. His Hawaii connection came when he acquired the private Honolulu Rapid Transit (HRT), forerunner of TheBus. He had also invested in transit in several Mainland cities.

Harry was one of the original "greenmailers." (Greenmail is a term used when an aggressive investor buys enough shares in a company to threaten a takeover or

Photo from 1996 American Bankers Association convention in Hawaii. I couldn't get Federal Reserve Chairman Alan Greenspan into an aloha shirt, but at least he gave up the tie.

other mischief, forcing the company to buy the shares back at a premium to fend off the attack.) Locally, he targeted both Dillingham Corp. and Alexander & Baldwin, among others.

Larry Mehau, former Land Board member and head of Hawaii Protective Association

I first met Larry when Eddie Sherman, the old *Honolulu Advertiser* columnist, asked me to work on the March of Dimes telethon. Eddie had been a song-and-dance man and was very close to Larry, who had ties to Don Ho and a lot of Hawaii entertainers. Larry is a big, strong man. At the telethon, Eddie had Larry take a phone book and rip it in two with his hands. That impressed me! I found out that Larry, who had a ranch on the Big Island and owned a security guard company called Hawaii Protective Association, was an ex-cop, and of course my dad was a cop, too.

Later, when I ran George Ariyoshi's 1970 campaign for lieutenant governor, Larry was the co-chair. One of my newspaper reporter friends called me up and said, "Do you know who your co-chair is? Are you aware he has ties to organized crime?" I had no knowledge of those rumors, so I went to see Ariyoshi. George said, "Those rumors have been around for years. He's a good friend of Governor Burns, a good friend of mine, and he's an honorable guy. I stand behind him 100 percent." I said, "That's good enough for me."

In the campaign, Larry ran the entertainment side; I ran the media strategy side. We got along well. Over the years I'd see him at social events, at political events. We were never close friends, but we had a respectful relationship.

There were occasional mentions in the paper connecting Larry to organized crime. Rick Reed, who was an aide to City Prosecutor Charles Marsland and later a candidate for Congress had at one point claimed that Larry was the "godfather of organized crime." Larry unsuccessfully sued Reed, Marsland and the city for defamation. Although he has never been convicted, Larry's name continued to be connected to organized crime accusations.

Years later, we had an incident at the bank. One of our customers was a payroll-processing company, and we discovered somebody at the company was kiting checks, basically running a Ponzi scheme. As a result, some of the payroll checks were bouncing. We called in the company boss to tell him what we had found, and he said he would investigate. He drove out of our bank, went to Hanauma Bay, jumped off the cliff and killed himself.

We were describing the incident in one of our training sessions later, to help people learn from history. It turned out that the company he had screwed was Hawaii Protective Association. Through no fault of Larry's, his payroll checks bounced, and he had to come up with money to pay his employees again. One employee trainee in the back row said, "The guy did this to Mr. Mehau? No wonder he jumped."

That quip shows the staying power of rumors, true or untrue.

Wallace (Wally) Fujiyama, prominent local attorney and former UH regent

Wally was rough and tough, a street fighter all the way. After he graduated from McKinley High School, his college education in engineering was interrupted by World War II service. He then worked briefly as a policeman before changing his focus to law and attending the University of Cincinnati Law School. (He was recommended for admission by William Richardson, a Cincinnati graduate who went on to become Hawaii's lieutenant governor and chief justice.)

Wally didn't put on airs. On purpose, he had a little platform in his office, and you would be sitting in the lower chair. He would be sitting up at his desk, stockings but no shoes, feet on the desk, picking his nose. When the big New York lawyers would come in, he would pick his nose and fart. But he was a smart SOB who prepared well for cases. In court, he played the "I am just a dumb local boy" to the jury, and it usually worked.

Wally Fujiyama and I at First Hawaiian offices.

He was highly opinionated. He got involved in politics. He wasn't a Democrat. His beliefs were more Republican, but he could get in with whomever he needed to get along with.

One thing he didn't have was credibility in the business community, because he was always on the other side and litigating against business. There's the famous case involving Sears in which somebody fell off of a ladder and was seriously injured. Wally sued for damages on the man's behalf. The Sears people brought in top litigators from around the country. In his summation to the jury, all locals, Wally brings out the pidgin and says, "Dey bring in dese high-priced Mainland lawyers. Dey give you all dis kine hype. All I know is da guy wen' on the ladder, the ladder fell and he broke his neck. Dese guys cannot get away with dat." The jury awarded a humongous verdict for Wally and his client.

From that day forward, Sears never used anybody but Wally Fujiyama, and the Mainland lawyers loved him even though they got their asses kicked by him. Although he was a rough guy, he had a good heart. I got a letter from him one Monday morning, saying, "I want to let you know, something happened to my heart and I am writing you this on Friday. I am sure everything is going to work out OK, but in case it doesn't, I really appreciate you giving me credibility in the business community." He died at the hospital during surgery in 1994, and I was honored to be asked to give one of his eulogies.

In my eulogy, I focused on his years as a very active member of the UH Board of Regents and how it typified his efforts to stand up for local people. I said that Wally asked, "What should the University of Hawaii's faculty workload be? Shouldn't the faculty be spending more time in the classrooms?" He accepted the furor that came with these questions. He asked, "Why aren't there more local professors on the UH faculty?" And he accepted the furor that came afterward. He asked, "Why aren't more local athletes being given scholarships at the university?" And he took the furor that came with that question. Wally was a giant in our community who often tweaked our consciousness, if not our nose

Wesley Park, educator, businessman and longtime First Hawaiian Bank director

Wesley came up from the streets of Kalihi. He had polio as a kid, lived in an iron lung for a while. He suffered, but after he got out of that, from his early years, he'd just fight every day. He knew no fear. He'd take on guys five times his size, get pounded down and just keep coming back. Finally the big guy would give up.

He was a very tough guy, but after graduating from Roosevelt High School, he went on to UH and got his master's and was given an honorary doctorate by a university in Korea. He ultimately ended up being dean of UH's College of Continuing Education, vice president of the East-West Center and later CEO of Hawaii Dental Service. On the side, he was entertainer Danny Kaleikini's manager.

Through all of this, he kept friends with the guys from the wrong side of the law from his days in Kalihi, while also becoming very close to people in the business community, the political community. He was one of those behind-the-scenes guys who are extremely knowledgeable and extremely powerful.

He is also a quiet collector of art. He is probably one of the best art connoisseurs in Hawaii, but you would never know that.

Jeff Watanabe, attorney, longtime friend and business associate

When I started at the bank, there was a small law firm downstairs that included George Ariyoshi and some other old-time big names. There were also two young upstarts in the firm, Bert Kobayashi Jr. (son of the former Hawaii attorney general and Supreme Court justice) and Jeff Watanabe. Through my relationships with Ariyoshi, I got to know both Bert and Jeff well, and we have been lifelong friends.

Jeff had interned with Senator Inouye, and so he knew my wife, Diane, who had also worked in the senator's office. When Jeff married Lynne, and Diane and I got married, we would go to each other's houses. We have been very good friends ever since. Later, Jeff became Inouye's chief legal adviser, taking him through difficult episodes. Jeff worked his way up to the corporate and business community and became very powerful.

Many people don't realize that he was on the board of the Smithsonian Institution and he was a chairman of the Children's Television Workshop that produces *Sesame Street*. Then, he got on a lot of the local boards like Hawaiian Electric and American Savings, and, of course, I nominated him years ago for the boards of A&B and Matson. Jeff is very successful and urbane. He is much more sophisticated than the typical local person. He has contacts and connections around the world.

Bert Kobayashi Jr., attorney, longtime friend and First Hawaiian Bank director

Like Jeff, Bert became a very successful lawyer. At one time, they were partners, but after a while they had a friendly split. Jeff was more a corporate lawyer and Bert more of a litigator.

Bert was a strong Ariyoshi guy, as Jeff and I were. Bert and I ended up helping George select his first cabinet in 1974, when the two of us were still barely 30. I don't know why George trusted us so much to do that, but we did all the vetting of applicants, just the two of us.

Bert had recommended this one guy to be the tax director, Gordon Wong. In the middle of the conversation of the vetting, Bert said, "We always have to ask the same question. Is there anything that's going to embarrass you if you join the administration?" He said, "Yes, I voted for (Republican) Randy Crossley." That was pretty funny. I said, "We can live with that."

Another time Bert and I were in the old executive dining room at the bank and interviewing a woman applicant, an attractive lady. We went through the whole interview and got down to our last standard question, "Is there anything that would prove embarrassing to the governor that you want to tell us about?" She looked at Bert and me, both of us much younger than she, and said, "Well, I *have* had a few affairs." Bert and I were so embarrassed. We didn't know how to respond. We laughed about that for years.

George Chaplin, former editor-in-chief of *The Honolulu Advertiser*

George and I became good friends on the Governor's Commission on the Year 2000, which took place in 1970. He was a co-chairman and, at age 29, I was the youngest on the planning committee. The running joke was that I was picked because I might still be around in the year 2000. I became the go-to guy on the committee because I was the whippersnapper and could get press releases written up and have brochures printed.

George kind of adopted me after that. When I got promoted over the years, he'd write fabulous stories about me every time. We served on several subsequent committees and commissions and, much later in his career, he wanted to do one of these futures committees like Year 2000 all over again. "George," I said, "those kinds of things aren't working anymore." I think he was disappointed in me.

I liked that he was an activist newspaper editor. He'd take positions. None of this "We can't get involved in the community because we're reporting on the community" kind of stuff. George would get out there and take strong positions on issues.

We also worked together big time on endorsement editorials when *The Advertiser* would endorse a political candidate, usually one I was working for like George Ariyoshi or Dan Inouye. Or when it involved Frank Fasi, with whom he had a continuing feud. When the paper was going to endorse someone, George would be writing it, but I'd be feeding the info to him.

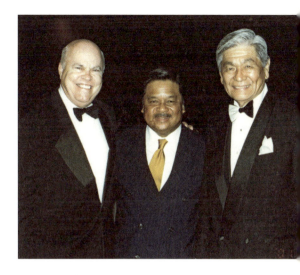

Two guys from Kalihi and one from Kuliouou. I worked with Governors Ben Cayetano and George Ariyoshi, among many Island leaders.

Sheridan C.F. (Sherry) Ing, business executive, developer, longtime First Hawaiian Bank director

Sherry Ing was a major influence on my business career, someone who always gave me wise advice. He had a very unusual background; he was from Molokai, graduated from Roosevelt High in Honolulu, and then went to college at MIT. He was extremely smart, had very strong convictions and was a champion of things local. He really fought for giving local kids a chance and fought for local companies. He was a top executive and one of the driving forces behind Aloha Airlines, along with Hung Wo Ching.

As I wrote in Chapter 8, he was one of the key board members who helped me to become CEO after Johnny Bellinger died. As a matter of fact, he had been a classmate of Johnny's at Roosevelt. He was a quiet mentor of mine. I would go to Sherry for advice whenever I had hard decisions as CEO. He was a strong supporter of building First Hawaiian Center.

In his own right, he also built quality developments on Oahu—condos such as Royal Iolani, Admiral Thomas, Yacht Harbor Towers. He and Bruce Stark did some of those projects together.

Sherry died way too young, at 70, of cancer.

The Power Issue
Hawaii Business magazine, 2002.

CHAPTER 21

Most powerful? Nah!

Who's most powerful in Hawaii?

"Who are the most powerful people in Hawaii?. . . The fact that Walter Dods was the top vote-getter in our poll was no surprise. But the margin between Dods and second place was eye-opening. Everyone (among 50 prominent community leaders surveyed) mentioned Dods, and everyone except two. . . had him on top of their list. He was prominently mentioned in all three categories (No. 1 in business, No. 5 in politics and No. 4 in community affairs).

"Under Dods' 13-year leadership, (First Hawaiian's) shareholder value and presence in the community have increased exponentially. But that's not the only reason for his influence. Possessing an uncanny ability to put a finger to the winds of change, Dods has been sought after for his advice by governors, senators and leaders of many stripes. In addition, a reputation for honesty and loyalty has won him friends throughout the business community."

(Following Dods on the magazine's Top-10 "Power List" were U.S. Sen Dan Inouye, UH President Evan Dobelle, Gov. Ben Cayetano, Mike O'Neill of Bankoh, gubernatorial candidate (later, governor) Linda Lingle, Warren Haruki of Verizon Hawaii, House Speaker Calvin Say, developer Bert A. Kobayashi and UH coach June Jones.)

Hawaii Business *"Power Issue,"* 2002

Back in 2002, *Hawaii Business* magazine polled 50 community leaders and wrote, "Walter is the most powerful guy in the state." I find "Most Powerful" lists hilarious, but I guess it sells magazines. My theory has always been, "If you say you got power, you ain't got power."

In 1967, when my wife Diane (then Diane Nosse) was a senior in political science at the University of Hawaii, she wrote an honors thesis in which she tried to identify Honolulu's "community power structure" of the day. She asked a cross-section of leaders for their opinions, narrowed the list to the 21 with the most votes, then asked those 21 for their own lists. That narrowed her analysis to a "Top 12."

People were fascinated by the topic then, as they are now. Her report used fictitious names; only by promising them anonymity would people freely talk to her. However, *Honolulu Magazine* couldn't resist trying to guess the 12 she was writing about. The *Honolulu Star-Bulletin* also devoted a page to her study, with a dozen tantalizing mug shots. Was "Adam Montgomery" really Gov. Jack Burns? Was "Percy Weston" actually Lowell Dillingham? Maybe "Fred Chow" was businessman and *Star-Bulletin* owner Chinn Ho?

To this day, Diane has never revealed to me who's who. (Interestingly, no bankers made the top tier of her 1967 power list.) The point is that the attempt to generate a list generated publicity and speculation. (She concluded that the former Big Five power structure had been replaced by multiple "power pyramids"—different people with power for community planning, for politics, for education. No one person led all three.)

Anyway, it's ironic that, long before we ended up as a couple, she became well known as a young scholar for analyzing local power. Then, years later, I'm on that silly power list in *Hawaii Business*.

Thirty years ago, I could get maybe three guys in the bank to follow me and help me on a political campaign, but Takumi (Crabby) Koyama, a shoe store manager who was one of the foot soldiers for the Burns and Ariyoshi campaigns, could get 600 people to follow him to go get votes. That, to me, was power.

I have never considered myself really powerful. Did I have the ability to pick up the phone and call certain people? Yes. But you earn that ability by spending 40 years going out, doing grassroots campaigns, fundraising for charity, making hard business decisions. If you do that long enough, when you call somebody, they say, "Yeah, you want that? No questions asked, I'll help you."

That happens because you've laid the groundwork with hard work, not because you're CEO of a major company. There are lots of CEOs of major companies around town. If you ask, "Are they powerful?" I think the answer would be, "Probably not." A head of a major union like HGEA has 10 times more political power than I ever had. Maybe I have had power in terms of economic power, through the ability to make loans and help projects happen—or not. However, you have to exercise it soundly or you'll take your bank down the tubes.

I guess if you're active in the community, active in politics and active in business, through that networking you'd have some ability to get things done. However, I never ever believed I had much actual clout. Jeff Watanabe's comment (quoted right) about the existence of "perceived power" takes me down a peg in a subtle way. I accept his theory that sometimes perceived power becomes real. People perceive Walter has power, therefore, I guess he did sort of have it.

However, even if you have power in a certain realm, it's only good if you don't wield it. It's a resource that can be diminished through overuse. People resent it and start trying to find ways to knock you down.

I think you can say that there's power in ideas, so perhaps there is a certain amount of power in my commitment to express my ideas and advocate for them. In my case, maybe people say I have—or had—power because I was never shy about voicing my opinions. So many people hide behind masks. How many business executives put their ass on the line outside of their own companies? Very few.

One can make a case that business shouldn't go out and take stands on state or local issues. It's perfectly legitimate to argue, "Their job is to make their product, sell it and take care of their employees and their shareholders." I just don't happen to believe that philosophy. I agree with the approach George Chaplin took when he was editor of *The Advertiser* and was very active in the community, too.

Business is part of the community. Business gets its income from the community. You ought to be invested in the community. Giving back also means standing up. Maybe part of perceived "power" is being willing to stand up and be counted on a regular basis.

Of course, if you stand up, you risk being knocked down. My classic example is something I put together in 1995 that turned into an embarrassment for me. I persuaded business executives to donate money for an ill-fated marketing program called "Thumbs Up, Hawaii!" I had a lot of successes over the years, but that was my biggest flop.

Here's how it happened. Hawaii was in a severe economic slump that lasted for years, brought on in large measure after the Japanese asset bubble burst. Gov. Ben Cayetano called me over to the Capitol to meet with a group of political leaders. Ben said, "We need help. We need to get the economy going." I told him I'd try to come up with ideas.

My marketing guy at the bank was an old pro named Norwood "Red" Pope who had worked for major banks around the country. Red had been in a similar situation in Florida and helped come up with a campaign—"Thumbs Up, Florida"—to help people understand how to improve their local economy. The idea was to

---

"In Hawaii where you have a highly centralized, heavily regulated environment, a relationship with the governor is not insignificant. Walter's successful leadership in political campaigns with George Ariyoshi gave Walter and Johnny Bellinger and the bank the perception of power.

"In this town, perception is more important than reality. You want to tangle with Walter, you are not only going to tangle with him, you are going to tangle with the governor, you're going to tangle with his cabinet, and you have to tangle with a whole bunch of other people, too. So over time, I think, Walter generated a huge amount of perceived power."

—*attorney Jeff Watanabe*

> "Walter is clearly the most influential single person in the business community and probably the broader community in this state. Why is he so influential? Because he's the first guy you think of calling for so many different things.
>
> "If you have a business question or problem, you're going to go to him. If you have a political question or an issue, you're going to go him. Every day people call him to look for mentoring about their life or their career. Speaking engagements? He's always asked. When nonprofits are looking for directors, they all want him. Even for public companies, he's top of the list. Those are the ones who pay money for you to sit on their board, so it's real important who they select.
>
> "If you're going to have dinner in public, and you want to prove you're an important guy in town, invite Walter."
>
> —*Stan Kuriyama, CEO of Alexander & Baldwin*

get people to have confidence in themselves and in their state, boosting local spending as a result. One local example might be: If more people in Hawaii vacationed on the Big Island and Maui and spent money in the Islands instead of going to Las Vegas, we could have a self-help recovery. The same concept had worked in Florida.

I went to the governor and business leaders and told them, "Originality is undetected plagiarism. Let's steal a good idea from Florida." I raised $300,000 around town in two days for ads. (Maybe all my *power* scared people into contributing.) All the big business players chipped in. Unfortunately, the public was in no mood yet to feel better. Our ads débuted on the eve of Cayetano's re-election campaign, and his critics came out in force. The "outs" used the campaign as a way to slam the "ins." Critics said, "People have no food in their mouths, and you're running an advertising campaign!"

Also, our execution of the ads wasn't so hot. I had competing CEOs, such as Larry Johnson from Bank of Hawaii and me, do commercials together cooperatively promoting "Thumbs Up." I should have done man-on-the-street ads instead because people were in no mood to follow the leadership. The ultimate low point was somebody saying, "Tell Dods to put one thumb up in his mouth and one up his ass. Every hour, change thumbs."

I personally don't think "Thumbs" was a bad idea, even to this day. Yet the campaign was a dud, which was pretty depressing because I was just trying to do something helpful. I don't regret doing it, but I wish I had executed it better. We pulled the plug after a few months.

Larry Johnson of Bank of Hawaii joined me in the "Thumbs Up, Hawaii!" Campaign. Unfortunately, most of the public turned thumbs down on the idea.

"I've known Walter a long time. I've never seen him exercise any 'power.' Walter's not about power. Walter's about taking care of his employees, his customers and his community. He enjoys those accolades with a sense of humor because I can tell you he does not take them seriously."

—Don Horner,
retired First Hawaiian Bank chairman & CEO

Some people say, "Dods screwed up on that." I say, "I let my community down." I didn't do a good job of getting our message across and I took a kick to the shin, but I don't think it ultimately affected my reputation. A few years later, *Hawaii Business* named me "most powerful," so putting yourself out there and taking a risk doesn't necessarily hurt you long-term.

In the end, however, I expect "Thumbs" will be featured prominently in my obituary.

The Dods family met the Obamas at a local political fundraising event. Left to right are my daughter-in-law, Starr Wedemeyer Dods; son Walter III (Trippy); Barack; my wife, Diane; son Peter; Michelle; son Chris; and me.

CHAPTER 22

Local Boys and Girls *Can* Succeed. Here's How:

It would be a shame to make it through seven decades without learning something useful. Fortunately, I've absorbed a few lessons along the way. As a kid, I never thought of myself as a future leader. However, my early days in the Jaycees interested me in the subject of leadership, and I've added to my list of lessons learned over the years.

This chapter is aimed squarely at young local kids who are today where I was a half-century ago—nowhere near the top of the heap and not quite sure how to get there. A few tips from an old guy:

Be local, brah, but be confident!
There was a great phrase Gov. Jack Burns coined in a speech almost 50 years ago. He said many local people have "a subtle inferiority of spirit," a feeling that he said is completely unwarranted but which keeps local youngsters from aspiring to climb the ladder.

One example: Over the years I've made a lot of speeches to young people in Hawaii. When I'm finished, I ask for questions. Usually I get none. It's not because they aren't smart, but many of us in Hawaii were brought up not to raise our hand in class because we risk making ass. We were conditioned not to be a showoff. We may not have the confidence to speak out, though we may go up quietly after the meeting and ask a good, tough question.

Hopefully, it's a cultural trait that is disappearing, because it can get in the way of local kids reaching their potential. I tell college classes that this behavior holds local kids back—and I'm as local as they come. Some are ashamed of pidgin. I had a hard time getting away from pidgin myself as a young guy and speaking co-called "Standard English." My wife says I still haven't learned how. Kids don't have to ban pidgin from their vocabulary; they can do both.

What we consider "showing off" is just putting your point out there because it's as good as (or better than) anybody else's point. Hawaii kids need to learn that. Our verbal skills are still weak. I beg young people in Hawaii, if they take nothing else from this book, to start working on verbal skills. Don't be afraid to express your thoughts and opinions. Making good first impressions is hard for many local kids because they hold back. I'd like to see that change, and I do see it changing. Once employers know your work ethic and how solid you are, you will do fine.

When local kids who have gone away to school come back looking for jobs, we see dramatic change. They've been exposed to the bigger world and gained confidence. Some of the best employees we ever hired are kids from Hawaii who've gone away, gotten roughed up a little bit, then came back. They're terrific people.

A good side of being local is—no talk stink!

Back in 2003, Central Pacific Bank CEO Clint Arnoldus, in town barely a year, publicly criticized First Hawaiian for not being "local." He said we were "owned by a French parent, not the most popular foreign ownership to have right now" (because of French opposition to the Iraq War). Normally, I would have ignored it, but I saw it as a cheap shot from a *malihini* at our bank's 2,000 local employees. So I had a little fun. I told the media, "I was born and raised here. I didn't just get off the boat from California and learn the *shaka* sign. If Clint really understood what 'local' means, he'd know local people don't make hostile attacks on honorable competitors. Anytime he wants to debate in pidgin on 'local,' I'm available." Needless to say, he didn't accept the offer. He left town a few years later, just before Central Pacific needed a federal bailout during the Great Recession.

The lesson? To succeed in business in Hawaii, understand the local culture and way of operating. Being "local" doesn't mean you have to be born here. It does mean you have to adapt to local ways of living together on small islands.

Dream big dreams.

People sometimes laugh at big dreamers, but they're the ones who make things happen. My favorite example is in downtown Honolulu, 429 feet tall. When I first dreamed of building First Hawaiian Center and we began designing it, the city's height limit was only 350 feet. We hadn't yet approached the City Council about raising it.

The architect was starting drawings, $8 million worth of work, and I had to tell him whether to design it at 350 or 450 feet. I made the decision to go with the higher number. I thought it was a nice dream, a better-looking building, better for the downtown community. Had I not finally rounded up the Council votes to raise the height limit, I would have been an *ex*-executive at First Hawaiian.

But the dream did come true. When we sealed a time capsule in its cornerstone, we invited leaders to send us their dreams about what Hawaii would be like when the capsule is reopened in 2058, the 200th birthday of First Hawaiian Bank. We got

> "Walt is perceptive, bright and loyal to his friends to a fault, and he's totally colorblind. He has a great love for Hawaii and vision, and he has the capacity of thinking big, thinking beyond insular Hawaii. He has ridden the wave of Hawaii's transition from an English colonial agrarian society to what it is today. He has shown that a local boy can make it here and on the big stage on the Mainland."
>
> —*Glenn Kaya, former First Hawaiian director*

a lot of visionary ideas. U.S. Sen. Dan Akaka summed it up, writing to me that "leadership, by definition, begs a destination—a goal that needs achieving, a dream that needs realizing."

You don't make it come true without first dreaming it, then working for it. Don't be afraid to dream big dreams, whether you come from Waianae High School or Farrington or Saint Louis or Punahou or Iolani.

Say "Yes" to community service.
You make your money from this community and you should put time and effort back in. If you do, you will go a lot further than the genius at the next desk who is only one-dimensional. To get ahead in our bank, you need talent as a banker, but you also need to do the right thing for our community. Do your day job well, but also devote time as a director of nonprofits, or helping with charity fundraising. We want people who are great professionals and great public citizens, too.

I have tried to live up to the old advice about being generous with your time, talent and treasure. I'm proud of having served as a director of two-dozen nonprofits involved with education, social services, youth programs, the arts, historic preservation, international relations, environmental protection, and health. Over the years, I have played a leadership role in fundraising campaigns that have raised over $160 million for Hawaii charities and schools.

One of my earliest projects was chairing the four-month campaign that raised $1.6 million to build the Blood Bank of Hawaii building in Kalihi in 1979. The money was raised and the building designed and built in 16 months. The campaign taught me that if the cause is right, the community will respond. Co-chairing the drive to fund the $5 million Mamiya Theatre at my alma mater, Saint Louis, in 1986 was another great joy. Until then, Saint Louis had great athletes and zero culture. I know; I was there. When community groups used the theater, I wanted them to let students attend rehearsals for free to learn something beyond football.

When I was at First Hawaiian, the bank had an unmatched record of supporting United Way campaigns—as much as $1 million a year from the company and employees. Our teller's average gift was the same as a University of Hawaii professor's. We simply let everyone know from the top down that we believe in community service.

> "Walter is a dreamer. But he doesn't just dream, he acts, and we're all lucky that he does because he helps others' dreams come true in the process. Raising millions for social agencies and schools. Helping to rescue elderly depositors caught in despair by a finance company disaster. And keeping First Hawaiian a locally run bank that gives back to our community at a time when we need that more than ever.

> "Hawaii is lucky to have a man like Walter in the leadership ranks of business, community service and just plain common humanity."

—*U.S. Sen. Daniel Inouye, 2003*

Showing off the record Aloha United Way check with John Couch of A&B

If the bosses aren't committed, it won't happen. I led the 1989 Aloha United Way campaign that raised a record $16.1 million for Oahu charities.

Over the years, I've also had roles in raising money for the UH Campaign for Hawaii ($116 million), construction of Hawaii Children's Discovery Center ($16 million), a new Palama Settlement administration building ($3 million), the Daniel K. Inouye Fund at the Hawaii Community Foundation ($5 million), an endowed Dan Inouye chair at UH ($2.2 million) and a scholarship endowment at the university in honor of Dan Akaka ($1.1 million), among others.

If I'm going to ask other people for money for charities, I have to lead by example. That's one reason Diane and I gave $1 million to the University of Hawaii for undergraduate scholarships. The recipients must come from public schools and be immigrant children. Why? All my life I've seen immigrants sacrifice the most for their children and make education the top priority.

Teamwork trumps superstars.

Teamwork commands a higher premium than talent at First Hawaiian Bank. Our philosophy is: No matter how good you are, if you're not a team player, go elsewhere.

We don't say, "It's not my *kuleana*; it's somebody else's problem." When there's a problem, it *IS* my job. We're all in the same canoe. If somebody isn't paddling, we're going to lose the race. If there's a hole in the canoe, we don't say, "I didn't put the hole in the canoe." We work together to fix it, because my *okole* is going to get wet along with everybody else.

Does it work? Today, we're the largest bank in the state.

Draw a line of integrity. Don't cross it!

Johnny Bellinger called me in one day and said, "I want you to fire Tom Whittemore." I said, "Johnny, he's one of our best guys." He was running Kauai at the time. I said, "Let me check it out." Johnny was ticked at me for not agreeing with him right away.

Tom was a great banker and also a carpenter. Whenever we sent him to a different island, he would build his own home in his spare time. On Kauai, he went to a local building material house run by a cantankerous old guy who was Bellinger's buddy. The guy's prices were 30–40 percent above Oahu's, so Tom went to the Oahu City Mill to buy his materials and shipped them to Kauai.

LOCAL BOYS (AND GIRLS) CAN SUCCEED. HERE'S HOW:

This guy called Bellinger and said, "Whittemore insulted me bringing in material from Oahu. Get rid of him."

After I researched it, I said, "John, I can't fire Tom; he's doing a great job and he's done nothing wrong." Bellinger said, "He's embarrassed me and this bank. Either you fire him or I'll fire you." I said, "Well, I guess you'll have to fire me." He threw me out of his office. Whittemore and I didn't get a raise for a couple of years, but he didn't fire either of us.

Ironically, years later when Kauai had Hurricane Iwa, Tom did something I wouldn't have had the class to do. In the middle of the storm he went with his belt, hammer and carpenter's tools and nailed tarps to this guy's roof to save his house. *After* the guy tried to get him fired.

> "Walter has always been a firm believer in, and these are my words, matching up responsibilities and authority. If you are responsible for something, you better have the authority to do whatever needs to get done to fulfill that responsibility. Once you see a mismatch between authority and responsibility, you have a problem."
>
> —*Jeff Watanabe, attorney and longtime friend*

Senator Inouye joined me at a dinner that raised hundreds of thousands of dollars for the Boy Scouts in Hawaii.

"Walt's leadership style is collaborative. He delegated authority, did not micromanage. He believed you can't over-communicate. I think he was concerned about perception—looking at decisions not just on how they affect the bottom line but how they affect the community and our overall image. In our industry, image is critical. Every competitor has the same color of money, and you're all insured by the FDIC. How the customer perceives an institution is important.

"He was a mentor to me; I learned a lot about being a banker and a lot about life. He is an outstanding father and an outstanding husband. Those are traits that employees also see that are important in leadership and in a business of trust. You could see the depth of his character by how he treated his wife, his kids, his friends, and how he treated the employees.

"You could fill a book with all the campaigns that he's run for the community. He encouraged the rest of us to do those things, too."

—Don Horner, retired chairman & CEO, First Hawaiian Bank

When bank trainees come to see me, I tell them the Tom Whittemore story as an example of how you have to draw an internal line of integrity. Once you cross that line, you're no good to yourself. You have to be able to look at yourself in the mirror every day.

Be humane, even when making tough decisions.

First Hawaiian Bank had 28 straight years of record profits before a slump hit Hawaii during the 1990s. In tough times for Hawaii's economy, a lot of local companies needed to cut costs. One bank—not ours—brought in an outside consultant who said, "This is what we are going to do. Here's the winners, here's the losers, and we are going to give them a blue slip or a pink slip Monday morning. The blue slip says you get to keep your job but you have to reapply and fight for it; the pink slip says you're out."

That's not the way we made cuts. We first tried to do everything we could without eliminating jobs. We froze top-level salaries, froze hiring, revised profit-sharing. We delayed capital investment projects. We didn't push an early retirement plan to nudge people out because it's not effective. The best people leave because they know they can find work elsewhere. We got some great folks from Bank of Hawaii that way.

In the end, First Hawaiian reduced payroll by several hundred employees almost entirely through attrition. In the end there were very few layoffs, in contrast to our competitors. You have to do it right. If you want to be a leader, treat your people well.

Don't be a slave to conventional wisdom.

It may be conventional, but it's not always wisdom. Sometimes it's better not to follow the pack. For example, the experts tell you the only way to make a merger work is to cram the cultures and the managements of the two companies together. I don't agree. We thought long and hard about that point after we acquired Bank of the West in 1998 and decided instead to keep both cultures.

First Hawaiian is the biggest fish in a small pond, with more than 40 percent of the bank market share in Hawaii. Bank of the West was then a smaller fish in a gigantic pond, California. At the time the banks merged, First Hawaiian was 25 percent bigger, but we saw no benefit in forcing our culture on Bank of the West. Now, 17 years later, First Hawaiian has $18 billion in assets, and Bank of the West has made a lot of acquisitions and is closing in on $75 billion, but they haven't forced their style on us, either. We still keep our unique Hawaiian brand, and the combined company has thrived.

Don't do business where you don't understand the language.
Or the culture, or the customs. A classic example is the early 1990s when our major competitor was expanding in Asia and a lot of tiny Pacific islands. I'm no financial genius, but I knew the language was different, the culture was different, the laws were different.

"All good leaders have a vision of where they want to go plus the ability to drag, kick, push and motivate others to share your vision. It wasn't easy to take a major company that had been independent and Hawaii-centric for a long time and make it a bigger company yet keep the great things about First Hawaiian. A lot of people wouldn't have had the imagination and flexibility and good humor to bring it off.

"When issues came up, he was the reasonable guy in the room who would help work it through. Walter is a very fair guy to deal with, a no-nonsense guy. You tell him what you want, and he'll say yes or no. He expected the same from me. He's a good guy . . . but a lousy golfer."

—*Don McGrath, retired chairman and CEO of Bank of the West and BancWest Corporation*

I kept getting attacked by the stock analysts asking me, "Why don't you have a Pacific Strategy like Bankoh?" Common sense told me that if you go out to Hong Kong, Taiwan, Japan and the Philippines, you're competing against Citicorp, Hong Kong Shanghai Bank, Chase Manhattan—the biggest of the biggest. What would make us unique to them? Most of the Pacific islands are the size of Molokai. Instead, we expanded east to the West Coast where we knew the rules and could make money. In the end, my friend Larry Johnson stepped down as Bank of Hawaii's CEO when their Asia-Pacific strategy—which had been put in place before he took over—didn't pan out. My competitor, which had gone west instead of east, had to retrench from a $15 billion bank to $9 billion in just a few years when they had to pull back from those markets.

"Walt was personally invested in the design of First Hawaiian Center. At the time, I was in charge of the branches, and I remember looking at the architects' layout of the main branch in the building. I'm very pragmatic. Every square inch is important in a branch—space for marketing platforms, business banking, personal banking, mass market, etc. There's a science to where you put safe-deposit boxes, how you lay out furniture—none of which was applied at the new branch.

"I leveled with Walt about how I felt: 'Boss, this branch, blah, blah, blah.' He was very gracious, allowed me to finish, and said, 'How many branches do we have?' I said 61. He said, 'How many report to you?' I said, 'At the moment, all of them.' He said, 'Think of it this way. This branch reports to me.' I said, 'Boss, I think I got it.' So we built the branch exactly the way it was laid out on the plan. Time will tell whether it was the most efficiently laid out branch, but it is certainly the most beautiful branch we have and probably one of the most beautiful in the country, if not the world."

—*Don Horner, retired chairman & CEO, First Hawaiian Bank*

People do business with people.

All the gurus said the wave of the future is technology, that banks should downplay brick-and-mortar branches. People thought ATMs plus online banking would kill branches. I've always thought that was bunk. Why would you want to eliminate the great strength of your industry—touching the customer?

People bank with people. When you make major financial decisions, you still have a great desire to look somebody in the eye and feel good about who you are doing business with. I have no doubt that's true in most other lines of work, too.

Banks have the great advantage of location, location, location. We have 57 branches in Hawaii. We encourage our branch managers to be active in their communities. They are the presidents of their community associations, the heads of fundraising drives. They are respected there.

That adage about doing business with people was proven again when First Hawaiian was acquired by BNP Paribas. When we did the deal, some of my managers worried we would lose customers because we're owned by a French bank. I didn't think so and I was right. People see the bank through the lens of the people in it—the branch manager, the tellers, the personal and business bankers who help them day in and day out. I knew that as long as they took care of their customers and stayed active in the community, we would do just fine. As a matter of fact, we gained market share.

Art is the soul of a community.

Art isn't just for the rich. It's for everybody, but with my background I didn't always feel that way. Fortunately, my good friend Wesley Park forced me to go to museums, and I got involved in supporting the local art scene. In First Hawaiian Center, we've made art accessible downtown by incorporating an art museum into the main branch. I've gotten letters from customers who wander through the gallery and write to thank me for giving them a way to enjoy local art on their lunch hour or when they come in to cash a check.

Candidly, the museum idea was not popular with most of my fellow bankers. They wanted a branch with posters and loan desks. I wanted a real museum, with loan officers pushed onto the second floor and no marketing materials in sight. I told them, "We have 60 other branches where you can put posters."

The bank's museum, originally part of the Contemporary Museum but now an arm of the Honolulu Museum of Art, hosts four shows a year. We subsidize it to encourage artists to produce work in the Islands. We show only artists with Hawaii connections. Proceeds from sales go 100 percent to the artists.

If you screw up, admit it.
You're going to have setbacks, especially if you dream big dreams and do big things. I've had plenty. I try to admit my mistake right away, learn from it, and don't repeat it.

In 1994, we discovered a problem in some trust accounts we were managing. When you manage accounts for pension funds, you have investment parameters. You can invest within these parameters without checking with the client; outside the parameter, you have to go to your client first. Somebody in our investment department made investments that were good investments, but outside the customers' parameters, without permission. When we found the issue, we announced it publicly right away to be totally transparent about the issue. We set aside $5 million for potential losses while we worked through the problem, but our ultimate loss was pretty small.

"I firmly believe that it is because of Walter Dods that the Hawaii Children's Discovery Center exists today. He played a key role on the committee that raised $16 million for our center in Kakaako. He even suggested that First Hawaiian and Bank of Hawaii work together on the campaign. He told me, 'Usually one bank or the other takes the lead with a major gift, but for this project, both Larry Johnson and I will make equal gifts and work together. It's for the children.'

"One more important thing Walter did for us was a gift that lasted for years. At one campaign committee meeting in our new but empty building, I greeted him at the door with a roll of toilet paper in my hands because I was cleaning toilets when he arrived. When I told him what I was doing, he called Jim Walters at Hawaiian Building Maintenance and told Jim that I needed help. Because he personally made that request, Jim donated janitorial services to the Discovery Center for almost 10 years!"

—*Loretta Yajima, chair of Hawaii Children's Discovery Center*

You can get lawyers who say, "Well, technically you kind of have their authority. They knew it's been in the accounts for a while." Yet I knew we had done wrong and needed to tell every client "We did wrong, we'll make it right." We made sure they didn't suffer any losses as a result. We were honest with the public and our customers, we were able to sleep at night, and in the end we lost very few clients.

I've already written in the previous chapter about the ill-fated 1995 "Thumbs Up, Hawaii!" campaign. We tried. We failed. We moved on. Don't let the bastards grind you down, though. Admit your error, shake it off, pick yourself up and keep going.

Mix insiders and outsiders.
For the most part, First Hawaiian has done very well by growing our managers in-house, but you can't always do that. It may grate on some people, but I have always felt you need to mix up your team so you don't get a culture that's all one way. Good bankers are very valuable, but I always believed you need non-bankers in the mix as well. The fact that I came from a non-banking background might have something to do with my approach. When Mr. Bellinger hired me, he said, "I have enough people who understand banking. I want people who understand the community and the customers."

Occasionally, I went outside the bank to find smart, quick studies who would think big and work hard. The first was Gary Caulfield. When I hired him, he was still young but one of the top guys in Governor Ariyoshi's office. We had worked together on George's campaigns. His state job crossed all boundary lines. One day he would be handling prison outbreaks, the next day an economic development project and three days later dealing with poison in the milk system. He was really good under stress. I told him, "This is George's last term. Take your nose out of the public trough and come earn a real living."

After a year as my administrative assistant, troubleshooting all kinds of projects for me, he said, "I want to go into operations." I told him, "Gary, that's a hard, messy job, and you don't know anything about banking." He insisted, so I put him under Ken Bentley, our top operations guy. Gary is now vice chairman and chief information officer, one of the top guys in the bank.

In the early 1990s, I brought in Red Pope from the Mainland to run marketing. When I went to bank marketing school in Colorado as a young guy, he was an instructor. We became good friends, so I knew he was a top-notch bank marketer. We didn't have anybody ready to assume the top job. He was getting toward the end of his

> "Walt has a vision and looks for the right people to execute that vision whether we're odd ducks or not. He'll tell you what he wants and expects you to get it done. If you have a problem, come back to him. If you're not talking to him, he's expecting it to get done. That's been his management style."
>
> —*Gary Caulfield, First Hawaiian Bank vice chairman*

career, but his bank had been acquired and he was willing to come to Hawaii on a five-year contract.

Red didn't know Hawaii, but he really knew marketing. Red ran some great campaigns including the Karate Kid, Pat Morita, and the "High-Y" ads. He changed the "The Bank That Says Yes" to "Yes You Can." (He kept the "Yes" part, which was non-negotiable with me.) Red stayed until he retired.

Of course, Bob Harrison did the ultimate mix-and-match when he hired Eric Yeaman, who had never been a banker, away from Hawaiian Telcom to become president at First Hawaiian. That surprised a lot of people inside and outside the bank, but it's going to be a home run.

Give people room to fail.

Johnny Bellinger was a tough, exacting boss, but he always gave me room to succeed or *fail*. I especially stress "fail" because many bosses don't allow this important learning experience. Even though he may not have had faith in a particular project, he had faith in me. He understood that the only way for me to learn and to help our bank grow was to give me the opportunity to fail all by myself.

One time, back in the early 1970s, I had the idea for a discount brokerage service. I ran the numbers, and they said all we needed was to get 1 percent of the market to make a lot of money. We ran ads. We printed brochures. We hired people. We lost money. But I didn't lose my job, and I became better for it.

When I became CEO, I would tell people, "Go ahead. Make a decision. If you make a mistake, I'll back you."

No single leadership style works for everyone.

When I was getting ready to retire and Don Horner was going to take over, I started hearing, "We're going to miss you, Walt. The other guy isn't like you. He no put his arms around me." But successful leadership comes in many forms. No two leaders are alike. I wasn't like Bellinger; Don wasn't like me. If you set the basic culture of your organization deep, if you believe in community service and you believe in caring, the system will work fine even though the personalities differ.

> "I worked directly with Walt for 18 years. I never saw him lose his temper. Walt never micromanaged, just demanded the best of everybody and expected you to do your job well. He was a good sport. On his 50th birthday, we put a wheelchair in his parking stall so he would see it when he got to work. He arrived at the same time as Jack Hoag. Walt hopped in the wheelchair, and Jack wheeled him up in the elevator to his office."
>
> —*Audrey Karr, Walt's longtime administrative assistant*

> "He's a bit of a Renaissance man. It's surprising the things that interest him—architects and architecture, local contemporary artists and, of course, cars. We'll watch old movies, and he can name the makes, models and years of every single car. He's really into the latest technology. He has to have the latest iPhone. He has the iWatch. He tries to convince you he knows what he's doing with it. It all adds up to a very interesting person."
>
> —*Stan Kuriyama, CEO of Alexander & Baldwin*

It's important for the people who work for you to see you have a sense of humor. I dressed up as a sheik and danced with a belly dancer at this employee party.

Have fun, laugh. Especially at yourself.
If you're happy, you do a better job. People you work with are inspired to do better, too. It doesn't cost you any more to have fun, be nice and smile. A sense of humor is very important. You can still get the job done and have fun. Sometimes we go out after work and have a *lot* of fun.

When I was elected to the Bank Marketing Association's Hall of Fame in 1997, I rode in on rollerblades for my acceptance speech. My teenaged daughter Lauren and I had started rollerblading together in the neighborhood. I thought it would be a cool gimmick, but I didn't count on the uneven flooring. Try riding in-line skates on carpet and all of a sudden hit wood. You go really fast! Fortunately, I was able to keep my balance. I just thought it would be a fun thing to accept the award and then cruise off. Maybe kind of stupid to do at age 56, though.

Finally, balance work and family.
I'm the worst person to give this crucial advice because I didn't do it. My family paid a price for my being over-committed. I try not to, but I guess it's in my genes. What success means is different from one person to the next. Success doesn't mean you have to become a CEO. One of my Saint Louis classmates became a pressman at *The Honolulu Advertiser*. I was the best man at his wedding. He played baseball with his kids every day, has a happy family life and he's successful—in his own eyes and in mine.

If you're going to go all the way to the top in a big company, however, you have to make sacrifices. You can't do it all. I've been blessed with a wonderful spouse, Diane, who kept the family together. I have a great relationship with my kids, better than I deserve because I didn't put in the time on that side of life.

> "I remember when Walter got the Marketer of the Year award one year, and he's talking about how happy he was. He started crying because he knew the sacrifices Diane and his family had made for him to do that."
>
> —investment partner Bill Mills

I'm sometimes asked if I would do it all over again. In fact, I would do very little differently. I've had a wonderful career, experiences of more than one lifetime. I have met and sometimes worked with state, national and world leaders. I've run successful campaigns for governor and for Dan Inouye, the greatest political figure in Hawaii's history. (Unfortunately, I ended my political career by losing that Hanabusa-Schatz Senate race I discussed earlier. That was very hard.)

My one regret is not paying enough attention to my family. If I could go back and change anything, I would have tried to cut out some of the community service and spend more time with them. In this book, you'll notice I've said very little about Diane and our four wonderful kids—Trippy (that's our nickname for Walter III), Chris, Peter and Lauren. That's because the Dods name has been in the public spotlight for a long time, and they had to live with the fallout, so I didn't want to put them in public view again with this book. They are the most important part of my life.

I love you all!

Diane and me.

ACKNOWLEDGMENTS

A lot of people graciously shared their time and memories with us as we worked with Walt on this book. Thanks to:

Sen. Dan Akaka, Gov. George Ariyoshi, Sharon Shiroma Brown, Gary Caulfield, Philip Ching, Suzanne Dods Chong Kee, Matt Cox, Bobby Dods, Tommy Dods, Larry Fish, Bob Fujioka, Paul Ganley, Kim Gennaula, Alan Goda, Doug Grigsby, U.S. Rep. Colleen Hanabusa, Bob Harrison, Jack Hoag, Don Horner, Tom Huber, David Hulihee, Audrey Karr, Howard Karr, Glenn Kaya, Myra Kirby, Bert Kobayashi Jr., Dorri Kuriki, Stan Kuriyama, Dr. Fujio Matsuda, Colbert Matsumoto, Don McGrath, Bill Mills, Jack Myers, Nick Ng Pack, Ray Ono, Wesley Park, Dick Rosenberg, Jennifer Goto Sabas, Kit Smith, Donna Tanoue, Jack Tsui, Jeff Watanabe, Jim Wayman, Leslie Wilcox, Al Yamada, Lily Yao, and Eric Yeaman.

We also owe a debt of gratitude to John Strobel, Jeff Portnoy, Beverly Creamer and Karen Keir for reviewing and editing the narrative and suggesting corrections and improvements; to Luana Perry, Walt's trusty assistant, for finding files and pictures and keeping his schedule (and ours) organized; to Stacey Leong Mills and Karyn Yasui Lau for creative layout and design; and to Jackie Aweau, who patiently and accurately transcribed dozens of hours of tape.

We two and Walt are responsible for any remaining errors.

Gerry Keir & Jerry Burris

APPENDIX A

FAMILY TREE ON MY FATHER'S (DODS) SIDE

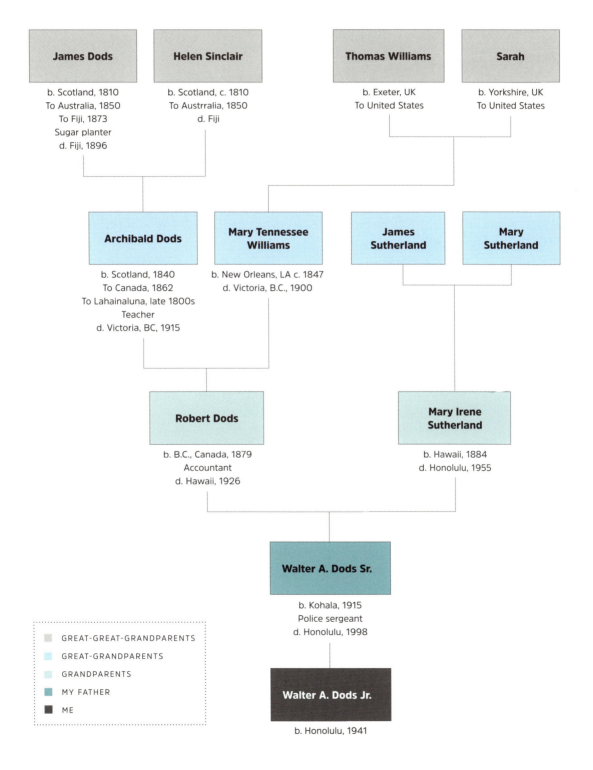

FAMILY TREE ON MY MOTHER'S (PHILLIPS) SIDE

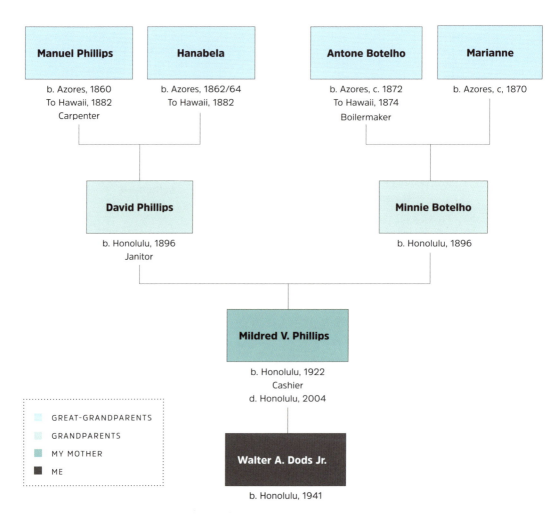

WALTER A. DODS JR. CAREER HIGHLIGHTS

1941	Born May 26, Honolulu
1959	Graduated from Saint Louis School
1959–65	Dead-files clerk, mail boy, underwiter at Home Insurance (which later became First Insurance Co. of Hawaii)
1965–68	Community relations specialist, advertising manager at Dillingham Corp.
1967	Graduated from University of Hawaii, Bachelor's in Business Administration
1968	Age 27, Hired by First National Bank of Hawaii as Director of Advertising & Public Relations
1969	Age 28, Bank renamed First Hawaiian Bank. Assistant Vice President, Marketing Division
1970	Age 29, Vice President, Marketing Division
1973	Age 32, Senior Vice President, Marketing & Research Group
1976	Age 34, Executive Vice President, Marketing & Research Group
1978	Age 37, Executive Vice President, Retail Banking Group
1984	Age 43, President, First Hawaiian Bank
1989	Age 48, Chairman & CEO, First Hawaiian, Inc. (holding company) and First Hawaiian Bank
1998	Age 57, Chairman & CEO, BancWest Corporation (new holding company name)
2004	Age 63, Retired as CEO of First Hawaiian Bank, Remained BancWest chairman until 2007 and chairman of the bank through 2008

POLITICS

1970	Co-chair, George Ariyoshi for lieutenant governor
1974	Co-chair, George Ariyoshi for governor
1978	Co-chair, George Ariyoshi for governor
1982	Co-chair, George Ariyoshi for governor
1992	Chair, Dan Inouye for U.S. Senate
1998	Chair, Dan Inouye for U.S. Senate
2014	Chair, Colleen Hanabusa for U.S. Senate

SELECTED HONORS

1963	Age 22, Outstanding Jaycee in the Nation
1980	Saint Louis School's Outstanding Alumnus Award
1987	American Marketing Association, Marketer of the Year
1992	Sales & Marketing Executives of Honolulu, Inc., Salesperson of the Year
1993	University of Hawaii Distinguished Alumni Award
1997	Bank Marketing Association Hall of Fame
1998	Hawaii's Distinguished Citizen, Aloha Council, Boy Scouts of America
2000	Bishop Museum Robert J. Pfeiffer Medal
2004	Order of the Rising Sun, with Gold and Silver Star, imperial honor from Government of Japan

APPENDIX C

LET'S MAKE A DEAL

Over a quarter-century as an executive, corporate board member and investor, Walter Dods Jr. was involved in more than two dozen mergers and acquisitions valued at nearly $10 billion. Some of the significant deals:

FIRST HAWAIIAN BANK/BANCWEST DEALS

1991   First Hawaiian Bank acquired First Interstate Bank of Hawaii (20 branches, $858 million in assets) for $143 million.

1993   First Hawaiian acquired Pioneer Federal Savings Bank (19 branches, $600 million in assets) for $87 million.

1996   First Hawaiian acquired 31 branches with $700 million in deposits from U.S. Bancorp in Oregon, Washington and Idaho for $38 million, creating a new subsidiary, Pacific One Bank, a platform for future Mainland expansion.

1998   First Hawaiian merged with Bank of the West, a California bank owned by Banque Nationale de Paris (BNP), leaving BNP with 45 percent ownership of BancWest Corporation, parent of the merged banks. Transaction was valued at $1.03 billion, largest stock deal in history for a Hawaii company.

1999   BancWest acquired Sierra West Bank ($900 million in assets and 20 branches in Northern California and Nevada) for $180 million.

2001   BancWest acquired 30 branches in New Mexico and Nevada from First Security Bank.

2001   First Hawaiian bought Union Bank of California branches in Guam and Saipan, acquiring $200 million in deposits.

2001   BNP Paribas acquired the remaining 55 percent of BancWest stock for $2.5 billion, largest deal in Hawaii history.

2002   BancWest acquired United Bank of California (largest L.A.-based bank with assets of $11 billion and 117 branches) from UFJ Bank of Japan for $2.4 billion in cash.

2004   BancWest acquired Community Bankshares (parent of Community First National Bank, with assets of $5.5 billion and 156 branches in 12 Western and Midwestern states) for $1.2 billion.

2004   BancWest acquired Union Safe Deposit Bank ($1.2 billion assets and 19 branches in central California) for $245 million.

(When Dods became chairman and CEO in 1989, First Hawaiian had $5 billion in assets and 46 branches. When he retired in 2004, BancWest—the former First Hawaiian Inc.—had $49 billion in assets and 530 branches in Hawaii, Guam, Saipan and 16 Mainland states from California to Minnesota.)

AFTER RETIRING AS FIRST HAWAIIAN CEO

2004　Dods assembled a group of local investors who put in $30 million as part of the acquisition by Carlyle Group of Verizon Hawaii, as the local phone company was then called. The local investors lost the entire $30 million when the company, now known as Hawaiian Telcom, went into bankruptcy.

2007　Dods and partners Bill Mills and David Hulihee, teaming together as Kokooha Investments Inc., acquired Mid Pac Petroleum, owner of Union 76 gas stations and convenience stores in the Islands, for $44 million. In 2015, Mid Pac was sold to Par Petroleum for $107 million.

2012　Dods was board chairman of Alexander & Baldwin, Inc. (A&B) when it spun off its subsidiary, Matson Navigation Co., as a separate company. Within three years, that deal helped to create $2.5 billion in additional market capitalization for the two companies combined.

2013　A&B acquired Grace Pacific, a construction company, for $277 million. Dods, an investor in Grace and a member of the boards of both companies, recused himself from involvement in the transaction.

2014　Bill Mills' company, with Dods as a minority investor, acquired Ameron Hawaii, Oahu's largest producer of concrete, and Island Ready-Mix Concrete Inc. from California-based Ameron International Corp. in a $100 million transaction. The acquisition returned century-old Ameron Hawaii to local ownership, with management staying in place.

2015　Dods was board chairman of Matson Navigation Co. when it acquired the Alaska operations of Horizon Lines in a transaction valued at $456 million.

INDEX

A

Abercrombie, Neil 64-65, 70, 186-187
Ackerson, Dan 199-200
Adair, Dick 138, 144, 160
Aina Haina Chevron 17
Aina Haina Chop Suey 17, 24
Aina Haina Foodland 17, 24, 180
Aina Haina Service Station 17, 19, 24, 171
Akaka, Dan 194, 218, 235, 246
Akaka, Millie 218
Akamine, Richard 25
Alexander & Baldwin Inc. (A&B) 32, 94, 118, 176, 203-205, 207-208, 210, 213-214, 220-221, 224, 230, 236, 244, 252
Almeida, Johnny 206
Aloha Airlines 36, 172-174, 200, 225
Aloha United Way 32, 42, 174, 235-236
American Bankers Association (ABA) 40, 42, 127, 138-145, 147-148, 171, 213, 220
American Factors (Amfac) 32, 204
American Savings 101, 224
American Security Bank 100-101
Ameron Hawaii 206, 252
Amfac Financial 57
Anderson, D.G. "Andy" 179-181
Anderson, Eileen 217
Aoki, Dan "Balloon" 76
Aoki, Harriet 98, 109
Arellano, Mel 127
Ariyoshi, George 58, 61-62, 68-69, 71-80, 84, 88, 179-180, 215-218, 221, 223-225, 228-229, 242, 246, 249
Arnoldus, Clint 234
Attwood, Jim 198
Aweau, Jackie 246

B

Baird, Tom 38
Baker, L.M. "Bud" 140
Bank Marketing Association 38, 44, 244, 250
Bank of America 40, 44, 101, 104, 106, 141, 147, 151, 163
Bank of Hawaii (Bankoh) 24, 40-44, 48-49, 51-52, 84, 89, 99-100, 104-105, 109-110, 117-118, 129-135, 147, 153-155, 158, 163-165, 168, 171, 173-174, 181, 219, 227, 230-231, 238-239, 241
Beam and Milici 24-25, 30
Beam, Jerry 25
Beam, Paul 24-25
Bellinger, Joan 48, 54-55, 93
Bellinger, John "Johnny" D. 34-36, 38-55, 58, 63, 66, 71, 74, 77, 79-85, 87, 91-96, 99-100, 103, 108, 129-130, 172-174, 181, 199, 204, 215, 220, 225, 229, 236-237, 242-243
Bellinger, Neil 181
Bentley, Ken 50, 111, 242
Berman, Steve 193
Big Five 32, 48-49, 204, 228
Bishop Bank 31
Bishop Estate 31
Bishop, Charles Reed 91, 118, 150
Blaisdell, Neal 12, 28, 217
Boggs, Hale 108
Boggs, Lindy 108
Boggs, Tommy 108
Borges, Jimmy 13
Borreca, Richard 181
Botelho, Antone 13, 248
Botelho, Marianne 13
Botelho, Minnie 13-14, 248
Boylan, Dan 183
Brother Aiu 16

Brown, Jerry 72
Brown, Pat 72
Brown, Sharon Shiroma 42, 129, 246
Burns, Jack 12, 24, 28, 32-33, 44, 71–73, 76–77, 84, 216, 221, 228, 233
Burris, Jerry 246
Bush, George W. 193
Buyers, J.W.A. "Doc" 130-131

C

C. Brewer & Company 32, 48-49, 131, 204
Cades Schutte 58, 60, 62
Camara, Norman 30
Cameron, Gerry 147
Campbell Estate 108
Carter, Jimmy 72, 212
Case, Ed 73, 179–181
Castle & Cooke 32, 48-49, 204, 206
Caulfield, Gary 77, 110–111, 180, 242, 246
Cayetano, Ben 64-65, 77, 87, 179–180, 225, 227, 229–230
Central Pacific Bank 89, 101, 135, 219, 234
Chaplin, George 224–225, 229
Charan, Ram 110
Cheney, Dick 193-194
Ching, Hung Wo 173–174, 225
Ching, Philip 50, 82–83, 85–86, 88, 94, 246
Chow, Norm 216
City Bank 89, 101
City Mill 236
Clark, Charlie 77
Clinton, Bill 141–142, 144, 194, 198
Coffman, Tom 72
Coppa, Bruce 186
Correa, Butch 15
Correa, Naomi "Sister" 15
Costco 41
Couch, John 236
Cox, Matt 204, 206, 246
Creamer, Beverly 246

Crossley, Randy 78, 224
Czarnecki, Gerry 106

D

D'Amato, Al 194
Dahl, Richard 131
Daly, Don 50
Damon Estate 67
Damon Haig, Christopher 121
Damon, Samuel M. 121
Deng, Xiaoping 213
Devine, Andy 34
Dillingham Corporation 30–33, 35–36, 114, 221, 249
Dillingham, Benjamin Franklin 31
Dillingham, Lowell 31-33, 228
Dillingham, Walter 31
Doane, Allen 214
Dobelle, Evan 216–217, 227
Dods Chong Kee, Suzanne 21, 24, 246
Dods, Archibald 11–12, 247
Dods, Bob "Bobby" 16, 21, 31, 246, 247
Dods, Chester 12-13, 28
Dods, Chris 91, 232, 245
Dods, Diane (Nosse) 48, 73, 91, 93, 114, 139, 181–182, 185, 187, 212, 215, 223, 227–228, 232, 236, 245
Dods, James 11, 247
Dods, Lauren 91, 123, 127, 194, 244-245
Dods, Mildred "Millie" Vivian Phillips 13–15, 18–20, 248
Dods, Peter 91, 211, 232, 245
Dods, Robert 11-12
Dods, Starr Wedemeyer 232
Dods, Tommy 17, 20, 180, 246
Dods, Walter "Buster" Sr. 5, 11–16, 18, 20–21, 28, 35, 247
Dods, Walter III "Trippy" 91, 232, 245
Dole, Bob 187
Dorman, Dan 45
Duty Free Shoppers 108

INDEX

E

Easy Music 211
Ellerbee, Linda 145
Equitable Life Insurance Company 32

F

Farrington High School 235
Fasi, Frank 72, 77–78, 119–120, 217, 225
Father Louis Boys' Home 12
Finance Factors 58, 119
First Federal Savings & Loan 99–100, 105
First Interstate Bank of Hawaii 98, 100–103, 105, 108–111, 149, 152, 251
First National Bank of Hawaii 33, 35, 44, 249
Fish, Larry 143, 167, 246
Flamson, Dick 87
Fletcher Pacific Construction 113
Foodland 17, 24, 280, 215
Ford, Gerald 101
Freitas, George 94
Fujioka, Bob 134-135, 246
Fujiyama, Wallace "Wally" 49, 85, 216, 222–223

G

Ganley, Paul Mullin 14, 51, 246
Gas Company 209
Gay & Robinson 204
GECC Financial Corporation 57, 66–67
GEM 41, 95
General Electric 57
General Motors (GM) 200
Gennaula, Kim 174, 246
Gill, Gary 119
Gill, Tom 44, 73, 78
Giugni, Henry 184, 188–191, 193
Go! Airlines 174
Goda, Alan 82–83, 86, 246
Goldman Sachs 164
Goo, Ah Chew 12
Gore, Al 142
Grace Brothers 206

Grace Pacific 206–208, 210, 252
Graham, Don 31
Great Hawaiian Financial 60–62
Green, Harry 88
Green, Steven 209–210
Greenspan, Alan 127, 213, 220
Grigsby, Doug 153, 155, 169, 246
GTE Corporation 198
GTE Hawaiian Tel 198
Guerrero, Tony 98, 110, 134–135

H

Haig, David 123
Halekulani 19, 23
Hall, Jack 32
Hanabusa, Colleen 69–72, 185–187, 245–246, 249
Harper, John C. 123
Harris, Jeremy 179, 181
Harrison, Bob 43, 108, 135, 198, 207, 243, 246
Hart, Peter 78
Haruki, Warren 227
Hashimoto, Ron 30
Hata, Frank 76
Hata, George 44, 50, 53
Hawaii Business magazine 166, 226–228, 231
Hawaii Community Foundation 48
Hawaii Dental Service 223
Hawaii Government Employees Association (HGEA) 70, 180, 228
Hawaii Protective Association 221
Hawaii Public Television (PBS Hawaii) 176
Hawaii Reserves, Inc. 130
Hawaii Thrift & Loan 58–59, 62, 81, 149
Hawaii Visitors Bureau 36
Hawaiian Airlines 175
Hawaiian Commercial and Sugar (HC&S) 204
Hawaiian Dredging & Construction Company 31–32, 114
Hawaiian Electric Company 111, 200, 224

Hawaiian Telcom 111, 141, 176, 198–201, 207–208, 210, 243, 252
Hawaiian Telephone Company 25
Heen, Walter 28
Helfer, Ricki 127
Hemmeter, Chris 87, 214
Hill, Dave 66
Hilo Boarding School 12
Hilo Electric Light Company 39
Hilo High School 12
Hirano Inouye, Irene 186-187, 193
Hirono, Mazie 179–180, 182, 217
Hitch, Dr. Tom 39
Ho, Chinn 40, 228
Ho, Don 221
Ho, Stuart 188
Hoag, Jack 16, 19, 39, 43, 52, 92, 96, 100, 108, 128–131, 158, 165, 243, 246
Hoag, Jeanette 39, 53, 129–130
Home Insurance Company of Hawaii (First Insurance Company of Hawaii) 24–25, 30, 36, 249
Honfed Bank 101, 103, 106, 119
Hong, Buzzy 180
Honolulu Advertiser, The 50, 123, 131, 181–182, 221, 224–225, 229, 245
Honolulu Board of Water Supply 77
HONOLULU Magazine 219, 228
Honolulu Museum of Art 241
Honolulu Police Department 12
Honolulu Rapid Transit (HRT) 220
Honolulu Star-Advertiser 138, 160, 172, 178
Honolulu Star-Bulletin 55, 181, 228
Horio, Don 76
Horner, Don 43, 49–50, 55, 108, 110, 130, 132, 134–135, 168, 171, 197, 230, 238, 240, 243, 246
Howard Hughes Corporation 33
Huber, Tom 60, 62, 65–66, 101, 149, 246
Hulihee, David 202–203, 206–211, 246, 252

Humphrey, Hubert 72
Hutaff, G. Harry 34, 129

I

Ige, David 53, 187
International Longshore and Warehouse Union (ILWU) 23, 32, 180
Inaba, Norman 60, 62
Ing, Sheridan "Sherry" C.F. 94–95, 225
Inouye, Dan 63, 69–70, 73, 141, 174, 180, 183–191, 203, 209–210, 218, 223, 225, 227, 235, 237, 245, 249
Inouye, Maggie 184, 192-193
Iolani School 21, 134, 208, 235
Island Insurance Company 89
Ito, Lance 194

J

J.C. Penney 32
Jack, Wayne 99–100
Japan-America Institute of Management Science (JAIMS) 216
Japan-Hawaii Economic Council 80–81, 84–88, 104
Jensen, Don 38
Johnson, Larry 130–131, 135, 181, 219, 230–231, 239, 241
Jones, June 227
Junior Chamber of Commerce (Jaycees) 25, 28, 250

K

Kalakaua, King 13, 31
Kaleikini, Danny 223
Kamehameha, King 16
Kamehameha Schools 200
Kappock, Tom 131
Karr, Audrey 243, 246
Karr, Howard 47, 59, 93, 102–104, 110, 120, 153, 168, 246
Kaya, Glenn 41–42, 94–95, 234, 246

Keir, Gerry 180–181, 246
Keir, Karen 246
Kellner, Jack 73
Kelly's Drive-In 19
Kennard, Bill 198
Kennedy, Robert 72
KHON-TV 30, 180
Kiehm, Joe 25
Kimura, Shigeru 81–82
King Dom Luis 13
King Hussein 213, 215
King, Sam 73
Kirby, Myra 246
Klenske, Charles 57
Kobayashi, Bert Jr. 83, 223–224, 227, 246
Kohl, Helmut 213
Koizumi, Junichiro 88–89
Kona 44
Koyama, Takumi "Crabby" 76, 228
Kuhaulua, Jesse "Takamiyama" 104
Kuliouou 6, 14–15, 225
Kupau, Walter 219
Kuriki, Dorri 180, 199, 205, 246
Kuriyama, Stan 203, 207, 230, 244, 246
Kwock, Lenore 192

L

Lahainaluna 11
Landon, Allan 147
Lau, Karyn Yasui 246
Lee, Tom 24
Leilehua High 95
Liberty House 32, 40
Lingle, Linda 174, 179, 182, 217, 227
Louie, David 186
Ludwig, Eugene 142
Lurie, Herb 151
Lyman House 12
Lynch, Russ 55

M

MacArthur, Roger 51
Magoon Estate 119
Manoa Finance 56–67, 88
Marcos, Ferdinand 72
Mariani, Pierre 161–162
Marsland, Charles 221
Maryknoll School 13
Matson Navigation Company 176, 203–205, 207, 213, 224, 252
Matsuda, Fujio 216, 246
Matsuhashi, Isao 87
Matsumoto, Colbert 89, 91, 246
Mauka Arterial 19
McCann Erickson Worldwide 140
McClung, David 78
McGrath, Don 146, 149–156, 159, 161–162, 168, 170–171, 197, 239, 246
McGregor, Don 101, 109
McGuire, Buster 12
McKenzie, Bill 39
McKinley High School 12, 94-95, 191, 222
McPhee, Rod 94
Mehau, Larry 71, 221
Mercado Kim, Donna 119
Merrill Lynch 102-103
Mid Pac Petroleum 152, 209–210, 252
Mid-Pacific Institute 44
Midweek 183
Milici Valenti (Milici Valenti Ng Pack) 36, 38, 119
Milici, Ray 24, 36
Mills, Bill 66, 78, 202–203, 206–211, 245–246, 252
Mills, Stacey Leong 246
Minami, Wayne 59–60
Mink, Patsy 28
Minute Chef 14, 20
Mizumoto, Lance 135
Moana Hotel 23

Moanalua 52
Mondale, Walter 72
Morgado, Arnold 219
Morinoue, Hiroki 122
Morishita, Yasumichi "Mamushi" 82–83
Morita, Akio 89
Morita, Pat 243
Morita, Yoshiko 89, 91
Muheim, Harry 72
Mulholland, Brad 214
Muto, Masatoshi 88
Mutual Telephone Company (Hawaiian Telephone) 198
Myers, Jack 113–114, 118, 120, 215, 246

N
Nader, Ralph 141
Napolitan, Joe 71–73, 78
Ng Pack, Nick 36, 119, 246
Nixon, Richard 101, 213

O
O'Neill, Mike 147, 168, 227
Oahu Country Club 14
Oahu Railway & Land Company 31
Oasis 19
Obama, Barack 77, 232
Obama, Michelle 232
Ocean Properties/Castle & Cooke Land 208
Okata, Russell 180
Ono, Ray 52, 134, 157, 246
Ono, Tiare 52
Onodera, Peter 82, 85
Osano, Kenji 81, 83-84, 86
Oshiro, Bob 72–73, 76

P
Pacific Concrete and Rock 206
Pacific Construction 94
Pacific International Center for High Technology Research (PICHTR) 216

Pacific One Bank 148–150, 159, 251
Pan American Financial 59
Pang, Wendell 119
Par Petroleum Corporation 152, 210, 252
Park, Wesley 11, 103, 180, 223, 240, 246
Parsky, Gerald 101–102
Patterson, Patt 33
Pauahi Bishop, Bernice 150
Pebereau, Michel 151, 154, 162–163, 168, 171
Peck, Rod 156
Pedersen, Bill 117–119
Perry, Luana 246
Pfeiffer, Robert "Bobby" 48, 94, 213, 220
Pflueger, Jimmy 39
Phillips, David 13–14, 248
Phillips, Manuel (Filippe/Felipe Manual) 13, 248
Phillips, Mildred "Millie" Vivian 13–15, 18–20, 248
Pingree, Hugh 34, 50, 52–53, 83, 94, 96
Pioneer Federal Savings and Loan 106–111, 149, 152, 251
Pope, Norwood "Red" 229, 242–243
Porteus, David 67
Porteus, Hebden "Heb" 67, 94, 100
Portnoy, Jeff 246
Price, Larry 20, 216
Princess Kaiulani Hotel 14
Punahou School 12, 21, 134, 235

Q
Queen Liliuokalani 11
Queens Hospital 14

R
Radcliffe, John 175
Randall, Kennedy 40, 42, 129
Reed, Ricky 192, 221
Rexall Drugs 14
Reyes, Norman 30
Richardson, William 222

Roberts, Cokie 108
Rogers, Glenn 214
Ronson, Larry 35
Roosevelt High School 42, 48, 58, 95, 223, 225
Rosenberg, Barbara 44
Rosenberg, Dick 44, 101, 104, 141, 163, 246
Royal Contracting 206
Royal Hawaiian Hotel 23

S

Sabas, Jennifer Goto 184–185, 192, 246
Sacred Hearts Academy 16
Saint Louis School 7, 16, 19, 21, 23–24, 28, 31, 94–95, 158, 235, 245, 249–250
Santos, Alexandrina Augusta (Hannabela) 13, 248
Sarah 247
Satoh, Yoshiharu 89, 91
Say, Calvin 227
Schall, Peter 87–88
Schatz, Brian 70–71, 186, 245
Schuman Carriage 39
Schumer, Chuck 194
Schutte, Fred 58
Scotty's Drive Inn 19
Sears 31–32, 40, 222
Security Pacific Bank 87
Seigle, Jack 73
Shapiro, David 182
Sherman, Eddie 221
Shinseki, Eric 77
Silan, Alex 39
Simmons, Harris 149
Simon, William "Bill" E. 101–102, 104
Simpson, O.J. 194
Sinclair, Helen 247
Smith, Kit 50, 246
Sofos Realty Company 115
Sofos, Steve 115
Sony, Suntory and Meiji Yasuda Insurance 85
St. Stephens Seminary 16

Steele, Dwayne 206–208
Steinbrenner, George 189
Stephenson, Howard 100, 130–131
Stevens, Ted 194–195
Strobel, John 246
Sullivan, Maurice "Sully" 215
Sutherland, James 247
Sutherland, Mary Irene 12, 247

T

Takayama, Gregg 180
Takefuji 88
Takei, Yasuo 81, 84, 86
Takushi, Jimmy 72
Takushi, Tokuichi "Dynamite" 76
Tanoue, Donna 61–62, 64, 192, 194, 246
Territorial Mental Hospital 12
TheBus 220
Theo H. Davies & Company 32, 48–49, 204
Tojio, Lois 42–43
Treca, Laurent 155
Trinidad, Corky 178
Trotter, Fred 188
Tsuchida, Kazuko 105
Tsuchida, Terumichi 88, 104–105, 149
Tsui, John K. (Jack) 47, 128–136, 168, 213, 246
Tsutsumi, Yoshiaki 88

U

University of Hawaii 20, 24, 28, 42, 44, 197, 206, 216–217, 222–223, 227, 235–236, 249–250

V

Valenti, Frank 36
Vericella, Tony 87–88
Verizon Hawaii 198–199, 201, 227, 252

W

Wahiawa Water Company 12
Wahl, Jacques 169
Waialae Country Club 49, 65, 218

Waianae High School 235
Waihee, John 179
Walters, Jim 241
Watanabe, Jeff 48, 77, 164, 181, 186–187, 191–192,
    203, 206–207, 223–224, 228–229, 237, 246
Watanabe, Lynne 223
Watts, Denny 113
Wayman, Jim 109, 117, 118, 123–124, 246
Weinberg, Harry 220
Weyand, Fred 151
Whittemore, Tom 236–238
Wilcox, Leslie 176, 246
Williams, Mary Tennessee 11
Williams, Thomas 247
Willows 41
Winer, Andy 70
Winton, David 162
Wo, Bob 94
Wong, Gordon 224
Wong, Marvin 186

Y

Y. Hata & Company 76
Yajima, Loretta 241
Yamada, Al 110, 246
Yamamoto, Hirotoshi 60, 65
Yamasaki, Minoru 114
Yamashita, Diane 180
Yannell, Donnie 109
Yao, Lily 106, 108–110, 246
Yates, Jim 209–210
Yeaman, Eric 200–201, 207, 243, 246
"Yes" ads for First Hawaiian Bank
    (The Bank That Says Yes; Yes You Can)
        6, 38, 49, 243
Yee, Ken 86
Yuen, George 77

Z

Zell, Sam 210–211
Zhang, Zemin 213